Contents

Inside Out
Course Study Guide

produced by

with contributions by

Jean P. Volckmann, Ph.D.
Pasadena City College

Inside Out is a video-, print-, and web-based course designed and produced by INTELECOM Intelligent Telecommunications

Psychology, 8th Edition, and Psychology Eighth Edition in Modules, by David Myers, published by Worth Publishers, are designated for use with this course.

Printed in the United States of America

ISBN: 1-58370-005-6

Introduction

Inside Out is a comprehensive introduction to psychology. The video, textbook, and this study guide combine to provide you with basic concepts and insightful glimpses into the science and humanity of psychology. Interviews with noted psychologists bring you face to face with the major debates and topics in the field of psychology and help penetrate the mysteries of the mind and body from the "inside out." You will explore neuroscience, genetic and environmental influences on behavior, memory, learning, personality, psychological disorders, and more in the evolving world of psychological science. Case studies further enrich the story of psychology from a human perspective.

This guide is only part of the *Inside Out* course you will be embarking upon with the help and guidance of your campus instructor. The 22 half-hour videos are closely integrated with David Myers' texts, *Psychology* and *Psychology in Modules*. Your instructor will let you know which text has been selected. The newest editions of these books offer increased coverage of cultural and gender diversity as well as greater emphasis on biological, psychological, and social/cultural influences on behavior.

Each of the half-hour video episodes is accompanied by a corresponding lesson in this guide and an optional online component. And both this study guide and David Myers' textbooks employ the SQ3R (survey, question, read, review, reflect) study principles discussed in the text.

Follow the steps below as you begin this exciting study.

Steps to Learning Success

STEP 1: Before you begin any reading, preview the Learning Outcomes and skim the Active Review exercises to formulate questions in your mind about the upcoming assignment.

STEP 2: Complete the reading assignment in the textbook as assigned by your instructor.

STEP 3: View the assigned Video Episode for this lesson from the video series *Inside Out: An Introduction to Psychology*. Watch the episode in its entirety without attempting to take notes the first time you view it. When you watch it or the review segments a second or third time, notes become useful. If you have the DVD, you not only have designated review segments for each lesson, but also additional opportunities to explore areas of interest to you, called Find Out More.

STEP 4: Complete the Active Review exercises in this Study Guide, referring to your textbook and video segments as needed. Consult the Answer Key for the Active Review after you have finished the exercises.

STEP 5: Take the Self Test, and then check your answers with those listed in the Answer Key for the Self Test.

STEP 6: Finally, go back to the Learning Outcomes for each lesson and check carefully to make sure you have successfully accomplished these outcomes as a result of your study process.

Lesson 1 (The Story of Psychology)

The Magic of the Mind

Assignments

Reading: "Prologue: The Story of Psychology" in *Psychology* by David Myers (Module 1 in the modular version of *Psychology*)

If you have not already done so, read the Introduction on page v of this guide, especially the Steps to Learning Success.

Video: Episode 1, "The Magic of the Mind"

LEARNING OUTCOMES

Familiarize yourself with the Learning Outcomes for this lesson before you begin the assignments. Return to them to check your learning after completing the Steps to Learning Success. Careful work on these materials should equip you to accomplish the outcomes.

Psychology's Roots (Module 1)

1. Summarize the key ideas of historically prominent philosophers and biologists who considered questions related to psychology.

2. Describe the events that defined the transition from prescientific psychology to scientific psychology, and discuss important movements in early psychology, including **structuralism** and **functionalism**.

3. Define **psychology**, explaining each term in the current definition, and discuss how the definition has changed since psychology emerged as a separate discipline.

4. Name several historically important psychologists who contributed to the development of the field of psychology, summarizing their contributions.

5. Discuss the past and present status of women in psychology, citing specific cases and statistics to support your points.

Contemporary Psychology (Module 1)

6. Summarize the opinions of the various experts who commented in the video about what makes psychology especially fascinating and challenging.

7. Explain the **nature-nurture issue** in psychology, and discuss the position of the textbook author on this issue.

8. Explain **Darwin's** concept of **natural selection** and describe the impact of **evolutionary theory** in psychology.

9. Identify the points of emphasis of the seven complementary **perspectives**, or **levels of analysis**, in psychology and explain their interrelationship to one another and to the **biopsychosocial approach** in psychology.

10. Distinguish between **basic research** and **applied research**, and provide an overview of the various basic and applied subfields of psychology.

11. Compare and contrast **clinical psychologists**, **counseling psychologists**, and **psychiatrists**.

12. List the five study techniques students can use to enhance their own learning and academic performance.

ACTIVE REVIEW

Each item in this section is based on material presented in the video or the textbook assignment for this lesson, or both. Complete this section, referring as needed to your notes or the source materials themselves. Answers are provided at the end of this lesson.

Psychology's Roots

1. The science of psychology developed primarily from **biology** and _____ .

2. Psychology is currently defined as the **scientific study of** _____ (observable actions) and _____ _____ (thoughts, feelings, beliefs, and perceptions that can be inferred from behavior).

3. The textbook author emphasizes that the science of psychology is distinguished most of all by its *(methods / findings / authorities)*.

4. To be scientific in their efforts, psychologists must *(have faith in / test / reject)* their hunches and theories.

5. Among the prominent ancient Greek philosophers, *(Socrates / Plato / Aristotle)* stands out today as one who believed in relying on careful observation and data to arrive at explanations, qualifying him as an important forerunner of today's scientists.

6. *(Socrates / Plato / Aristotle)* insisted that knowledge, rather than being innate, comes from experiences stored in our memories.

7. Seventeenth century French philosopher **René** _____ held several key ideas that essentially *(agreed / conflicted)* with those of Socrates and Plato—namely, that the mind and body are *(separate / interconnected)* forms of existence and that ideas are *(innate / based on experience)*. Descartes went on to propose that the specific location in the brain where the mind or soul could interact with the body was the *(pineal gland / pituitary gland / thyroid gland)*.

8. British philosopher **John** *(James / Bacon / Locke / Kant)* held that all knowledge comes from experience, a view that underlies modern _____

(reliance on observation and experimentation) in science.

9. Review some of the major contributors to *prescientific psychology* by choosing the name from the Key List that best matches the descriptions in items a–e. Write your choice in the blank next to the description.

Key List
Aristotle
Darwin
Descartes
Locke
Plato
Socrates

a. _____ *and* _____
Ancient Greek philosophers who contemplated the relationship between the mind and the body, concluding that mind and body are separate and distinct.

b. _____ British philosopher who believed that all knowledge comes from experience, and who was accordingly associated with empiricism.

c. _____ Biologist whose concept of natural selection and theory of evolution strongly influenced early functionalist psychologists and today's evolutionary psychologists.

d. _____ Seventeenth century French philosopher who developed the concept of the reflex and promoted the idea that mind and body are separate forms of existence that are able to interact at the pineal gland in the brain.

e. _____ Greek philosopher who believed that knowledge is based on experience and that the mind and body are interrelated.

10. Because he established the first scientific laboratory for the study of psychology in *(Russia / Poland / Germany / the U.S. / Canada)* in *(1678 / 1798 / 1879 / 1921)*, historians credit _____ _____ with being the founder of scientific psychology.

11. One of the earliest branches of scientific psychology, founded by **Edward Titchener**, was

_____. Titchener trained his research participants to use the method called _____ (looking within oneself to report on conscious experiences) as a means of searching for the fundamental elements of mind or consciousness.

12. As psychology progressed, the **structuralism** movement soon *(expanded / declined),* primarily because the method of **introspection** was found to be highly *(reliable / unreliable).*

13. Another early branch of psychology, which focused more on the functions of the mind than the structure of the mind was called _____. This movement, which was influenced by the evolutionary theory of **Charles** _____, was started by **William** *(Watson / Skinner / James / Whiton / Wundt).*

14. Early in its history, the field of psychology was dominated by *(men / women).* One important woman in psychology, **Mary** _____ _____, who worked in William James' laboratory, completed the requirements for a Ph.D. degree in psychology and was *(awarded / denied)* the degree by Harvard University in the early 1900s. In the U.S. and Canada today, about *(one-tenth / one-third / two-thirds)* of the doctoral degrees in psychology are granted to women.

15. Another historically important pioneer in psychology was **Margaret Floy Washburn**, who in 1921 was voted into office as the *(first / second)* woman president of the _____ _____ _____, the largest professional organization of psychologists.

16. Review some of the major *early pioneers in scientific psychology* by choosing the name from the Key List that best matches the descriptions in items a–e. Write your choice in the blank next to the description.

Key List
Mary Whiton Calkins
William James
Edward B. Titchener
Margaret Floy Washburn
Wilhelm Wundt

a. _____ The philosopher and physiologist who is credited with being the founder of scientific psychology, because he set up the first laboratory for scientific research in psychology in Leipzig, Germany in 1879.

b. _____ The first woman to be awarded a Ph.D. degree in psychology, and the second woman to be elected president of the American Psychological Association.

c. _____ American philosopher who was strongly influenced by Darwin's theory of evolution; began the functionalism movement in psychology.

d. _____ Studied under Wundt, and later founded the structuralist movement in psychology; sought to describe the mind and consciousness, based on use of the method of introspection.

e. _____ Denied a Ph.D. in psychology from Harvard, even though she completed all the qualifications for the degree; in 1905, became the first woman to be elected president of the American Psychological Association.

17. Review some additional *historically important people in psychology* by choosing the name from the Key List that best matches the descriptions in items a–d. Write your choice in the blank next to the description.

Key List
Freud
Pavlov
Piaget
Skinner
Watson

a. _____ Austrian physician who developed psychoanalysis as a talk therapy treatment for emotional problems, and who also formulated a controversial theory of personality.

b. _____ Swiss biologist whose careful observations of young children led to an influential theory of the development of thought processes in children.

c. _____ and _____ Two American behaviorists, both described in the textbook as provocative, who insisted that psychology must be made scientific by adopting a focus on observable behavior, *not* the mind or consciousness.

d. _____ Russian physiologist whose studies of salivary conditioning in dogs earned him the Nobel prize.

Contemporary Psychology

18. Over many years, psychologists engaged in vigorous discussions about the extent to which built-in mechanisms and experience each contributed to human characteristics, taking positions in the _____-_____ **debate**. In addressing this issue, the textbook author takes the position that **nurture** *(is far more important than / is far less important than / works on what is endowed by)* **nature**.

19. Each person is a complex system existing within a larger social system. Accordingly, it makes sense to seek explanations of thought and emotion from various **perspectives**, or stated another way, at various **levels of analysis**. For example, as textbook author David Myers mentions in the video episode, questions about human happiness can be posed and answered using various perspectives. Match each research question (a–g) with the appropriate *level of analysis (perspective)* from the Key List. Write the correct term in the blank provided.

Key List
neuroscience
evolutionary
behavior genetics
psychodynamic
behavioral
cognitive
social-cultural

a. _____ What kinds of facial expressions, actions, and verbalizations distinguish happy people from less happy people? What kinds of observable conditions in the environment seem to have an influence on a person's reported level of happiness?

b. _____ How do an individual's expectations, perceptions, and inter-pretations of their circumstances affect their level of happiness?

c. _____ Do people from different countries around the world vary in their average level of happiness? In what ways do people's expressions of their level of happiness or unhappiness vary according to cultural influences?

d. _____ Do happy and unhappy people have differences in their patterns of brain chemistry or brain activity?

e. _____ Is there a selective survival advantage in being relatively happy most of the time? Are happy people more likely than unhappy people to notice and correct problems that threaten their survival? Do happy people attract mates more readily and reproduce more offspring?

f. _____ Might people be happy or unhappy for reasons they cannot fully know, based on influences at an unconscious level of the mind?

g. _____ To what extent do hereditary factors contribute to happiness? Do twin studies reveal greater similarities in the level of happiness of identical twins than of fraternal twins? Does the happiness level of an adopted person correspond more closely to the happiness of their biological parent or their adoptive parent?

20. The textbook author and various experts interviewed in the video suggest that although each perspective or level of analysis has its limitations, the various levels of analysis tend to be *(complementary / contradictory)*. If we integrate our explanations from various levels of analysis, we arrive at what is known as a _____ perspective.

21. Psychology is not only a science but is also a helping profession. At times, psychologists conduct _____ **research** in which the goal is simply to increase our knowledge about behavior and mental processes (as in biological, developmental, social, personality, and cognitive psychology). However, when they use research to solve practical problems, psychologists are said to be doing _____ **research**, as in the case of _____-_____ psychologists, whose research finds direct applications in workplace settings.

22. Various professionals apply psychology in assisting people with personal and relationship issues, or in treating those with problems such as depression or anxiety. Match each description given in items a–c with one of the types of *helping professionals* listed in the Key List.

    Key List
    clinical psychologists
    counseling psychologists
    psychiatrists

    a. _____ Medical doctors who are licensed to prescribe medications and to use psychotherapy and/or medical treatments for psychological disorders.

    b. _____ Provide assistance to people seeking help with challenges and transitions in dealing with school, work, or family life.

    c. _____ Professionals who are trained to administer and interpret psychological tests, diagnose disorders, and conduct therapy with people who seek help for depression, anxiety, or other disorders.

23. To study more effectively, the textbook author recommends that students use the **SQ3R technique**, whose steps (in order) are to first S_____ the assigned material, then formulate Q_____s about the information the assignment will cover, then R_____, R_____, and finally R_____.

24. The author also recommends that students *(distribute / concentrate)* their study time, because research has shown that *(massed / spaced)* study promotes better learning than *(massed / spaced)* study sessions.

25. **Overlearning** involves devoting extra study time, *beyond* what is required merely to understand while going through the assigned material. Overlearning *(improves / decreases)* retention of the information.

26. **Smart test-taking tips** from the textbook author include the advice to read over any essay questions *(before / after)* completing the multiple choice section of the test, and to treat a multiple choice question as though it is a *(fill-in-the-blank / true-false)* item, formulating an answer in your mind before looking at the answer choices.

SELF TEST

Read each question and circle the letter of the best answer. When you have completed the Self Test, check your answers against the key at the end of this lesson. If you have answered any items incorrectly, review the appropriate materials to correct misunderstandings and cement your knowledge.

1. Philosophers in ancient Greece, including Socrates and Plato,
   a. used all of the same scientific tools as today's psychologists, but arrived at different conclusions.
   b. were entirely unaware of the kinds of issues and questions that concern today's scientific psychologists.
   c. had nothing in common with today's psychologists.
   d. offered ideas on many of the same matters as are studied scientifically by today's psychologists.

2. Which of the following philosophers rejected the notion of inborn ideas, insisting instead that experience is the source of all knowledge?
   a. Aristotle and Locke
   b. Plato and Descartes
   c. Socrates and Bacon
   d. Plato and Aristotle

3. Which of the following philosophers advocated the idea that the mind or soul is separate from the body?
   a. Socrates, Plato, and Aristotle
   b. Socrates, Plato, and Descartes
   c. Aristotle, Socrates, and Plato
   d. Aristotle, Socrates, and Descartes

4. René Descartes' philosophy
   a. influenced Socrates' and Plato's philosophical ideas.
   b. held that the mind (soul) and body are separate, but that the mind can influence the body.
   c. held that soul and body are not separable.
   d. did not take any position on the issue of the relationship between mind and body.

5. According to W.V.O. Quine's comments in the video, French philosopher René Descartes proposed that the mind or soul could affect the body at an area of the brain known as the
   a. prefrontal cortex.
   b. temporal lobe.
   c. thalamus.
   d. pineal gland.

6. Which movement in the early history of psychology was most strongly and directly influenced by the evolutionary theory of Charles Darwin?
   a. Functionalism
   b. Structuralism
   c. Behaviorism
   d. Introspectionism

7. A person who is trained in the techniques of introspection would have expertise in
   a. objectively observing and recording events as they occur in the external environment.
   b. designing carefully controlled experiments and surveys for gathering scientific data.
   c. reflecting on and reporting their own inner sensations, images, and feelings in a particular situation.
   d. using logical analysis to arrive at reliable and valid conclusions about the world around them.

8. The origin of the science of psychology as we know it today is generally traced back to
   a. the opening of Wundt's laboratory in Germany in the late 1800s.
   b. Skinner's publication of *The Behavior of Organisms* in the 1930s.
   c. Darwin's theory of evolution and the publication of *On the Origin of Species by Means of Natural Selection* in 1859.
   d. Freud's publication of *The Interpretation of Dreams* in 1900.

9. Early in its history, psychology was defined as the scientific study of ____; but from about 1920 to 1960 leading thinkers, including Watson and Skinner, argued that psychology should be redefined as the scientific study of ____.
   a. animals; humans
   b. humans; animals
   c. the mind or consciousness; observable behavior
   d. observable behavior; the mind or consciousness

10. In the textbook, author David Myers emphasizes the point that psychology is defined primarily by its
    a. findings–the collection of facts and opinions accepted by professionals in the field.
    b. methods–an insistence on testing ideas and opinions with rigorously designed scientific observations and experiments.
    c. authorities–the credibility and respect awarded to important people who have contributed to the field of psychology over its history.
    d. traditions–the history and ways of thinking built up over many hundreds of years, as educated people have contemplated what makes people act as they do.

11. William James was a major contributor to the early development of psychology who
    a. developed the functionalism school of thought and authored the first textbook in psychology.
    b. opened the first laboratory for the scientific study of psychology.
    c. formulated the theory of psychoanalysis and conducted investigations of the unconscious mind.
    d. developed the first widely used intelligence test.

12. The first woman to be elected president of the American Psychological Association was
    a. W. James.
    b. B. F. Skinner.
    c. M. W. Calkins.
    d. J. B. Watson.

13. In his comments in the video, psychologist and Nobel laureate Daniel Kahneman traces his fascination with people back as early as his childhood, when a frightening and confusing encounter he had with a German soldier during World War II made him realize that
    a. people have no control over their own actions.
    b. people are innately good, but cultural experience can distort us and bring out negative and destructive behaviors.
    c. nurture is far more important than nature in determining our actions.
    d. people are complex, and they can possess both good and bad characteristics.

14. In regard to the "nature-nurture" issue, textbook author David Myers takes the position that
    a. "nature" determines our physical makeup, but "nurture" determines our behavior.
    b. "nature" is far more important than "nurture" in determining our behavior.
    c. "nurture" is far more important than "nature" in determining our behavior.
    d. "nurture" works on what "nature" endows.

15. Which of the following statements best captures the basic idea of Darwin's concept of natural selection?
    a. Those inherited characteristics which contribute to survival and reproduction will be more likely to be passed on to succeeding generations.
    b. Changes in the environment force individuals to make rapid adaptations directly in response to those changes.
    c. Humans naturally select from the environment those things which meet their personal needs and naturally reject the things they do not like.
    d. The most physically fit members of the species survive, and this process brings overall improvements in the species over generations.

16. A psychologist who researches changes in brain activity, blood pressure, heart rate, and adrenal hormone levels when a person is angry would be using the ____ perspective or level of analysis in psychology.
    a. psychodynamic
    b. social-cultural
    c. neuroscience
    d. evolutionary

17. Professor Miura explains to her students the theory that powerful unconscious motives underlie our preferences for certain types of romantic partners, and that such preferences relate to unresolved conflicts we had with our parents during our very early childhood years. This explanation fits most closely with the ____ perspective or level of analysis.
    a. psychodynamic
    b. behavior genetics
    c. neurosciences
    d. evolutionary

18. Dr. Chavez's research involves conducting surveys of adults in several countries (United States, Canada, Mexico, Chile, and Argentina). The research is aimed at comparing the expectations of adults in these different countries about the role of fathers in childrearing. Dr. Chavez's work fits best with the ____ perspective or level of analysis.
    a. psychodynamic
    b. social-cultural
    c. behavioral
    d. neurosciences

19. Research with identical and fraternal twins, aimed at determining how strongly our hereditary material and our experiences influence individual characteristics, is an especially important tool for psychologists whose research fits with the _____ perspective or level of analysis.
    a. behavior genetics
    b. cognitive
    c. social-cultural
    d. psychodynamic

20. In the biopsychosocial approach to psychology, the various levels of analysis or perspectives that can be used to understand behavior are viewed as
    a. inadequate.
    b. complementary.
    c. contradictory.
    d. indistinguishable

21. Which of the following subfields of psychology is most focused on *applied research* (rather than basic research)?
    a. personality psychology
    b. social psychology
    c. biological psychology
    d. industrial/organizational psychology

22. Which kind of psychologist is trained to study, diagnose, and treat people who have psychological disorders?
    a. social psychologist
    b. personality psychologist
    c. clinical psychologist
    d. developmental psychologist

23. Which of the following describes counseling psychologists?
    a. They are trained as medical doctors and are licensed to prescribe medications.
    b. They help to improve well-being in people who are coping with challenges in daily living such as with work, school, or family issues.
    c. They most often work in an industrial setting, helping employers to select, train, and boost productivity of employees.
    d. They diagnose, test, and conduct psychotherapy with patients who have serious mental and emotional disorders.

24. The letters in the SQ3R method
    a. remind the student to complete two important preliminary steps before beginning to read, and to follow reading with additional steps, including reviewing.
    b. stand for the importance for students of answering Study Questions as they Read, Read, and Read again.
    c. stand for "Simplify, Quote, Research, Read, and Repeat."
    d. remind students to "Stay Quiet, and to demonstrate Resourcefulness, Respect, Responsibility" during class sessions.

25. Which of the following is NOT one of the textbook author's study recommendations for students taking a psychology course?
    a. Overlearn the material.
    b. Use the SQ3R method while studying.
    c. If a test contains both multiple-choice questions and essays, turn first to the essays and jot down just a few notes before you work on the multiple-choice questions.
    d. In scheduling your study sessions, use massed rather than spaced practice.

ANSWER KEY FOR THE ACTIVE REVIEW EXERCISES

In the Answer Key for the Active Review Exercises throughout this study guide, the correct answers are given first, followed by the learning outcome number in [ ], and finally the source of the material.

1. philosophy; [3] Textbook, Video 1
2. behavior; mental processes; [3] Textbook, Video 1
3. methods; [2, 3] Textbook
4. test; [3] Textbook
5. Aristotle; [1] Textbook
6. Aristotle; [1] Textbook
7. Descartes; agreed; separate; innate; pineal gland; [1] Textbook, Video 1
8. Locke; empiricism; [1] Textbook
9. (a) Plato; Socrates; [1] Textbook (b) Locke; [1] Textbook (c) Darwin; [1] Textbook (d) Descartes; [1] Textbook, Video 1 (e) Aristotle; [1] Textbook
10. Germany; 1879; Wilhelm Wundt; [4] Textbook, Video 1
11. structuralism; introspection; [4] Textbook
12. declined; unreliable; [4] Textbook
13. functionalism; Darwin; James; [4] Textbook
14. men; Whiton Calkins; denied; two-thirds; [5] Textbook
15. second; American Psychological Association; [5] Textbook
16. The achievements of most of these individuals are summarized not just in the assigned reading, but also in the "Story of Psychology: A Timeline" provided in the front cover of your textbook. To assist you in reviewing, next to each name this answer key provides a date from the Timeline, under which you can find the person's name and major achievements listed. (a) Wilhelm Wundt *(1879);* (b) Margaret Floy Washburn *(1894);* (c) William James *(1890);* (d) Edward Titchener; (e) Mary Whiton Calkins *(1893, 1905);* [4] Textbook (and Video 1 for item a)

17. (a) Freud *(1900);* (b) Piaget *(1923);* (c) Watson *(1913),* Skinner *(1938);* (d) Pavlov *(1905);* [4] Textbook
18. nature-nurture; works on what is endowed by; [7] Textbook
19. (a) behavioral (Point of focus: Observable events) (b) cognitive (Focus: How we encode, process, store, and retrieve information) (c) social-cultural (Focus: How behavior and thinking processes vary across situations and cultures) (d) neuroscience (Focus: Physical processes of the body, including brain activity); Textbook (e) evolutionary (Focus: How natural selection promotes the perpetuation of one's genes) (f) psychodynamic (Focus: The role of unconscious drives and conflicts in behavior) (g) behavior genetics (Focus: The contribution of our genes and our environment to our individual differences); [9] Textbook, Video 1
20. complementary; biopsychosocial; [9] Textbook, Video 1
21. basic; applied; industrial/organizational; [10] Textbook
22. (a) psychiatrists; Textbook (b) counseling psychologists; Textbook (c) clinical psychologists; [11] Textbook
23. Survey; Question; Read; Review; Reflect; [12] Textbook
24. distribute; spaced; massed; [12] Textbook
25. improves; [12] Textbook
26. before; fill-in-the-blank; [12] Textbook

ANSWER KEY FOR THE SELF TEST

Item #	Answer	Learning Outcome #	Source	Item #	Answer	Learning Outcome #	Source
1.	d	1	Textbook	14.	d	7	Textbook
2.	a	1, 6	Textbook	15.	a	8	Textbook
3.	b	1	Textbook	16.	c	9	Textbook, Video 1
4.	b	1	Textbook, Video 1	17.	a	9	Textbook
5.	d	1	Video 1	18.	b	9	Textbook, Video 1
6.	a	2	Textbook	19.	a	9	Textbook, Video 1
7.	c	2	Textbook	20.	b	9	Textbook, Video 1
8.	a	2	Textbook, Video 1	21.	d	10	Textbook
9.	c	3	Textbook, Video 1	22.	c	10, 11	Textbook
10.	b	3	Textbook	23.	b	11	Textbook
11.	a	4	Textbook	24.	a	12	Textbook
12.	c	5	Textbook	25.	d	12	Textbook
13.	d	6	Video 1				

Lesson 2 (Critical Thinking and Research)

Endless Questions

Assignments

Reading: Chapter 1, "Thinking Critically with Psychological Science," in *Psychology* by David Myers (Modules 2 and 3 in the modular version of *Psychology*)

Video: Episode 2, "Endless Questions"

LEARNING OUTCOMES

Familiarize yourself with the Learning Outcomes for this lesson before you begin the assignments. Return to them to check your learning after completing the Steps to Learning Success. Careful work on these materials should equip you to accomplish the outcomes.

Thinking Critically with Psychological Science (Module 2)

1. Explain how errors of common sense judgment such as **hindsight bias** and the **overconfidence phenomenon** make it important to rely on careful observations and measurements in reaching conclusions.

2. Discuss the **scientific attitude** and its relationship to the elements of **critical thinking**.

3. Describe the relationship between **theories**, **hypotheses**, and the process of research.

4. State what **operational definitions** are, explain why they are important, and give examples.

5. Discuss the importance of **replication** of research.

Frequently Asked Questions about Psychology (Module 2)

6. Discuss issues regarding the pertinence of laboratory research to real life, and the generality of psychology principles across the boundaries of culture and gender.

7. List reasons for the use of non-human species in psychology research, and discuss some of the ethical issues involved in animal research.

8. Describe some of the benefits of using virtual reality (the **immersive virtual environment** or **IVE**) as a tool in psychological research.

9. Discuss issues related to the use of deception in psychological research.

10. List and explain psychologists' major ethical obligations to human research participants.

Description (Module 3)

11. Distinguish between **case study**, **surveys**, and **naturalistic observation**, and discuss the advantages and limitations of each.

12. Explain how surveys involving appropriate **sampling** from a **population** can counteract the **false consensus effect**, and discuss **random sampling** as a means of arriving at a **representative sample**.

Correlation (Module 3)

13. Explain how **correlational research** is conducted.

14. Compare and contrast **positive** and **negative correlation**, and describe what a **correlation coefficient** and a **scatterplot** can reveal.

15. Explain why it is a mistake to conclude that **correlation** reveals cause and effect.

16. Explain how an **illusory correlation** may develop and how illusory correlations can be counteracted.

Experimentation (Module 3)

17. Describe how an **experiment** is conducted, and explain how experiments allow researchers to draw conclusions about cause and effect.

18. Explain the importance of a **control condition** in an experiment, and state why experimenters often use **random assignment** of participants to **experimental** and **control conditions**.

19. Identify and distinguish between the **independent variable** and the **dependent variable** in an experiment, and provide examples of each.

20. Explain the **placebo effect** and use of the **double-blind procedure** in experiments.

Statistical Reasoning (Module 3)

21. Explain why it is important to look carefully at scale labels and values before drawing conclusions about data displayed in a graph.

22. Compare and contrast the **mean**, **median**, and **mode** as **measures of central tendency**, and be able to calculate each of these statistics when given a simple list of numbers.

23. Identify and distinguish between the **range** and the **standard deviation**.

24. Summarize principles that can guide decisions about whether to generalize on the basis of a sample.

25. Explain the concept of **statistical significance**, and distinguish between statistical significance and practical significance.

ACTIVE REVIEW

Each item in this section is based on material presented in the video or the textbook assignment for this lesson, or both. Complete this section, referring as needed to your notes or the source materials themselves. Answers are provided at the end of this lesson.

Thinking Critically with Psychological Science

1. Common sense and intuition can often be misleading. For example, whether given either a summary of actual research findings or a summary that runs opposite to the real result, people tend to view *(the real result / the opposite result / either result)* as obvious common sense. This tendency is known as the _____ **bias**, which has sometimes been called the *(I-knew-it-all-along / who-would-have-known)* phenomenon.

2. Another pitfall of common sense is the **over-confidence phenomenon**—our tendency to be *(more confident than correct / more correct than confident / neither confident nor correct)* in our judgments.

3. To avoid some of the limitations of relying on common sense, psychologists need to make careful and objective measurements, basing their conclusions on *(intuition / evidence / logic)*.

4. List and explain the characteristics of the **scientific attitude**. _____

_____

_____

_____

_____

_____

_____

5. Describe the relationship of the **scientific attitude** to **critical thinking**._____

_____

_____

_____

_____

_____

6. A research study typically begins with the formulation of a testable proposition, known as a *(hypothesis / theory)*, which can be based on an informal hunch, on previous research, or might be derived from a *(hypothesis / theory)*.

7. Before a researcher can conduct a test of a particular **hypothesis** (such as the idea that there is a the relationship between people's happiness and their

health), _____ **definitions** are needed, specifying exactly how each major concept is to be *(explained / measured / labeled)* within the research study. For example, out of the many possible ways to define "happiness," a researcher might choose measurements such as: _____

_____

_____

_____

_____

_____

8. In addition to clarifying communication, operational definitions make it *(easier / harder)* for scientists to _____ (repeat) others' research, increasing *(confidence / doubt)* in the reliability of findings when the results of the **replication** match what was originally found.

Frequently Asked Questions about Psychology

9. David Myers emphasizes the point that underlying principles of behavior are sufficiently *(different / similar)* across different cultures that research on one cultural group often has *(considerable / limited)* relevance in another cultural group.

10. While most research in psychology involves human participants, some psychologists study other species. List several advantages or benefits of animal research.

_____

_____

_____

_____

_____

_____

_____

11. According to a survey conducted in 2000, 98 percent of animal researchers *(favored / opposed)* government regulations protecting primates, dogs, and cats, while a *(majority / minority)* of these animal researchers favored "regulations providing for the humane care of rats and mice."

12. Some researchers have used technology to stretch the bounds of research with human participants. Jim Blascovich explains in the video that he uses computer-generated virtual reality in the form of the IVE (which stands for the _____

_____ _____)

to create ecological realism while exerting a high degree of experimental control in social psychology experiments. The IVE allows researchers to manipulate a specific variable (such as personal distance), while other factors are *(held constant / also varied)*. Because a given IVE is the same each time it is presented, the use of the **Immersive Virtual Environment** *(simplifies / complicates / prevents)* the process of **replication** of research.

13. According to ethical principles formulated by professional organizations of psychologists in the United States and Britain, psychologists conducting research with humans should:

   a. *(reveal / conceal)* in advance enough information about the research that participants can provide *(informed / uninformed)* consent to participate;

   b. conduct the research in a way that *(minimizes / disregards / maximizes)* the potential for harm or discomfort to research participants;

   c. treat information gained from individual participants as *(confidential / open and public)*; and

   d. offer participants *(full / deceptive / partial)* explanation of the research after it is over.

14. Deception in psychology research with humans is *(always / sometimes / never)* considered permissible. Briefly explain why deception may be necessary in some types of psychology research, and describe the ethical obligations of researchers who design research involving deception. _____

_____

_____

_____

_____

15. Universities and other research institutes have ethics committees composed of specialists in the field *(as well as / instead of)* people from the community, who must approve a research study before it can be conducted. David Myers comments in the video that ethical guidelines for research today are *(much stricter / less strict)* than was the case 20 years ago.

Description

16. Psychologists have *(two / three / many)* research methods available to them, and each of these methods has specific *(strengths / limitations / strengths and limitations)*.

17. Psychologists use **case study**, **surveys**, and **naturalistic observation** as ways to arrive at *(descriptions / predictions / explanations /control)* of behavior.

18. Using the **case study** method, scientists study *(one or a few / many)* individuals at a time, usually in *(less / more)* depth than with other research methods. In contrast, **surveys** generally provide data in *(less / more)* depth on *(fewer/ more)* individuals.

19. The wording or ordering of survey questions is important, because minor changes can exert *(no / a minor / a major)* impact on survey results. However, carefully designed **surveys**, using a *(representative / biased)* **sample** from the **population** of interest, can provide solid statistics to help combat the _____ _____ **effect**—our tendency to assume that others' beliefs, attitudes, and opinions resemble our own.

20. The larger target group whose attitudes or opinions a surveyer wishes to characterize is called the _____, while the set of individuals actually selected from that group to participate in the survey is termed the _____. According to the textbook, a smaller **representative sample** with only 100 participants would be *(better than / equivalent to / worse than)* a nonrepresentative sample including 500 participants, because the *(size / representativeness)* of a sample is most critical to the ability to generalize results from the sample to the population of interest. The most common method of drawing a representative sample is _____ **sampling** from the target population.

21. Researchers who observe and record behavior in its natural setting are using the method known as

_____ _____.

List some of the advantages and limitations of this method.

Advantages:_____
_____
_____

Limitations:_____
_____
_____

Correlation

22. Researchers investigate the naturally occurring associations between different things by means of *(correlational / experimental)* studies. When one thing is found to vary in association with another, we can say that these two variables _____. The degree to which one variable (such as health) varies along with another (such as happiness) can be expressed with a statistic called the _____ _____. If two variables are found to **correlate**, then we can say that a change in one of these *(causes / describes / explains / predicts)* a change in the other.

23. Given that taller people generally tend to weigh more and shorter people tend to weigh less, we would probably find that there is *(positive / negative / zero)* **correlation** between height and body weight. But because there are some short people who are unusually heavy, and some tall people who are unusually thin and light, the **correlation coefficient** relating height and weight *(is / is not)* a perfect positive correlation of +1.0.

24. A **negative correlation** would be present when we see that one variable increases as another variable *(increases / decreases / remains constant)*. For example, if higher levels of emotional depression are associated with lower levels of self-esteem, we can say that there

is a *(positive / negative / zero)* **correlation** between depression and self-esteem.

25. According to comments by David Myers in the video, research has demonstrated that age is generally unrelated to a person's happiness, suggesting a *(positive / negative / zero)* **correlation** between these two variables.

26. Indicate what kind of correlation (positive correlation, negative correlation, or zero correlation) is suggested by the *hypothetical relationships* described in items a–f below. Write your answers in the blanks provided.

    <u>Key List</u>
    positive correlation
    negative correlation
    zero correlation

    a. _____ Among people diagnosed with heart disease, the lower the annual income, the higher the annual death rate is found to be.

    b. _____ The age at which human infants first stand alone and walk is generally unrelated to the amount of time their parents spend encouraging them to stand and take steps with assistance.

    c. _____ Among adolescents, increased time spent viewing violent television programming is associated with increased frequency of aggressive behavior.

    d. _____ In adults, the lower the level of education attained, the lower the annual income tends to be.

    e. _____ The greater the amount of time mothers spend reading to their children, the more advanced the childrens' language development tends to be.

    f. _____ The greater the body weight for women of a given height, the lower is their level of annual earnings from fashion modeling.

27. When a correlation between two variables is discovered, knowing one of the variables allows us to *(explain / predict)* the other variable; but the correlation does <u>not</u> provide a(n) *(explanation / prediction)*.

28. The existence of a correlation suggests the *(presence / absence / possibility)* of a cause-and-effect relationship between the variables (A and B) under study. But as strongly emphasized in the video and the textbook, a key point in critical thinking is that **correlation** *(rules out / proves / does not prove)* causation, and that various alternative interpretations are possible when we find that two variables are correlated. For example, if variables A and B correlate, it could be that a change in A causes B to change, <u>or</u> that a change in B causes a change in A. Finally, there could be a _____ **variable problem**–the complication that the association between A and B might have arisen because some entirely different variable (variable C, which was not measured or considered in the research) may have caused both A and B to change, independently of one another.

29. If a researcher were to find a positive correlation between alcohol use (variable A) and depression (variable B), several different explanations of this finding could be proposed. To arrive at a specific explanation for this correlation, further research *(would/ would not)* be necessary.

30. Suggest three plausible explanations for increased rates of depression among people who consume greater amounts of alcohol, including one explanation that involves a third **variable**.

    _____
    _____
    _____
    _____
    _____
    _____
    _____
    _____

31. If we strongly suspect that a correlation exists between two things, we tend to notice and remember instances that fit with our preconceptions, and fail to notice cases that do not fit. Under such circumstances, we have the makings of a(n) _____ _____, which reflects our inclination to perceive patterns where none exist.

Experimentation

32. **Experiments** require far *(more / less)* researcher control over variables than do descriptive or correlational research studies. David Myers states in the video that scientists love to do experiments wherever they can, because experiments allow them to sort out *(cause and effect / correlations / the laundry / the sheep from the goats)*.

33. In an experiment, a researcher actively manipulates a variable of interest (known as the _____ _____), while equalizing other variables or holding them constant, and then measures the _____ _____ to see if the previous experimental manipulation had any effect. If only one variable was manipulated by the researcher while every other relevant variable was equalized or held constant, it is logical to conclude that any change measured in the _____ **variable** must have been caused by the change the researcher made in the _____ **variable**. Thus, a properly designed experiment *(is / is not)* an appropriate way for researchers to identify cause-and-effect relationships.

34. The best way to evaluate the effectiveness of a particular treatment for a disorder is with evidence from a(n) *(anecdote / correlational study / experiment / naturalistic observation)*, precisely because this research method *(allows / does not allow)* cause-and-effect conclusions.

35. To conduct an experiment to investigate whether a new antidepressant medication effectively relieves depression, participants in the research should be *(voluntarily / randomly)* **assigned** to either a(n) _____ **condition**, in which participants would receive a particular dose of the new medication, or a(n) _____ **condition**, in which participants would receive no medication. Ideally, this no-medication group should be given a _____, an inactive substance that looks just like the real medication and is administered in exactly the same way.

36. Explain why researchers testing the effects of a treatment for depression would need to include a **control condition** in which participants receive a **placebo**.

_____
_____
_____
_____
_____
_____

37. In experiments testing the effects of a medication on depression, the *amount of medication* received (the dose of an active substance versus a placebo) is the _____ **variable**, manipulated by the researcher under controlled conditions. Participants' *level of depression* after treatment would constitute the _____ **variable**, measured to see if the researcher's manipulation of the independent variable had any effect.

38. Explain why experimenters investigating treatments for depression would randomly assign participants to **experimental** and **control conditions**.

_____
_____
_____
_____
_____
_____
_____

39. To review the various *research methods*, match items a–e with the appropriate term from the Key List. Write your choices in the blanks provided.

Key List
case study
correlational research
experiment
naturalistic observation
survey

a. _____ Two different variables of interest are measured within each of a number of research participants, and the researcher checks for a systematic relationship between these two variables. If the two variables are found to be associated, knowing the value of one of these variables allows prediction of the other.

b. _____ An in-depth study of only one or a few selected individuals, this type of research yields a rich amount of descriptive detail. It is difficult to draw general conclusions from such studies, as the individuals may not be representative of any broader group; however, this type of research can be a valuable source of hypotheses for more controlled research studies.

c. _____ Observations are made under carefully controlled conditions, with the researcher manipulating one variable while holding other variables constant and observing the outcome of the manipulation. This research method permits researchers to identify cause-and-effect relationships.

d. _____ This research method involves collecting the responses of many people to carefully worded questions, typically inquiring about their thoughts, attitudes, and opinions. If random sampling is used to assure that the participants are representative of the larger population, the researcher can use the data from the sample of participants to draw conclusions about the larger population.

e. _____ The researcher observes and records events as they occur within their natural setting, and without manipulating or controlling conditions. This research method allows description of events of interest, but does not provide explanations.

Statistical Reasoning

40. Research data can be organized and summarized through graphs, or with statistical **measures of central tendency** and **measures of variation**. Explain why it is important to scrutinize the scale labels along the axes of a bar graph before drawing conclusions. _____
_____
_____
_____
_____
_____

41. The three statistical **measures of central tendency** used to summarize data are the _____ (the arithmetic average of all the scores), the _____ (the middle score when all the scores have been arranged in order), and the _____ (the most frequently occurring of all the scores). Of these three measures, the _____ is the most sensitive to the value of each score, and therefore can be pulled in toward an extreme score when the distribution of scores is **skewed**.

42. Developmental psychologists have conducted research to reveal the average age at which children take their first steps, walking without assistance. For the following list of hypothetical ages (in months) at which nine infants from one extended family first walked alone, calculate the descriptive statistics requested below:

Ages in months: 9, 12, 15, 12, 11, 13, 12, 11, 10

mean = _____ months

median = _____ months

mode = _____ months

43. Two statistical **measures of variation** in a set of data include the _____ and the _____
_____. An average based on data having a smaller **range** and/or a smaller **standard deviation** would be *(more / less)* reliable than an average for a set of data having a larger value for its statistical measures of variation.

44. David Myers admonishes us in the textbook not to be too *(impressed / interested / skeptical)* when we hear anecdotes. To arrive at solid generalizations, it is safer to rely on data from research conducted on a *(larger / smaller)* number of *(representative / hand-picked)* cases.

45. If the difference between two sets of measurements (e.g., the average height of adults in Japan and the U.S.) is large and reliable, we could say that this difference has **statistical** _____, meaning that this difference is *(likely / unlikely)* to be based simply on chance variation between the two samples.

46. Psychologists consider a result to be **statistically significant** if it appears to have *(less / more)* than a 5 percent probability of having occurred by chance alone. It is important to recognize that statistical significance of a result *(is / is not)* the same as practical importance.

SELF TEST

Read each question and circle the letter of the best answer. When you have completed the Self Test, check your answers against the key at the end of this lesson. If you have answered any items incorrectly, review the appropriate materials to correct misunderstandings and cement your knowledge.

1. In the video, Daniel Kahneman describes an experience in the military when he was assigned the task of observing people during challenging leaderless group activities and using his common sense to judge their qualifications for officer training. Kahneman stated that even when he confidently believed he could pick out people with the best qualifications for leadership, his predictions turned out to be essentially worthless. This tendency to believe our common sense judgments are correct is known as
   a. hindsight bias.
   b. the intuition gap.
   c. the overconfidence phenomenon.
   d. the confirmation bias.

2. Hindsight bias contributes to
   a. our tendency to view either an actual research result or its opposite as obvious common sense.
   b. our exaggerated confidence in the correctness of our judgments.
   c. both the above.
   d. none of the above.

3. According to the textbook, a scientific attitude incorporates
   a. curiosity, skepticism, and humility.
   b. cynicism, stubbornness, and amazement.
   c. hindsight, overconfidence, and false consensus.
   d. certainty, close-mindedness, and self-importance.

4. In science, a theory
   a. is a hunch based on intuition.
   b. organizes facts and can suggest hypotheses for future research.
   c. is the same as a hypothesis.
   d. has no evidence to support it.

5. Professor Porter thinks there could be a relationship between hours of sleep and irritability, with sleep-deprived people hypothesized to exhibit greater irritability. Before she can test her hypothesis, she must
   a. develop an operational definition of irritability.
   b. develop a theory to explain why such a relationship would be suspected.
   c. design a case study.
   d. all of the above.

6. When a researcher repeats research that was done before to find out whether the same result occurs again, we say that the researcher has ____ the previous research.
   a. reverberated
   b. replicated
   c. simulated
   d. plagiarized

7. The aim of most laboratory psychology research is to
   a. observe precisely the same behaviors as those that occur in everyday life.
   b. observe behaviors that are unlike any that could ever occur in real life outside the laboratory.
   c. test general theoretical principles under simplified and controlled conditions, rather than to recreate real life.
   d. test individual behavior in isolation, without any social influences whatsoever.

8. Which of the following practices would raise serious ethical problems, according to the guidelines of the American Psychological Association and the British Psychological Association?
   a. Coercing people to participate in research.
   b. Withholding information that could affect the person's decision about whether to participate in the research.
   c. Exposing people to conditions that would be likely to produce lasting harm or injury.
   d. All of the above.

9. A researcher who wants to find out more about happiness might choose to study one or two very happy individuals in depth, finding out about their life conditions, daily activities, family backgrounds,

upbringing, and significant life experiences, for example. Research such as this would be an example of
a. a case study.
b. an experiment.
c. a correlational research study.
d. naturalistic observation.

10. One advantage of a case study is that it
a. reveals causal relationships between variables because every relevant factor except the independent variable has been carefully controlled.
b. involves precise measurement under controlled conditions, making it the best research method for identifying cause-and-effect relationships.
c. yields results that can easily be generalized to the population at large because it involves drawing a random sample from the population of interest.
d. provides a great deal of rich and complex information, which can be a source of hypotheses for further carefully controlled research.

11. To choose a representative sample for a survey on attitudes toward alcohol consumption among the students attending one particular state university, a researcher would need to
a. advertise in the campus newspaper, soliciting student volunteers who are concerned with drinking habits at the university.
b. make efforts to include in the sample each and every individual enrolled at that university.
c. use random sampling from a list of all registered students at that campus.
d. base the sample on the latest national census.

12. To assure that survey results will be useful in reflecting characteristics of the population of interest, researchers should take steps to assure that their samples are
a. as large as possible.
b. reprehensible.
c. rational.
d. representative.

13. Students working on a project for a course in nutrition take turns sitting in a fast-food restaurant, observing and recording the amounts and types of food purchased by everyone patronizing the restaurant from 11 a.m. to 1 p.m. each weekday. The research method they are using is
a. a survey.
b. naturalistic observation.
c. an experiment.
d. a correlational study.

14. A researcher observes and records events on a downtown street as a homeless person asks for money from people passing by. After each request, the researcher marks down whether the passerby complied with or ignored the request, and later examines the data to see overall rates of compliance with the request. This research qualifies as
a. naturalistic observation.
b. a correlational research study.
c. a case study.
d. an experiment.

15. A correlation coefficient is useful because it provides statistical evidence of _____ between two variables, such a self-esteem and depression.
a. a cause-and-effect relationship
b. a false consensus
c. an illusory correlation
d. the strength and direction of a relationship

16. When a researcher has found a strong correlation between amount of exercise and mood, the researcher can safely conclude that:
a. exercise causes a change in mood.
b. exercise could not possibly cause a change in mood.
c. exercise patterns are associated with mood, but this association does not prove that there is a cause-and-effect relationship between the two.
d. changes in mood cause changes in exercise.

17. Parents who spend more time in conversation with their children are found to have toddlers with larger vocabularies. What would a critical thinker conclude upon finding out that this result had emerged from carefully conducted large-scale correlational research?
a. Language stimulation from a parent causes a child's vocabulary to develop more rapidly.
b. More rapid vocabulary development in a toddler encourages parents to spend more time talking with the child.
c. Some third factor, such as genes for above average language ability, are the cause of both the toddler's more rapid language development and the parents' greater inclination to engage in conversation.
d. Because correlation does not reveal causation, all we can conclude is that knowing parents' conversational habits at home could help us to predict the size of the toddler's vocabulary.

18. In an experiment, the researcher measures the _____ after a systematic manipulation of the _____ under controlled conditions.
    a. dependent variable … independent variable
    b. independent variable … dependent variable
    c. control condition … experimental condition
    d. placebo effect … participants

19. Why is random assignment of participants to conditions so commonly used in the design of experiments?
    a. It serves to equalize groups prior to the manipulation of the independent variable.
    b. It ensures a double-blind procedure.
    c. It confuses participants so they don't feel cheated if they fail to receive beneficial treatment.
    d. It prevents illusory correlations from forming.

20. A researcher studies peer influence on teenagers' risk-taking behavior by using a driving simulator, observing how often teen drivers speed up and how often they apply the brakes when faced with a green traffic light changing to a yellow caution light. Each research participant brings a friend to the laboratory. Half the participants are randomly assigned to be tested on the driving simulator with the friend present during the driving trials, and the other half are tested without the friend present. The hypothesis for the research is that teens who complete the driving trials with a friend present will be more likely to speed up in response to the yellow caution light than those who are tested with no friend present. In this research, the *independent variable* is
    a. the percentage of times the teen drivers speed up after the light changes to yellow.
    b. whether a friend is present or not during the driving simulator trials.
    c. the age of the teen driver.
    d. the group tested without a friend present.

21. A pharmaceutical firm is planning clinical trials of a newly developed medication that is anticipated to work effectively in relieving anxiety. The researchers need to give the new medication to a group of research participants to measure its effects on anxiety. However, they also need to
    a. give these same participants a placebo along with each dose of the medication.
    b. track anxiety in another group that is given a placebo instead of the newly devised medication.
    c. put the medication into the participants' food without telling them they will be consuming a medication.
    d. include all of the above procedures.

22. Which of the following descriptive statistics represents the arithmetic average of all the scores in an array?
    a. the mean
    b. the median
    c. the mode
    d. the range

23. Choose the *median* of the scores given here: 10, 80, 20, 20, 70, 30, 20, 30, 80.
    a. 40
    b. 70
    c. 20
    d. 30

24. Lisa and Lindsay, twin sisters, have similar body types. But when they weigh themselves each week, the scales show that Lisa's weight fluctuates somewhat more than Lindsay's. Accordingly, Lisa's weight data would show a larger _____ than Lindsay's.
    a. mean
    b. mode
    c. standard deviation
    d. statistical significance

25. When an average difference between groups is large and reliable and is judged to be statistically unlikely to have occurred on the basis of chance variation alone, psychologists would refer to this result as
    a. a false consensus.
    b. statistically significant.
    c. a random sample.
    d. a representative sample.

ANSWER KEYS FOR THE ACTIVE REVIEW

1. either result; hindsight; "I-knew-it-all-along"; [1] Textbook, Video 2
2. more confident than correct; [1] Textbook, Video 2
3. evidence; [1] Textbook, Video 2
4. *Your answer should include the following concepts:* 1) curiosity: an enthusiastic desire for exploration, aimed at developing understanding; 2) skepticism: a doubting or questioning attitude; a tendency to look for clear definitions of terms, consistency of logic, and sound empirical evidence; and 3) humility: an open-minded willingness to be proven wrong; [2] Textbook
5. *Your answer should reflect these ideas:* A scientific attitude promotes critical thinking. Critical thinking entails carrying scientific attitudes over into day-to-day living—for example, scrutinizing claims to uncover assumptions and biases, asking questions and checking for evidence behind claims encountered in conversation or presented in the news media, and considering alternative interpretations of facts; [2] Textbook
6. hypothesis; theory; [3] Textbook, Video 2
7. operational; measured. *To be correct, your answers should refer to several specific things that can be measured objectively, such as:* 1) the ratings people provide on survey items asking them to report on their own happiness; 2) facial expressions, monitored by trained observers or through measurement of the tension in certain facial muscles that produce a smiling expression; 3) posture (erect or slumped); 4) the EEG activity in certain brain areas that regulate emotion, such as the left and right frontal lobes; [4] Textbook, Video 2
8. easier; replicate; confidence; [5] Textbook, Video 2
9. similar; considerable; [6] Textbook
10. *Your answer should touch on several of these points:* 1) Many psychologists have an interest in other species as well as in humans. 2) There is great similarity in human and animal physiology; enough that research discoveries with animals have provided important treatments for human disease. 3) Some types of research would be difficult or impossible to do on humans. 4) Research with animals allows greater simplicity and greater control over variables (genetic background, developmental history, diet, living conditions); [7] Video 2
11. favored; majority; [7] Textbook
12. Immersive Virtual Environment; held constant; simplifies; [8] Video 2
13. a) reveal, informed; b) minimizes; c) confidential; d) full; [9] Textbook
14. sometimes; *Your answer should include these ideas:* Deception can help researchers to capture human behavior in its purest form, without the distortions that might come with full awareness of what the researcher is looking for. At the end of the research, participants are debriefed, at which time they are informed of the true purpose of the procedures, including the reasons for the deception; [9] Video 2
15. as well as; much stricter; [9] Textbook, Video 2
16. many; strengths and limitations; [11] Textbook, Video 2
17. descriptions; Textbook, [11] Video 2
18. one or a few; more; less; more; [11] Textbook, Video 2
19. a major; representative; false consensus; [12] Textbook, Video 2
20. population; sample; better than; representativeness; random; [12] Textbook, Video 2
21. naturalistic observation; *Advantages:* Provides an objective description of behavior; realistic because behavior is observed in its usual environment. *Limitations:* Gives no information about people's thoughts, attitudes, or past behavior; does not provide an explanation of the behavior that is observed.; [11] Textbook, Video 2
22. correlational, correlate; correlation coefficient; predicts; [13] Textbook, Video 2
23. positive; is not; [14] Textbook, Video 2
24. decreases; negative; [14] Textbook, Video 2
25. zero; [15] Textbook, Video 2
26. (a) negative correlation (b) zero correlation (c) positive correlation (d) positive correlation (e) positive correlation (f) negative correlation; [14] Textbook, Video 2
27. predict; explanation; [14] Textbook, Video 2
28. possibility; does not prove; third; [15] Textbook, Video 2
29. would; [15] Textbook, Video 2
30. *Your answer should include ideas similar to those suggested here:* 1) Increased levels of alcohol consumption could cause increased depression; 2) depression might make people more likely to drink more alcohol; or 3) some third variable, such as difficulties with personal relationships, poor health habits, a genetic factor, or variations in brain chemistry, might contribute to a tendency toward heavier alcohol use and might also independently cause a person to be vulnerable to depression.; [15] Textbook, Video 2
31. illusory correlation; [16] Textbook
32. more; cause and effect; [17] Textbook, Video 2

33. independent variable; dependent variable; dependent; independent; is; [17, 19] Textbook, Video 2
34. experiment; allows; [17] Textbook
35. randomly; experimental; control; placebo; [17, 18, 20] Textbook, Video 2
36. *Your answer should include these ideas:* Depressed people can sometimes improve naturally over time, and the placebo control group would serve as a point of comparison, to check whether any greater improvement occurs in the experimental (medication) condition. The placebo is important to the double-blind procedure, keeping both the participant and the research assistant who gathers the data uninformed about who is getting the real medication. This permits a check on the specific effects of the medication, above and beyond the nonspecific effects exerted by peoples' expectations; [18, 20] Textbook, Video 2
37. independent; dependent; [14] Textbook, Video 2
38. *Your answer should include these ideas:* Random assignment of a large enough pool of participants would make the two groups similar at the beginning of the experiment. After random assignment, factors such as participants' ages, socioeconomic levels, overall health, history of depression, attitudes about medications, and enthusiasm about the research would be likely to average out as roughly equal for the two groups. If the two groups are balanced in this way at the outset, any difference between them at the end of the experiment is likely to be an effect of the independent variable, not a result of a pre-existing difference between the groups; [18] Textbook
39. (a) correlational study (b) case study (c) experiment (d) survey (e) naturalistic observation; [11, 13, 15, 17] Textbook, Video 2
40. *Your answer should include the main ideas presented here:* When scale values along the axes of graphs are spaced farther apart, the appearance of differences between bars of different sizes may be magnified or minimized. This can lead to a misjudgment of the actual size of differences if the reader fails to notice the precise scale values along the axis; [22] Textbook
41. mean; median; mode; mean; [22] Textbook
42. 11.67; 12; 12; [22] Textbook
43. range; standard deviation; more; [23] Textbook
44. impressed; larger; representative; [24] Textbook
45. significance; unlikely; [25] Textbook
46. less; is not; [25] Textbook

ANSWER KEY FOR THE SELF TEST

Item #	Answer	Learning Outcome #	Source	Item #	Answer	Learning Outcome #	Source
1.	c	1	Textbook, Video 2	14.	a	11	Textbook
2.	a	1	Textbook, Video 2	15.	d	14, 15, 16	Textbook
3.	a	2	Textbook	16.	c	13, 14, 15	Textbook, Video 2
4.	b	4	Textbook	17.	d	13, 15	Textbook, Video 2
5.	a	3	Textbook, Video 2	18.	a	17, 18, 19, 20	Textbook, Video 2
6.	b	5	Textbook, Video 2	19.	a	18	Textbook
7.	c	6, 7, 8	Textbook, Video 2	20.	b	19	Textbook, Video 2
8.	d	9	Textbook	21.	b	18	Textbook, Video 2
9.	a	11	Textbook, Video 2	22.	a	22	Textbook
10.	d	11	Textbook, Video 2	23.	d	22	Textbook
11.	c	12	Textbook, Video 2	24.	c	23	Textbook
12.	d	12, 24	Textbook, Video 2	25.	b	25	Textbook
13.	b	11	Textbook, Video 2				

Lesson 3 (Neuroscience and Behavior)

The Most Amazing Machine

Assignments

Reading: Chapter 2, "Neuroscience and Behavior," in *Psychology* by David Myers (Modules 4 and 5 in the modular version of *Psychology*)

Video: Episode 3, "The Most Amazing Machine"

LEARNING OUTCOMES

Familiarize yourself with the Learning Outcomes for this lesson before you begin the assignments. Return to them to check your learning after completing the Steps to Learning Success. Careful work on these materials should equip you to accomplish the outcomes.

Introduction (Module 4)

1. Describe philosophers' and phrenologists' prescientific efforts to understand the biological underpinnings of behavior and mental processes.

2. Define **biological psychology** and explain its focus.

Neural Communication (Module 4)

3. Explain what a **neuron** is, and list the parts of a typical neuron and their functions.

4. Compare, contrast, and describe the relationship between the **resting potential** and the **action potential** in neurons. Explain the chemical basis of these electrical activities.

5. Describe how neurons communicate with one another, explaining the relationship between **synapses**, **neurotransmitters**, and **receptors**.

6. List some of the best known neurotransmitters, and describe some of their normal functions and some of the conditions related to abnormalities in these neurotransmitters.

7. Explain the mechanisms by which certain drugs can affect **synaptic transmission**, citing specific examples.

The Nervous System (Module 4)

8. Outline the divisions and subdivisions of the **nervous system**, listing their functions and explaining the interrelationships among them.

9. Explain what a **reflex arc** is and how it functions, and compare this with complex **neural networks** in the nervous system.

The Endocrine System (Module 4)

10. Compare the **endocrine system** and the nervous system, and explain the idea that the brain and the endocrine system are closely connected entities.

The Brain (Module 5)

11. List and compare various methods for studying the brain, providing examples of research findings based on some of the more recently devised methods.

12. Compare and contrast the human **brain** with the brains of other species.

13. Describe the main functions of the brain structures reviewed in the textbook, including the **medulla**, **reticular formation**, **thalamus**, **cerebellum**, structures of the **limbic system** (**amygdala**, **hippocampus**, and **hypothalamus**), **cerebral cortex**, and **corpus callosum**.

14. Locate the four **lobes** of the **cerebral hemispheres** and list their functions.

15. Discuss **reward pathways** in the brain and the role of **dopamine** in reward and addictive behavior.

16. Discuss the involvement of the five specific brain areas in language.

17. Summarize evidence supporting the idea that some regions of the human brain possesses remarkable **plasticity**.

18. Describe **split-brain surgery**, the reasons for its use, and its effects. Explain how research studies on split- brain patients and people with intact brains have advanced our understanding of the **specialized functions of the left and right hemispheres**.

19. Compare patterns of hemispheric specialization for language in left- and right-handed people, and discuss research on what determines **handedness**.

ACTIVE REVIEW

Each item in this section is based on material presented in the video or the textbook assignment for this lesson, or both. Complete this section, referring as needed to your notes or the source materials themselves. Answers are provided at the end of this lesson.

Neuroscience and Behavior

1. Early efforts to illuminate the biological basis of behavior and cognition included Aristotle's idea that the mind emanated from the *(brain / eyes / heart / pancreas)*. By the 1800s, Franz Gall had devised *(biobumpology / physiology / phrenology / physiognomy)*, which promoted the idea that human abilities and personality traits correspond to specific bumps on the *(feet / hands / skull)*. Today we know that such bumps *(are / are not)* valid indicators of the traits they were claimed to reflect. But **phrenology** is credited with having advanced the idea that various aspects of behavior are controlled by different regions of the _____.

2. Researchers who study the connections between biological processes and behavior are known as

   _____ _____.

   David Myers places great importance on this specialty area of psychology by stating in the video that "Everything psychological is ultimately *(behavioral / biological / emotional / mental / futile)*."

Neural Communication

3. The individual cells that form the communicating networks of the nervous system are known as _____. The cell body of a typical **neuron** has a number of bushy fibers extending from it, known as _____, which *(receive / send)* information and then typically pass that information directly to the *(cell body / axon / other neurons)*. Another kind of extension of the neuron sends messages away from the **cell body** toward other neurons or to muscles or glands; this extension, the _____, can be very long indeed.

4. Some neurons have their **axon** insulated by a fatty substance called _____, which *(speeds / slows)* the passage of impulses along the axon. There is a(n) *(degeneration / overgrowth)* of the **myelin sheath** in the disease known as _____ _____, which is associated with a(n) *(increase / decrease)* in the speed of communication in some areas of the nervous system.

5. When the axon of a neuron is resting, not firing, the fluid inside the neuron has more *(positively charged / negatively charged / uncharged)* ions than does the fluid outside the neuron. During the neuron's **resting state**, positively charged _____ **ions** are kept outside of the axon. When the neuron fires, sodium ions *(rush in / are pumped out)* through open gates in the axon membrane, causing the one part of the axon to be *(depolarized / hyperpolarized)*.

6. In the video, Susan Greenfield describes signals sent within a neuron—the firing of impulses—as "little blips of electricity" called _____ _____, which can "zap down" the length of the *(axon / cell body / dendrite / myelin)*, sometimes at speeds in excess of *(20 / 200 / 2000)* miles per hour.

7. At any given time, the input signals to a neuron may have _____ effects, which encourage the neuron to fire, or _____ effects, which discourage firing. If the **excitatory** signals outweigh the **inhibitory** signals, resulting in the neuron's _____ being reached or exceeded, the neuron will produce **action potential** that is conducted along the entire length of the *(axon / dendrite)*. This reaction *(is / is not)* an **all-or-none** response, meaning that a stimulus beyond the minimum strength needed to trigger an action potential *(would / would not)* change the magnitude of the resulting action potential.

8. An area containing a tiny gap, where one neuron can communicate with another neuron, is known as a _____. Here, molecules of chemical messengers, called _____ , are released from axon terminals after an action potential has occurred. These molecules move across the gap, where they can encounter and bind to specially configured **receptor sites** on the surface of the *(sending / receiving)* neuron, causing a reaction in the receiving neuron.

9. The brain contains *(two or three / many)* different **neurotransmitter** chemicals. Research has revealed that the roles of specific neurotransmitters in behavior and mood are *(diverse / uniform)*, and that drugs that alter the availability or action of these neurotransmitters can affect such processes as movement, perception, mood, alertness, or memory.

10. For items a–j, select the name of the *neurotransmitter* from the Key List that best fits the description given. Write your answer in the blank. Note that some items may be used more than once.

Key List
acetylcholine
dopamine
endorphins
GABA
glutamate
norepinephine
serotonin

a. _____ Naturally occurring morphine-like chemicals in the brain that curb pain and induce pleasurable feelings.

b. _____ A major inhibitory neurotransmitter in the nervous system; some types of epileptic seizures may result from a deficiency of this substance in the brain.

c. _____ An excitatory neurotransmitter that plays a role in memory; too much of this substance can contribute to seizures or migraine headaches.

d. _____ Responsible for the pain relieving effects of acupuncture and for the natural "high" that can result from vigorous exercise.

e. _____ This substance plays a role in learning and memory, and is also released at the junctions between motor neurons and skeletal muscles to stimulate the muscle contractions required for body movements.

f. _____ A neurotransmitter known to affect mood, alertness, and arousal level.

g. _____ The antidepressant Prozac increases the availability of this neurotransmitter, which influences mood, appetite, and sleep.

h. _____ Brain neurons that produce this neurotransmitter degenerate in **Alzheimer's disease**.

i. _____ Botulin, the active compound in Botox, paralyzes muscles by blocking the release of this substance from neurons that stimulate muscle contractions.

j. _____ Helps to regulate movement and plays a role in emotion, attention, and learning. People with **Parkinson's disease** have too little of this substance, and schizophrenia is associated with an excessive level of activity of this neurotransmitter in the brain.

The Nervous System

11. The **brain** and **spinal cord** together form the
_____ nervous system (CNS), which
is linked to the body's muscles, glands, and sense
organs by the _____ **nervous
system** (PNS).

12. Bundles of peripheral nervous system axons that
carry neural signals toward or away from the central
nervous system are called _____. **Nerves**
that carry signals from the CNS out to muscles or
glands are made up of _____ **neurons**,
whereas nerves that carry signals from sense organs
in toward the CNS are made up of _____
neurons. The majority of neurons in the nervous
system function as intermediaries between sensory
and motor neurons, processing information entirely
within the CNS, and such neurons are called

_____.

13. Our ability to perform movements such as reaching,
grasping, walking, chewing, speaking, and smiling
depends on the division of the peripheral nervous
system known as the _____ **nervous
system**, which allows the brain to sense body
position and to deliver commands for skeletal
muscles to contract. The other main division of the
peripheral nervous system, the

_____ **nervous system**, regulates
certain glands (such as the sweat glands) and muscles
of internal organs (such as the heart, stomach, and
intestines). The autonomic nervous system consists of
two subdivisions that work together, exerting *(opposite
/ similar)* effects on basically the same organs. For
example, under stressful or alarming conditions, the
_____ **nervous system** speeds
up the heart rate, suppresses digestion, and elevates
blood sugar, preparing the body for vigorous activity.
Under more ordinary, nonstressful circumstances,
the _____

_____ **nervous system**
lowers the heart rate, promotes digestion, and

reduces blood sugar, promoting conservation of
energy. A simple way to remember the roles of these
autonomic nervous system subdivisions is "**s** for
stressful conditions, **s** = **s**ympathetic" and "**p** for
peaceful conditions, **p** = **p**arasympathetic."

14. The _____ _____ connects the
peripheral nervous system and the brain, and also
provides the neural pathways for _____
such as the knee jerk—an automatic response to a
stimulus. If an injury severs the **spinal cord** at a high
level, sensory signals from the area of the body below
the cut *(can / cannot)* reach the brain. After a severed
spinal cord, reflexes such as the knee jerk reflex can
(still / no longer) occur, even though the tap on the
knee *(would / would not)* be felt.

15. Neurons in the **brain** are organized into interconnected working groups called _____
_____. Each neuron in the human
brain is thought to be connected to an estimated *(100
/ 1000 / 10,000)* other neurons. The networks formed
by neurons in the brain are vast and complex, with an
area the size of a grain of sand containing an
estimated *(100 / 1,000 / 10,000 / 100,000)* neurons
and a *(thousand / million / billion)* synapses.

The Endocrine System

16. The glands of the **endocrine system** release their
secretions, called _____, into the
bloodstream, where they can be pumped around the
body to reach and affect other tissues and organs,
including the brain.

17. Although some **hormones** are chemically identical
to known neurotransmitter molecules, the hormones
travel to their target tissues more *(slowly / quickly)* than
do neurotransmitters. The effects of hormones also
tend to be *(briefer / longer-lasting)* than the effects of
neurotransmitters.

18. Hormones regulate a variety of body processes. For
example, the _____ **glands,** which

secrete _____ (adrenaline) and _____ (noradrenaline), elevate heart rate and blood pressure, and raise our level of blood sugar under conditions of stress or exertion. The _____ **gland** has been called the master gland because its hormones affect the activity of many other **endocrine glands**, including the reproductive organs. In fact, an intricate feedback system exists, involving the brain, the pituitary gland, and other hormones of the body. Pituitary hormones are released in response to signals from a neighboring brain area, the _____ _____, and the hormones whose release is triggered by pituitary hormones can in turn influence the brain's effect on the pituitary.

The Brain

19. Today's neuroscientists gather their data using a variety of tools, techniques, and resources. Match each description given in items a–h with the name of the appropriate *brain research method* in the Key List, writing your answers in the blanks provided.

    Key List
    clinical observation
    CT scan
    electroencephalogram (EEG)
    functional magnetic resonance imaging (fMRI)
    lesion
    microelectrode
    magnetic resonance imaging (MRI)
    positron emission tomography scan (PET scan)

    a. _____ An area of damage; can be surgically induced in a precise region of an animal's brain as a way to study the role of that brain area in behavior.

    b. _____ A scanner detects the distribution of a radioactive glucose-like substance that has been introduced into the body and absorbed by various brain areas in proportion to their metabolic activity; yields a color-coded map reflecting the activity of brain areas during a given task.

    c. _____ Introduced in the video as a method involving the use of X-rays to produce images of brain anatomy.

    d. _____ Tiny conductive device that can be placed in the brain to monitor the electrical activity of a single neuron at a time.

    e. _____ Careful study of patients with brain injury; early understanding of brain function was built primarily upon use of this approach.

    f. _____ Uses a strong magnetic field and pulses of radio waves to produce an image showing details of brain anatomy.

    g. _____ Based on magnetic resonance imaging techniques, but produces an image reflecting blood flow and thereby revealing the brain's pattern of activity.

    h. _____ Reveals the wave-like electrical activity of groups of neurons, using electrodes positioned on the scalp.

20. Among the brains of various species, the human brain *(is / is not)* the largest, and comparisons of species show that intelligence *(is / is not)* systematically related to the ratio of brain weight to body weight. The brains of primitive vertebrates function primarily to regulate basic *(survival / emotional / cognitive)* processes, whereas the human brain is *(more / equally / less)* complex. In regard to its basic functions, the **brainstem** of humans is quite *(similar to / different from)* the brainstem of our distant ancestors.

21. Match each description given in items a–i with the name of the appropriate *brain structure* in the Key List. Write your answers in the blanks provided.

    Key List
    medulla
    reticular formation
    thalamus
    cerebellum
    limbic system
    amygdala
    hippocampus
    hypothalamus
    cerebral cortex

    a. _____ This elongated brainstem structure regulates alertness and filters sensory inputs, sending important information to other brain areas; damage here reduces arousal, and its destruction results in a permanent coma.

b. _____ This brainstem structure regulates vital reflexes, affecting such functions as heart rate and breathing; damage here can be fatal.

c. _____ A "little brain" located at the back of the brainstem, responsible for coordinating sensory input with voluntary movements; damage here leads to the disruption of complex movements and problems with balance.

d. _____ A circuit of structures sometimes referred to as the "old mammalian brain," involved in emotions and basic drives; includes the amygdala, hippocampus, and hypothalamus.

e. _____ A component of the limbic system that is vital for our ability to remember new facts and experiences.

f. _____ The "bark" covering the outside of the cerebral hemispheres; most highly developed and most wrinkled in humans, endowing us with our superior adaptability and our distinctive ability to think abstractly and to use language; described in the textbook as "your body's ultimate information-processing center" responsible for sensory and motor processing, language, consciousness, imagery.

g. _____ A brain structure included within the limbic system that works with other brain structures to regulate emotional behavior and emotional experience, especially fear and rage; lesions in this area can blunt aggressive and defensive behaviors.

h. _____ Region lying not far from the top of the brainstem that receives incoming information from each sense except smell, and directs that information to other areas of the brain.

i. _____ A small area of the brain involved in regulating hunger, thirst, body temperature, sexual behavior, and the release of pituitary hormones that in turn affect a variety of other hormone levels. Electrical stimulation in certain parts of this structure can lead to a pleasurable effect.

22. Match each description in items a–f with the name of the appropriate *lobe of the cerebral hemispheres* from the Key List, writing your answers in the blanks pro-vided. Note that some items may be used more than once.

Key List
frontal lobe
parietal lobe
temporal lobe
occipital lobe

a. _____ An area at the back of the cerebral hemispheres containing the primary visual cortex.

b. _____ Located at the front of the cerebral hemispheres, this region contains the motor cortex, involved in the control of voluntary movements such as reaching, writing, and grasping.

c. _____ Contains areas important to judgment, planning, and the processing of new memories.

d. _____ Region of the brain that sustained major damage in Phineas Gage, the railroad worker whose personality underwent a dramatic change when he survived an accident in which an iron rod passed through his skull.

e. _____ In an area adjacent to the motor cortex, this lobe contains the sensory cortex, which receives incoming signals from receptors in the skin.

f. _____ Located at the sides of the brain, near the ears, this region processes auditory information; found to be highly active during auditory hallucinations in people with schizophrenia.

23. The **motor cortex** on one side of the brain controls movements primarily on *(the same side / the opposite side / both sides)* of the body, so damage to the left motor cortex would cause *(paralysis / loss of sensation)* on *(the right side / the left side / both sides)* of the body.

24. Within the **sensory cortex**, the size of the area that receives sensations from a particular area of the skin corresponds to the *(actual size / sensitivity)* of that particular body area. The greater the sensitivity of a body area, the *(smaller / larger)* is the amount of sensory cortex found to be devoted to processing signals from that area.

25. Damage to any of several important language areas of the brain can cause problems with language processing, known as _____. People with damage to _____ **area**, located in the left frontal lobe, have difficulty speaking but can sing familiar songs and understand what is said to them. A person with damage to _____ **area** speaks unintelligibly and has difficulty comprehending language. Those with damage to the **angular gyrus** lose the ability to *(speak / understand language / read)*.

26. Although some functions can be handled only in certain specialized areas of the brain, in other cases brain functions can be reshaped with experience or after injury. This modifiability of the brain is called _____. In deaf people, _____ **lobe** areas that would otherwise have processed auditory information are found to respond to visual and other non-auditory inputs. In blind people who learn to read Braille, brain areas devoted to processing of signals from the fingers are found to be *(larger / smaller)* than they are in sighted people.

27. New brain cells *(do / do not)* seem to form in some regions of the brain at later points in development, but the greatest plasticity of the brain is present in *(younger / older)* individuals, possibly because they possess a *(surplus / deficiency)* of neural connections. Perhaps the most surprising support for the idea of brain plasticity comes from cases of children who have grown up to function quite *(well / poorly)* after having had one entire cerebral hemisphere removed in a surgical procedure called a _____

_____.

28. Further evidence for brain plasticity can be seen in people who regain function after debilitating injuries to the brain. For example, while in high school, Matt Dykas became paralyzed on the left side of his body as a result of a *(stroke / seizure / blow to the head)* that occurred while he was participating in a track meet. With intensive physical therapy, Matt was *(successful /*

unsuccessful) in his efforts to reacquire the ability to walk, commenting that his physical therapy gave him the opportunity to *("use it or lose it" / "choose to snooze"/ "curse if it's worse")*.

29. We have long known that problems with language are more likely after damage to the *(left / right)* **hemisphere** than after damage to the other side. However, new knowledge about the specialized functions of the two hemispheres emerged from the study of split-brain patients, who have had the two hemispheres divided by surgical cuts made along the _____ _____ in the center of the brain.

30. The purpose of early split-brain surgery cases was to *(research / treat)* cases of people having uncontrolled *(epilepsy / schizophrenia / depression)*. The striking outcome was that seizures were essentially *(eliminated / unchanged / worsened)* by the split-brain operation, while follow-up studies showed that the patients' personalities and day-to-day functioning appeared to be *(normal / disrupted)* after the surgery.

31. In the intact brain, information reaching one side of the brain *(is / is not)* automatically relayed to the other side. Split-brain surgery *(prevents / does not affect / enhances)* communication between the two hemispheres.

32. Each eye ordinarily sends information to *(the left / the right / both)* hemisphere(s) of the brain. Because information from the right half of our field of vision passes through both eyes to *(the left hemisphere / the right hemisphere / both hemispheres)*, special tests show that a split-brain patient *(can / cannot)* restrict visual input to one hemisphere alone. Explain why the same kinds of tests in an intact individual *(would / would not)* restrict the visual input to one hemisphere.

_____

_____

_____

_____

_____

_____

33. If a researcher instructed a typical split-brain patient to fixate on a dot in the center of a screen and then watch while the stimulus ⎡BASE • BALL⎤ was flashed on the screen, the patient would report seeing *(BASE / BALL / BASEBALL / nothing)*. Explain this result.

_____

_____

_____

_____

_____

_____

34. However, if that same patient had been asked to use the left hand to point to what he or she had seen, the patient would select *(BASE / BALL / BASEBALL)*. Explain this result. _____

_____

_____

_____

_____

_____

35. Based on split-brain research, the right hemisphere could be described as having very *(well-developed / limited)* language and speech abilities, but it *(can / cannot)* perceive objects and it *(can / cannot)* comprehend and follow very simple verbal instructions. The *(left / right)* hemisphere excels at tasks such as face and picture recognition, perceiving and expressing emotion, and copying drawings. Furthermore, because each hemisphere exerts major control over the opposite side of the face, the *(left / right)* side of the face tends to be the more emotionally expressive side.

36. Studies of typical people with intact brains provide evidence that the pattern of specialization of the two hemispheres is *(similar to / different from)* that revealed in the split-brain studies. List a few of the research methods used to study hemispheric specialization in people with undivided brains. _____

_____

_____

_____

_____

37. Research on the effects of **strokes** has shown that deaf users of sign language rely primarily on the *(left / right)* side of the brain for language processing, as do hearing people, even though the *(left / right)* side does contribute some of the more subtle ingredients, such as the tonal modulation required for accurate interpretations of speech.

38. Given some of the widely disseminated exaggerations and oversimplifications of scientific findings on hemispheric specialization, it is important to note that for nearly any task the brain performs, *(the left hemisphere / the right hemisphere / both hemispheres)* make contributions.

39. The majority of right-handed people show evidence of *(left / right)* hemisphere specialization for language (about _____%). Left-handed people are *(more / less / just as)* predictable, with *(only a slight / an even larger)* majority showing left-hemisphere specialization for language. Nearly *(a quarter / half)* of all left-handed people process language in both hemispheres.

40. Genetic factors seem *(to be / not to be)* involved in **handedness**, and left-handedness is *(more / less)* common within certain occupational groups such as architects, artists, musicians, and some types of athletes. Inside and outside the scientific community, strong *(agreement / controversy)* has surrounded some reports of shortened longevity for left-handers as a group.

SELF TEST

Read each question and circle the letter of the best answer. When you have completed the Self Test, check your answers against the key at the end of this lesson. If you have answered any items incorrectly, review the appropriate materials to correct misunderstandings and cement your knowledge.

1. What group of investigators in the 1800s believed that an individual's traits and abilities could be discerned by measuring various protrusions on the skull?
   a. Phrenologists
   b. Biological psychologists
   c. Neurologists
   d. Scalpulists

2. In regard to the relationship between the biological and psychological domains, David Myers offers the comment in the video that
   a. "We are what we think, not what we eat."
   b. "The study of the brain is the only legitimate focus of study within the field of psychology."
   c. "Everything biological is ultimately irrelevant to psychology."
   d. "Everything psychological is ultimately biological–a manifestation of something that is happening at the level of the brain."

3. The fundamental communicating units making up the nervous system are
   a. neurons.
   b. glial cells.
   c. the cerebral hemispheres.
   d. hormones.

4. Which structure of the neuron serves as the zone where incoming information (from sense organs or from other neurons) is typically received?
   a. Axon
   b. Synapse
   c. Dendrite
   d. Myelin

5. A resting neuron has more _____ ions outside than inside its membrane.
   a. positively charged potassium
   b. negatively charged potassium
   c. positively charged sodium
   d. negatively charged sodium

6. An action potential is
   a. an all-or-none electrical event within a neuron.
   b. an electrical signal that travels along the length of the axon, away from the cell body and toward the axon terminal.
   c. an event that can trigger the release of neurotransmitter molecules at the synapse.
   d. all of the above.

7. How does one neuron typically communicate signals to another neuron?
   a. Special messenger molecules are released into the gap between the two neurons, affecting receptor sites on the receiving neuron.
   b. The sending neuron passes sodium ions to the receiving neuron.
   c. The sending neuron makes direct physical contact with the receiving neuron, and the electrical signal from one passes to the next.
   d. None of the above–neurons normally cannot affect one another.

8. A chemical messenger substance that passes across a tiny gap between one neuron and the next is a(n)
   a. hormone.
   b. action potential.
   c. receptor.
   d. neurotransmitter.

9. Which of the following disorders has been linked to a degeneration of neurons in certain motor areas of the brain that use dopamine as their neurotransmitter?
   a. Multiple sclerosis
   b. Parkinson's disease
   c. Epilepsy
   d. "Runner's high"

10. Which of the following is a list of neurotransmitters?
    a. Norepinephrine, serotonin, acetylcholine
    b. Dendrite, cell body, and axon
    c. Motor neurons, sensory neurons, and interneurons
    d. Sodium, potassium, chloride, and calcium

11. According to George Bigelow in the video, which neurotransmitter is involved in the brain's reward system and is affected by various drugs that are abused by some individuals?
    a. Acetylcholine
    b. Norepinephrine
    c. Morphine
    d. Dopamine

12. The brain and the spinal cord are the two main components of
    a. the central nervous system.
    b. the limbic system
    c. the somatic nervous system.
    d. the sympathetic nervous system.

13. As Tim sits in a relaxed position at the edge of the examining table, his doctor uses a rubber mallet to perform a simple test. The doctor taps the tendon just below Tim's kneecap and observes that a small but automatic jerk of Tim's leg quickly follows. Tim's knee jerk response is
    a. an autonomic nervous system reaction.
    b. a spinal reflex controlled by the spinal cord.
    c. a brain reflex, controlled by the vast and complex neural networks of the lower brain.
    d. an indication that Tim probably has Parkinson's disease.

14. Positron emission tomography can be used to
    a. detect the electrical activity of the brain, using electrodes placed against the scalp.
    b. produce images of brain activity using glucose-like radioactive isotopes that are absorbed more by active brain areas.
    c. produce images of the anatomy of the brain, but not brain activity.
    d. treat epileptic seizures.

15. Functional MRI (fMRI)
    a. detects the moment-by-moment electrical activity of the brain with electrodes placed against the scalp.
    b. shows details of the brain anatomy without revealing brain activity.
    c. uses magnetic fields and radio wave pulses to produce images representing brain activity, based on blood flow to different areas of the brain.
    d. can be used to treat various neurological disorders, including Parkinson's disease and schizophrenia.

16. What are the some of the functions associated with the limbic system, according to Daniel Siegel's description of the human brain in the video?
    a. Regulation of basic functions such as heart rate and breathing
    b. Language and abstract thinking
    c. Emotion, motivation, and social relatedness
    d. All of the above

17. According to Susan Greenfield in the video, the wrinkles of the cerebral cortex
    a. are more obvious in rats or rabbits than in humans.
    b. increase with age and wisdom in humans.
    c. allow an increased amount of surface areas to fit into the skull.
    d. All of the above.

18. Destruction of the brainstem area known as the reticular formation could be expected to result in
    a. a permanent coma.
    b. disruption of balance and difficulties in coordination complex movements.
    c. loss of the ability to remember recent experiences and new facts.
    d. disruption of appetite, body temperature, and reproductive cycles.

19. The cerebral cortex
    a. is the outer "bark" covering the outside of the cerebral hemispheres.
    b. contains the motor cortex, the sensory cortex, visual information, and auditory information.
    c. plays a critical role in our most human capacities for language and abstract thinking.
    d. all of the above.

20. Which neurotransmitter in the brain has become a focus of attention in efforts to explain the rewarding effects of brain stimulation and addictions to alcohol and other drugs?
    a. Serotonin
    b. GABA
    c. Acetylcholine
    d. Dopamine

21. When brain researchers speak of "plasticity" of the brain, they are referring to
    a. the soft, gooey, blob-like appearance of the brain.
    b. the rugged stability of brain connections, which are known to remain stable for a lifetime.
    c. flexibility of brain function, based in part on the ability of some brain areas to form and break connections, and to assume functions that were formerly handled elsewhere in the brain.
    d. extreme uncontrolled muscle contractions occurring after injury to the motor areas of the brain.

22. In the video, which of the following cases was cited in support of the idea that the brain can undergo some degree of reshaping with experience?
    a. London cab drivers, who have memorized a huge number of locations and routes, are found to have a larger than average hippocampus, an area of the brain whose activities are critical to working memory.
    b. Through intensive practice and rehabilitation therapy, Matt Dykas was able to regain his ability to walk and to pick up objects following a stroke that paralyzed one half of his body.
    c. Blind people begin to use the areas of the brain that would normally serve visual functions for other types of sensory processing.
    d. All of the above.

23. The early split-brain surgeries performed by Bogen and Vogel
    a. were intended to treat epilepsy, but actually worsened it.
    b. were intended to treat epilepsy, and were quite successful.
    c. were intended to treat schizophrenia, and were quite successful.
    d. were intended to treat schizophrenia, but actually worsened it.

24. Which of the following explains why a split-brain patient cannot easily name objects seen in the left visual field?
    a. The split-brain surgery makes the person blind in the left eye.
    b. Visual signals from the left visual field pass primarily to the right hemisphere of the brain, and this side of the brain typically does not possess sophisticated language skills.
    c. The corpus callosum contains the main language centers, and these have been destroyed by the surgery.
    d. Before any surgical procedure, epilepsy has destroyed the language centers of the brain.

25. In comparison to hormones, the effects of neurotransmitters tend to be
    a. faster and briefer.
    b. slower and briefer.
    c. faster and more long-lasting.
    d. slower and more long-lasting.

ANSWER KEY FOR THE ACTIVE REVIEW EXERCISES

1. heart; phrenology; skull; are not; brain; [1] Textbook, Video 3
2. biological psychologists; biological; [2] Textbook, Video 3
3. neurons; dendrites; receive; cell body; axon; [3] Textbook
4. myelin; speeds; degeneration; multiple sclerosis; decrease; [4] Textbook
5. negatively charged; sodium; rush in; depolarized; [4] Textbook
6. action potentials; axon; 200; [4] Video 3
7. excitatory; inhibitory; threshold; axon; is; would not; [4] Textbook
8. synapse; neurotransmitters; receiving; [5] Textbook, Video 3
9. many; diverse; [6] Textbook, Video 3
10. (a) endorphins (b) GABA (c) glutamate (d) endorphins (e) acetylcholine (f) norepinephrine (g) serotonin (h) acetylcholine (i) acetylcholine (j) dopamine; [6, 7] Textbook, Video 3
11. central; peripheral; [8] Textbook, Video 3
12. nerves; motor; sensory; interneurons; [8] Textbook
13. somatic; autonomic; opposite; sympathetic; parasympathetic; [8] Textbook
14. spinal cord; reflexes; cannot; still; would not; [9] Textbook
15. neural networks; 10,000; 100,000; billion; [9] Textbook, Video 3
16. hormones; [10] Textbook
17. slowly; longer-lasting; [10] Textbook
18. adrenal; epinephrine; norepinephrine; pituitary; hypothalamus; [10] Textbook
19. (a) lesion (b) PET scan (c) CT scan (d) microelectrode (e) clinical observation (f) MRI (g) fMRI (h) EEG; [11] Textbook, Video 3
20. is not; is not; survival; more; similar to; [12] Textbook
21. (a) reticular formation (b) medulla (c) cerebellum (d) limbic system (e) hippocampus (f) cerebral cortex (g) amygdala (h) thalamus (i) hypothalamus; [13] Textbook; Video 3
22. (a) occipital lobe (b) frontal lobe (c) frontal lobe (d) frontal lobe (e) parietal lobe (f) temporal lobe; [14] Textbook
23. the opposite side; paralysis; the right side; [14] Textbook, Video 3
24. sensitivity; larger; [14] Textbook
25. aphasia; Broca's; Wernicke's; read; [16] Textbook
26. plasticity; temporal; larger; [17] Textbook, Video 3
27. do; younger; surplus; well; hemispherectomy; [18] Textbook

28. stroke; successful; "use it or lose it"; [16] Video 3
29. left; corpus callosum; [18, 19] Textbook, Video 3
30. treat; epilepsy; eliminated; normal; [17] Textbook, Video 3
31. is; prevents; [18] Textbook, Video 3
32. both; left hemisphere; can; would not; *Your answer should include the following ideas:* In the intact brain, any information that reaches the right hemisphere, for example, is instantly shared with the left. (In the split-brain patient, the information cannot cross to the other side because the "bridge"–the corpus callosum–has been cut.); [18] Textbook, Video 3
33. BALL; *Your answer should include the following ideas:* Everything within the right half of the field of vision is signaled to the left hemisphere. Because the left hemisphere is specialized for language, the patient would report the word seen by the left hemisphere (BALL). The right hemisphere would be unaware of the stimulus in the right part of the visual field, because the cut in the corpus callosum prevents that signal from being passed from the left hemisphere across to the right hemisphere; [18, 19] Textbook, Video 3
34. BASE; *Your answer should include the following ideas:* The left hand is primarily connected to the less verbal right hemisphere, which saw what was in the left visual field (BASE), so the left hand could point to what the right hemisphere saw. (Each hemisphere experienced something different, and could indicate in its own way what stimulus it had received.); [18, 19] Textbook, Video 3
35. limited; can; can; right; left; [16, 19] Textbook; Video 3
36. similar to; *Your answer should include several of the following methods:* Monitoring brain waves, blood flow, and consumption of blood sugar (glucose) on each side of the brain during specific tasks; applying magnetic stimulation as a way to temporarily impairing the activity on one side of the brain and observing the results on performance; sedating one hemisphere at a time, and looking for interference with speech and/or picture recognition; (18, 19] Textbook
37. left; right; [16, 18, 19] Textbook, Video 3
38. both hemispheres; [18] Textbook, Video 3
39. left; 95; less; only a slight; a quarter; [16, 19] Textbook
40. to be; more; controversy; [19] Textbook

ANSWER KEY FOR THE SELF TEST

Item #	Answer	Learning Outcome #	Source	Item #	Answer	Learning Outcome #	Source
1.	a	1	Textbook	14.	b	11	Textbook, Video 3
2.	d	2	Video 3	15.	c	11	Video 3
3.	a	3	Textbook, Video 3	16.	c	12, 13	Video 3
4.	c	3	Textbook	17.	c	12, 13, 14	Textbook, Video 3
5.	c	4	Textbook	18.	a	13	Textbook, Video 3
6.	d	4	Textbook, Video 3	19.	d	13, 14	Textbook, Video 3
7.	a	5	Textbook, Video 3	20.	d	15	Textbook, Video 3
8.	d	5	Textbook, Video 3	21.	c	17	Textbook, Video 3
9.	b	6	Textbook	22.	d	17	Textbook, Video 3
10.	a	6	Textbook, Video 3	23.	b	18	Textbook, Video 3
11.	d	6, 7	Video 3	24.	b	16, 18	Textbook, Video 3
12.	a	8	Textbook, Video 3	25.	a	10	Textbook
13.	b	9	Textbook				

Lesson 4 (Behavior Genetics)

Codes of Life

> ## Assignments
>
> **Reading:** "Behavior Genetics" and "Evolutionary Psychology" in Chapter 3 of *Psychology* by David Myers (Module 6 in the modular version of *Psychology*)
>
> **Video:** Episode 4, "Codes of Life"

LEARNING OUTCOMES

Familiarize yourself with the Learning Outcomes for this lesson before you begin the assignments. Return to them to check your learning after completing the Steps to Learning Success. Careful work on these materials should equip you to accomplish the outcomes.

Behavior Genetics: Predicting Individual Differences (Module 6)

1. Describe human **chromosomes**, **DNA**, and **genes**, and explain the relationships of these elements to one another.

2. Compare the genetic similarity of humans to each other and of humans to chimpanzees and mice, and comment on the impact a tiny genetic difference can make.

3. Discuss the general idea that most human traits are the result of a complicated interaction between **gene complexes** and the **environment**. Include an explanation of the analogy between genes and the keys of a piano, as presented by Terry Sejnowski in the video.

4. Describe the kinds of influences **behavior geneticists** investigate and the major methods they use as they research individual differences.

5. Distinguish between **identical twins** and **fraternal twins**, and explain why twin studies have been so important in behavior genetics research.

6. Provide an overview of the findings that have emerged from a host of studies comparing the similarity of identical and fraternal twins.

7. Explain what studies of adopted individuals and their biological and adoptive parents have contributed to our understanding of genetic and environmental influences on behavior.

8. Compare the **Minnesota Twins Study**, the **Swedish Twins Study**, and the **Colorado Adoption Project** in terms of the methods used and the conclusions reached.

9. Summarize the results of research into how the home environment and parenting affect children's development, and describe the effects of adoption on adopted childrens' outcomes.

10. Define **temperament**, describe the classifications of newborn infants according to **temperament**, and summarize what research has suggested about factors that correlate with infant temperament.

11. Define **heritability** and explain what heritability estimates can and cannot reveal about the determinants of a particular characteristic.

12. Discuss gene-environment interactions, mentioning several common misconceptions about how genes exert their influence on behavior, including the failure to recognize that genes correlate with experience.

13. Discuss the potential contributions of **molecular genetics** in furthering our understanding of human diversity and solving human problems.

Evolutionary Psychology (Module 6)

14. Define **evolutionary psychology**, explaining the process of **natural selection** and its relationship to the evolution of behavior.

15. Give several examples of specific human behavior patterns for which evolutionary psychologists have offered explanations, and summarize those explanations.

16. Summarize what research has revealed about **gender differences** in sexual behavior, attitudes about sex, and **mate preferences**, and explain how evolutionary psychologists account for these differences between the sexes.

17. List the major criticisms of evolutionary psychology, and review some of the responses of evolutionary psychologists to these criticisms.

ACTIVE REVIEW

Each item in this section is based on material presented in the video or the textbook assignment for this lesson, or both. Complete this section, referring as needed to your notes or the source materials themselves. Answers are provided at the end of this lesson.

Behavior Genetics: Predicting Individual Differences

1. *(Genes / Chromosomes)* are like beads on a string—segments along the length of the molecules of

   _____ _____

   that constitute the hereditary material within every cell of the body. Every *(gene / chromosome)* carries many *(genes / chromosomes)*.

2. Each human being begins as a single cell having *(23 / 46)* chromosomes from the mother and *(23 / 46)* chromosomes from the father. During the process of cell division, these *(23 / 46 / 92)* chromosomes replicate themselves, so that each new cell that is formed contains a copy of the genetic instructions for the physical development of *(that new cell / the whole organism)*.

3. The human _____, consisting of the genetic instructions copied into the chromosomes within each cell of the body, is estimated to comprise about *(4,000 / 30,000 / 46 million / 100 billion)* genes.

4. In the video, Robert Plomin points out that we humans are *(70 / 80 / 90 / 95 / 99.9)* percent similar to one another, with only about a thousand of our DNA base pairs differing from one person to the next. Of course, small genetic variations can make for

differences that seem quite dramatic, as exemplified by the fact that, according to Plomin, the genes of chimps and humans are about *(70 / 80 / 90 / 99)* percent similar, and mice and humans have about *(70 / 80 / 90 / 99)* percent of their genes in common.

5. It appears that a tiny genetic difference can have a *(miniscule / huge)* impact. A mere 0.1 percent variation between the genes of one person and another can, *(entirely on its own / in interaction with differing environments)*, yield differences as great as those between a Nelson Mandela and an Adolf Hitler.

6. Terry Sejnowski emphasizes in the video that *(all / some / none)* of our behaviors and abilities have some genetic component, and that experiences interact with genes by determining whether certain genes are *(present or absent / turned on or off)*. Sejnowski likens the *(genes / environment)* to keys on a piano, saying that inputs to the cell can "play the keys on the piano," and in so doing, influence how the cell functions. David Myers explains that the effects of genes on behavior are *(direct / indirect)*. When activated, genes furnish the *("recipe" / ingredients)* for the making of certain proteins that are our bodies' fundamental building blocks.

7. Most human traits that interest psychologists (for example, characteristics such as intelligence, optimism, outgoingness, and aggressiveness) are the result of an interaction of the environment with *(a single gene / two genes / gene complexes)*.

8. The field of *(molecular genetics / behavior genetics / social psychology)* examines the roles of genes and experience in shaping individual differences in our behaviors and capacities.

9. List the two major methods behavior geneticists use to assess the contributions of genetic and environmental factors to behavior and cognitive processes in humans, and then explain the logic of these research methods. _____
_____
_____
_____
_____
_____
_____
_____
_____
_____
_____
_____
_____
_____
_____

10. In the video, Nancy Segal describes twins as "living laboratories," offering a simple and elegant way to study the influences that affect human behavior. Identical twins, formed from *(a single / two different)* fertilized egg(s), share *(all / most / half)* their genes in common. Fraternal twins, by contrast, are formed from *(a single / two different)* fertilized egg(s), and they share *(all / most / about half)* their genes. David Myers uses the term "nature's human clones" to describe _____ twins, but points out that _____ twins are genetically no more similar than ordinary siblings within the same family.

11. Studies of more than 20,000 pairs of twins in several countries around the world have revealed that basic personality traits, such as being socially outgoing and expressive or being emotionally unstable, are much *(more / less)* similar in identical twins than in fraternal twins. Other studies have yielded comparable

outcomes in regard to twins' risk of divorce. This pattern of results, repeated in study after study, offers a strong suggestion that when it comes to our personalities, interests, and attitudes, genes *(do / do not)* matter.

12. One alternative interpretation, however, is that a consistent pattern of results in twins research might not tell us as much as we think about the impact of genes because people may tend to treat identical twins *(differently / more alike)*. Given this possibility, studies of twins that grow up *(together / apart)* may offer a purer estimate of genetic influence. If identical twins reared apart are still found to be more alike than fraternal twins, the most obvious explanation would seem to be their shared *(genes / environments)*.

13. Mark Newman and Gerald Levey, who are featured in the video and whose photographs appear in the text, are identical twins who were adopted at birth by two separate families. This means that they have *(all the same / similar / different)* genes, but grew up in different _____ (surroundings). _____ geneticists are quite interested in cases such as these because they offer an opportunity to examine how differences in *(genes / environments)* affect the expression of a person's *(genes / environments)*, in turn influencing the development of behavioral and cognitive tendencies.

14. When Mark and Jerry were reunited at age 31, both were studied with a number of psychological and medical assessments in the Minnesota Study of Twins Reared Apart. Nancy Segal comments in the video that Mark and Jerry had many *(similarities / differences)* in their physical appearance: height, baldness, big noses, and mustaches. But they *(also had / did not have)* much in common in their habits, mannerisms, tastes, and attitudes. They liked *(none / few / many)* of the same types of food, beverages, and people. Furthermore, both had served as volunteer

_____.

15. The very first of the many sets of twins studied by Thomas Bouchard, lead researcher in the Minnesota Twins Study, were Jim Lewis and Jim Springer–

identical twin brothers separated at birth and brought back together 38 years later. In the "Jim twins," Bouchard identified a surpising assortment of *(similarities / differences)* in areas ranging from their vocal quality and speech patterns, personal habits and emotions, to their likes and dislikes, leisure activities, and talents and abilities.

16. The many striking parallels in the lives of separated identical twins *(are / are not)* enough to remove all doubt about the weight of genes in shaping personality. Robert Plomin points out in the video that the identical twins in Bouchard's research were *(selected randomly / volunteers who responded to newspaper ads)*, and for this reason, they might have been much more similar to one another than twins from a *(specially chosen / representative / volunteer)* sample would prove to be. Other critics have viewed Bouchard's case reports as anecdotal, and have called attention to the need for further data from *(additional anecdotes / studies with appropriate comparison groups)*.

17. Nancy Pedersen and colleagues sorted through nationwide registers in Sweden to locate several hundred pairs of separated *(identical / fraternal / identical and fraternal)* twins for their research. Her team of researchers compared those separated twins with identical twins reared together. In their personalities, the identical twins who had been separated early in life were found to be *(more similar than / just as similar as / less similar than)* identical twins reared together. But the separated identical twins were *(more similar than / just as similar as / less similar than)* fraternal twins who had grown up separately. This pattern of results suggests that genes play a *(significant / negligible)* role in shaping who we are.

18. Nancy Segal says in the video that every measured human trait has been found by behavior geneticists to have *(complete / some / little or no)* genetic influence, but the degree of genetic influence *(varies / is constant)* from one trait to another. If differences in genes account for about 50 percent of the variation in a particular personality trait, then this means that environmental differences account for *(none / about 50 percent / all)* of the variations observed in that trait.

19. In twins research, genetic influence is seen in *(nearly all / about half / almost none)* of the dimensions tested—personality, abilities, mental health, and child adjustment. Because this raises the question of whether twins research somehow generates misleading results, Robert Plomin sees benefit in studying the role of genes in behavior and personality not just through research on twins, but also through research on *(abused / adopted / institutionalized / neglected / talented)* children and their families.

20. In speaking about twins research and adoption research in the video, Plomin draws an analogy between using two diffferent research methods and putting on two different *(bathing suits with holes / wristwatches / socks that do not match)*. Each research method has its own unique *(strengths / limitations / strengths and limitations)*, and the strengths of one method are likely to *(worsen / compensate for)* the limitations of the other method. If the two complementary methods converge on the same conclusion, then we can be *(much more / no more / much less)* confident about the conclusion we draw.

21. Whereas most children grow up with parents who share both genes and environment with them, adopted children have *(genes / environment)* in common with their biological parents and *(genes / environment)* in common with their adoptive parents.

22. In the Colorado Adoption Project begun in 1974, Plomin conducted repeated assessments of adopted children, comparing them over time with their adoptive mothers, *(and also / but not)* with their biological mothers, who had *(no / very little / full)* contact with their child after three days of age. This research approach *(permitted / did not permit)* assessment of genetic influence, environmental influence, and the combined influence of genes and environment.

23. The adoption design is especially powerful because it entails a *(separation / blending)* of the major sources of genetic and environmental influence. On every characteristic tested, Plomin says that adoption studies reveal a *(minimal / moderate / huge)* genetic influence.

These findings, then, *(confirm / contradict)* what twins studies have revealed.

24. Although an adoptive parent is in a position to provide the *(genes / home environment)* that might be expected to shape the child's level of verbal abilities, for example, research findings reveal *(essentially no / a moderate / a great)* similarity in the verbal abilities of adoptive parents and their adopted offspring. In fact, people who grow up together are found not to be very similar in their personality traits (for example, how agreeable or outgoing they are), *(even if / unless)* they are related to one another.

25. Adoptees' personalities and abilities more resemble those of their *(adoptive / biological)* parents than their *(adoptive / biological)* parents. Shared home environment is found to exert almost *(no / complete)* influence over personality. Studies show, in fact, that as adopted children develop into adolescence and beyond, they become *(more / less)* like their biological parents. David Myers summarizes the results of this area of research by describing the effect of shared rearing environment as "shockingly *(powerful / modest)*."

26. So is good parenting pointless? In fact, there is evidence that parents do influence the *(attitudes, manners, beliefs, and values / outgoingness, emotional stability, and agreeableness)* of their children. Furthermore, intelligence test scores of adopted children are generally *(higher than / lower than / nearly identical to)* those of their biological parents, suggesting an advantage of growing up in an adoptive home headed by carefully screened and caring parents, whose risk of divorcing or becoming a child abuser is *(lower than / the same as / higher than)* in the general population. Overall, then, there is evidence that adoptions *(damage / benefit / do not affect)* children, and that in general, parenting *(does / does not)* make a difference in some important outcomes, even if it does not determine a child's personality.

27. In the video, Janet Shibley Hyde describes temperament as "the young version of" *(personality / emotion / aggressiveness)*—an individual's characteristic way of

reacting to the environment. Nancy Segal describes temperament as behavioral style, which is related less to what we're doing, and more to *(what we're not doing / how we're doing it)*. We can detect differences in babies' temperaments *(within the first few days of life / but not before age one year)*, and an individual's temperament is relatively *(stable / variable)* from one developmental period to another. Janet Shibley Hyde points out that temperament seems to have a *(negligible / weak / fairly strong)* genetic component. This conclusion emerges from several studies showing that *(fraternal / identical)* twins are more alike in temperament than are *(fraternal / identical)* twins.

28. Behavior geneticists use twin studies and adoption studies to estimate the degree to which differences in a trait within a group can be ascribed to genetic differences among them. If, for example, 68 percent of the variation in intelligence test scores were attributable to differences in genes within a particular group, then the _____ estimate for intelligence within that group would be 0.68.

29. Heritability estimates apply to *(individuals / groups / both individuals and groups)*, and the heritability estimate for a given trait (degree of dependability, for example) in one group *(can / cannot)* be generalized to another group *(and /or)* to other environmental circumstances beyond those in effect for the group used to obtain the heritability estimate.

30. As Stephen Hinshaw says in the video, whether a trait, such as a particular person's height, is a product of genes <u>or</u> environment is a *(meaningful / silly)* question, because any trait is a *(full / partial)* product of genes *(and / or)* environment. However, it is *(meaningful / silly)* to ask whether differences between the heights of the people in a particular group are attributable to differences in genes or differences in environment.

31. Very high heritability for a trait such as height *(means /does not mean)* that the environment is not influential. If we find that 90 percent of group differences in height can be traced to differences in genes, then height has *(low / moderate / high)* heritability. As a

society, we are a few inches *(taller / shorter)* on average than they we were a century ago, Hinshaw points out. This change in people over a span of just one hundred years (a period the textbook author describes in relative terms as "an eyeblink of time") is *(likely / unlikely)* to be based on changes in genes.

32. Travis Gibbs states in the video that genes *(determine / predispose)* certain traits, providing for a particular range or configuration. David Myers asserts that human differences are a product of *(genes / environment / both genes and environment)*, and that genes and environment work like *(a hand in a glove / two hands clapping / an audience clapping)*. For example, exposure of people to a new social context can bring out aggression that was not seen before, just as exposure of the feet to friction can bring out calluses, illustrating that genes *(overshadow / respond to)* environments.

33. It is *(accurate / a mistake)* to think of genes as blueprints that remain constant, given that different environments can trigger different outcomes from the same genes, and different genes can result in different reactions from the environment.

34. Robert Plomin stresses in the video the importance of gene-environment correlation, an idea that reaches somewhat beyond gene-environment interaction. Plomin explains that traits related to specific genes may steer the individual toward an exposure to certain *(other genes / specific environments)* that enhance those same traits. For example, parents may find it far more appealing to spend time singing songs with a child who *(loves / dislikes)* music. In this way, any genes predisposing the child to like music would be *(correlated with / independent of)* environmental exposure to music.

35. Plomin explains that he designs his research studies as *(longitudinal / cross-sectional)* studies, to enable him to track change as well as continuity in development. People often think of genetics as a constant, not a developmental factor; but as Plomin points out, a trait that is rooted in genes would *(necessarily / not necessarily)* be apparent throughout life. For example,

baldness *(is / is not)* genetically influenced, and is not observed until later in life.

36. _____ geneticists have recently been conducting explorations of peoples' DNA to identify genes that contribute to the risk for certain traits. Because gene complexes, rather than single genes, are generally involved in behavior, psychologist Robert Plomin says that these searches often target *(two or three / several dozen / several hundred)* genes that might each contribute a small amount of the variance to one particular trait, such as reading disability.

37. In his remarks in the video, Plomin primarily emphasizes the *(promise / perils)* that could come with genetic testing to detect risk factors for difficulties such as reading disabilities. The big advantage of DNA in psychology, he says, is that knowledge of specific genes could provide an early warning system, allowing *(prevention before / treatment after)* problems begin.

Evolutionary Psychology

38. While the field of behavior genetics focuses on how genes and experience make us who we are, *(evolutionary / cognitive / psychodynamic / sociocultural)* psychology takes a broader view over a longer span of time, stressing the functional role our *(behavior / anatomy / physiology)*, emotions, and cognitive processes play in our chances for surviving, reproducing, and passing our *(genes / learning)* on to the next generation.

39. At the core of evolutionary psychology is the application of the principle of _____ _____ to behavior. This principle, derived from the work of Charles _____, holds that from among the variety of gene combinations that exist (including those new genes that arise from _____–random changes in genes as they replicate), those genes that code for behaviors which enhance the chances for survival and reproduction are *(least / most)* likely to be passed on to further generations.

40. David Myers points out in the video that the role of genes is not simply to lock in specific behaviors, but

to predispose us toward *(flexibility / stability)* in our behavior, given the diverse and changing environments of humans and our need to adapt.

41. The textbook quotes Jared Diamond's idea that "virtually no contemporary scientists believe that Darwin was basically *(wrong / right)*," and describes evolutionary *(biology / psychology)* as "the second Darwinian revolution." Evolutionary psychologists are looking for keys to our widespread human patterns of mate selection, fears and phobias, devotion to our families, patterns of cooperation and aggression, and seemingly ordinary likes and dislikes.

42. Why do we seek out certain foods? Evolutionary psychologists point out that foods with a *(sweet / sour / bitter)* taste and those with a *(low / high)* fat content were in short supply over most of human history. In the past, those individual humans with the strongest preferences for these tastes were presumably *(more / less)* likely to survive and reproduce than those without such preferences. Perhaps our growing problem with *(obesity / starvation)* in today's Western societies represents the process of natural selection over many thousands of years favoring taste preferences that *(promoted / limited)* survival and reproduction in our ancestors. These same characteristics have been *(retained / lost)* in today's humans, many of whom live in environments where sweet and fatty foods are all too available.

43. Another evolutionary adaptation, described in the video by Paul Ekman, is the tendency to react more readily with fear toward the shape of a *(gun / reptile)* than to the shape of a *(gun / reptile)* because guns were not present to pose a threat throughout most of our ancestral past.

44. Cooperative behavior, as well as _____– seemingly unselfish actions that benefit others at our own expense–can also be viewed from the perspective of natural selection. The main idea, according to Dacher Keltner, is that with a few exceptions, all our actions, including our social behavior, ultimately stem from tendencies that further the propagation of *(our own / other people's)* genes. This general idea may explain why people often display more helpfulness toward relatives and others who are similar to themselves–those with whom they have a *(higher / lower)* proportion of genes in common. Nancy Segal suggests that this could be a way of getting our own genes into subsequent generations.

45. Evolutionary psychology has offered explanations for gender differences in sexual attitudes and behavior. Michael Baily states in the video episode that in general, *(men / women)*, regardless of their sexual orientation, are more interested in casual sex. Bailey adds that the majority of men are attracted to women and the majority of women are attracted to men because this is *(how we evolved / what we personally chose)*, meaning that these particular kinds of pairings were the ones that led to a greater likelihood of passing down one's genes.

46. The greatest gender difference in sexuality is that *(women / men)* are more likely than *(women / men)* to initiate sexual activity, and *(women / men)* tend to be more interested in and approving of casual, uncommitted sex.

47. As evolutionary psychologists point out, casual sex greatly *(expands / diminishes)* men's opportunities to spread their genes. But for women, because of the lengthy period of time required for pregnancy and care of one infant, preferences bend toward *(uncommitted / committed)* mates with the resources and willingness to cooperate in the parenting endeavor. As David Myers puts it, "Nature selects behaviors that *(increase / decrease)* the likelihood of sending one's genes into the future." And natural selection pressures for our ancestors seem to have been *(quite similar / somewhat different)* for men and for women.

48. In the video, Alice Eagly summarizes mate selection differences in pointing out that *(women / men)* in general have a stronger preference for status and resources in a mate, and *(women / men)* are more likely to be looking for nurturance and homemaker qualities in a mate. On average, women seek mates who are *(older / younger)* than themselves, and men

seek mates who are *(older/ younger)* than themselves. Explain how evolutionary psychologists have accounted for these differences. _____

_____

_____

_____

_____

_____

_____

49. Comparing cultures across the world, we find that as women and men become more equal, their criteria for selecting mates tend to *(converge / diverge)*. Alice Eagly states in the video that in cultures where women can have careers with reasonable income

potential, women are *(more / less)* likely to need an older man with lots of resources. Similarly, in cultures with a greater *(equality / disparity)* of opportunity for men and women, men's preferences for younger women with homemaker qualities are not as strong.

50. Critics have complained that evolutionary psychologists rely too heavily on *(hindsight explanations / predictions)*, starting with a result and working *(forward / backward)* toward an explanation. Critics also charge that evolutionary explanations may discourage people from taking _____ for their actions, and that evolutionary psychologists *(underestimate / exaggerate)* the importance of societal and cultural influences on behavior.

SELF TEST

Read each question and circle the letter of the best answer. When you have completed the Self Test, check your answers against the key at the end of this lesson. If you have answered any items incorrectly, review the appropriate materials to correct misunderstandings and cement your knowledge.

1. The set of coded instructions for making an organism is contained in that organism's
   a. G-proteins.
   b. sex-linked genes.
   c. chromosomes.
   d. gnome.

2. There are 23 chromosomes in
   a. a single molecule of DNA.
   b. the reproductive cells that a mother and a father contribute to their offspring at fertilization.
   c. every cell in the human body.
   d. every gene.

3. Humans are estimated to have about ____ genes.
   a. 30,000
   b. 10,000
   c. 99
   d. 46

4. According to Robert Plomin's comments in the video, humans share about ___ % of their genes in common with one another, and even mice and humans are about ____ % similar genetically.
   a. 90 … 60
   b. 90 … 75
   c. 99.9 … 75
   d. 99.9 … 90

5. The textbook author points out that genes guide our development by
   a. providing the instructions for cells to manufacture certain proteins.
   b. directly affecting our behaviors.
   c. both of the above.
   d. none of the above.

6. Behavior geneticists suggest that most human behavioral tendencies and characteristics are the result of an interaction between the environment and
   a. a single pair of dominant or recessive genes on a single set of chromosomes.
   b. the pineal gland, which Descartes long ago identified as the seat of the soul.
   c. groups of genes called gene complexes that act in concert with one another.
   d. prenatal nutritional influences.

7. Behavior geneticists conduct research on
   a. the structure of DNA.
   b. the relative impact of heredity and environment on differences in behavior.
   c. the anatomy of the reproductive system.
   d. the evolution of traits as species developed.

8. In twins research, behavior geneticists are most keenly interested in
   a. studying identical twins reared together.
   b. studying fraternal twins reared together.
   c. studying fraternal twins reared apart.
   d. comparing the degree of similarity of members of identical and fraternal twin pairs, especially when the twins have been reared apart.

9. Identical twins are
   a. formed when one fertilized egg splits, resulting in two individuals with copies of the same genes.
   b. formed when two fertilized eggs merge to form one individual.
   c. formed with two separate eggs are fertilized at the same time by separate sperm cells.
   d. genetically no more alike than ordinary siblings.

10. One of the most widely publicized studies of identical twins reared apart, conducted by Thomas Bouchard of the University of Minnesota, included separated identical twins Jim Lewis and Jim Springer. Upon being brought together after 38 years apart, these particular identical twins discovered that, they each had
    a. a wife named Betty.
    b. a dog named Toy.
    c. a circular white wooden bench built around a tree in the front yard.
    d. all of the above, and many other striking similarities as well.

11. Some critics of Bouchard's Minnesota Twins Study have contended that the data from this study amount to little more than a collection of interesting anecdotes, because
    a. the research lacked any comparison groups, consisting of pairs of people with a lesser degree of genetic relationship with which to contrast the data from the separated identical twins.
    b. Bouchard's sample of identical twins might not have been representative of identical twins in general, because many of these participants were solicited through newspapers.
    c. some of the twins who participated in the research had been reunited for as long as several years before they were assessed.
    d. all of the above.

12. Which of the following conclusions seems most reasonable, based on the substantial number of research studies comparing the personalities of twins reared together and twins reared apart?
    a. Contrary to popular belief, identical twins are no more similar than fraternal twins.
    b. Fraternal twins are typically more similar than identical twins, whether reared together or apart.
    c. It is obvious that identical twins are more alike than fraternal twins, but this has been shown to be true only because parents treat identical twins more alike.
    d. Identical twins are more alike than fraternal twins, and a tendency for parents to treat identical twins more similarly does not seem to explain this consistent finding.

13. In adoption studies, behavior geneticists are particularly interested in comparing the degree of similarity of adopted individuals to
    a. their adoptive parents.
    b. their biological parents.
    c. both their adoptive parents and their biological parents.
    d. none of the above.

14. Nate is a 23-year-old academically successful engineering student who was adopted into a loving family when he was only 2 days old. Based on a substantial number of research studies on adopted childrens' personalities, Nate's interests in technical subjects and his solid academic abilities are likely to be most similar to those of
    a. his adoptive parents.
    b. his biological parents.
    c. his college roommates, even though one of them is majoring in art history and the other is studying sociology but is barely passing his courses.
    d. all of the above, because genes and shared living environments have equal impacts on personality.

15. Which of the following is true of temperament in infants?
    a. Psychologists measure temperament by finding out how relaxed or emotionally reactive and intense an infant tends to be.
    b. In considering temperament, some babies can be classified as "easy" and others as "difficult."
    c. Knowing newborn babies' temperaments allows us to predict something about the degree of fearfulness and sociability they will display at later points in development.
    d. All of the above.

16. According to the textbook, an adopted child's
    _____ would be unlikely to be affected much by the
    adoptive parents' parenting practices.
    a. personality
    b. attitudes
    c. values
    d. manners

17. Baby Natalie, age 5 months, is somewhat fussy, does
    not have a very regular sleep schedule, and is not
    very quickly soothed when she starts to cry. Based
    on categories of babies described in the textbook
    and on Jerome Kagan's comments in the video, we
    would classify baby Natalie's temperament as
    a. easy.
    b. difficult.
    c. quick to warm up.
    d. depressed.

18. If we find that the heritability estimate for a
    particular trait is rather high, for example .80, this
    can be interpreted to mean that
    a. for each person in the group studied, 80% of that
       trait was shaped by genes, and the remaining
       20% by environmental factors.
    b. within the group studied, 80% of the variation in
       that trait is attributable to genetic differences
       within that group.
    c. 80% of the people with that trait got it from their
       genes.
    d. 80% of the people with that trait got it from their
       environment.

19. Perhaps the most accurate conclusion about genetic
    and environmental influences on behavior is that
    a. genetic factors usually overshadow
       environmental factors.
    b. environmental factors usually overshadow
       genetic factors.
    c. the effects of genes and the environment are
       additive.
    d. genes react in different ways to differing
       environments, and the environment reacts in
       different ways to differing genes.

20. Which of the following would be the clearest
    example of gene-environment correlation of the sort
    explained by Robert Plomin in the video?
    a. Ten-year-old Nancy hates to read, but her
       teacher has assigned her to a special after-school
       reading enrichment program. Although she
       rebelled strongly at first, over the past month she
       has become increasingly cooperative, and now
       seems on her way to stronger reading skills.
       Reading may never be her favorite activity, but

her parents are quite pleased that she is no longer
in the bottom reading group in school.
    b. Lila, age 8, is very shy, especially around
       strangers. Over the past year, her parents have
       been trying to help by encouraging plenty of
       social activities. They began by inviting
       classmates from school over to their house, one at
       a time, and they will soon move on to planning
       small group activities for Lila, with a focus on
       craft activities Lila has always loved doing on her
       own. Lila still prefers solitary activities, but her
       parents plan to keep up the effort to help her
       social adjustment.
    c. Cliff is an active, outgoing 22-year-old guy who
       has always craved excitement and novelty. At
       least since his teenage years, he has always easily
       attracted other active, outgoing people into his
       life. He and his friends have had dozens of
       exciting travel adventures together, and these
       have nurtured Cliff's love of new and thrilling
       experiences.
    d. At a very young age, Randall displayed a good
       sense of rhythm and could sing a variety of songs,
       staying perfectly on key. Knowing that it is very
       difficult to make a living in the music business,
       Randall's father has made a strong effort to
       discourage Randall from any involvement with
       music in the home, hoping that he will develop
       an interest in the field of law or medicine instead
       of music.

21. Researchers in the field of _____ have been working
    to develop sophisticated genetic tests to reveal
    precisely which genes may put an individual at risk
    for a variety of conditions, such as depression,
    violent behavior, alcohol abuse, and reading
    disabilities.
    a. molecular genetics
    b. evolutionary psychology
    c. behaviorism
    d. neuropsychology

22. The general point of focus of evolutionary
    psychology is the study of
    a. genetic similarities and differences among
       members of twin pairs.
    b. racial and ethnic diversity, and conflict and
       harmony in relation to our human differences.
    c. the importance of personal growth and self-
       fulfillment in improving personal happiness and
       social relationships.
    d. how specific behaviors and cognitive capacities
       affect the chances for survival and reproduction,
       thereby influencing which genes are passed to the
       next generation.

23. What explanation do evolutionary psychologists offer for the fact that so many humans initially have a more intense and immediate fear reaction to the sight of a spider or a snake than to guns or electricity?
    a. Guns and electricity can be a force for good as well as evil, and we innately know this.
    b. Spiders and snakes can survive and reproduce and pass down their genes to their offspring.
    c. Our human ancestors who displayed fear and avoidance of spiders and snakes were more likely to survive and reproduce than those humans that did not fear and avoid spiders and snakes, and the genes that influenced these fear tendencies were passed down to us.
    d. Those of us who have a strong fear of spiders and snakes are poorly adapted to the current environment, and those with fears of guns and electricity have more emotional control.

24. Evidence suggests that gender differences in mate preferences are
    a. explained entirely by genes.
    b. a product of natural selection, and are unaffected by social structure.
    c. a product of natural selection, but are also influenced by social structure.
    d. entirely a product of social structure.

25. In cultures where gender equality has increased, gender differences in mate preferences have
    a. decreased.
    b. increased.
    c. shifted, but in different directions in each individual culture.
    d. remained constant, because these mate preference patterns are a matter of long-standing cultural tradition.

ANSWER KEY FOR THE ACTIVE REVIEW EXERCISES

1. Genes; deoxyribonucleic acid (DNA); chromosome; gene; [1] Textbook, Video 4
2. 23; 23; 46; the whole organism; [1] Textbook
3. genome; 30,000; [1] Textbook
4. 99.9%; 99%[1]; 90%; [1, 2] Video 4, Textbook
5. huge; in interaction with differing environments; [2, 3] Textbook
6. all; turned on or off; genes; indirect; "recipe"; [3] Textbook, Video 4
7. gene complexes; [3] Textbook, Video 4
8. behavior genetics; [4] Textbook, Video 4
9. *Your answer should include the following ideas:*
   a. Twin studies: Comparisons of the degree of similarity of identical and fraternal twins permit us to see how differences in genes relate to behavioral differences. If genetic differences are important, identical twins reared together (same environment, same genes) should be significantly more similar to one another on the trait being measured than are fraternal twins reared together (same environment, different genes). Twins separated at birth show another angle on the same question: How similar are identical twins (same genes, different environments) and fraternal twins (different genes, different environment)? In either case, if identical twins resemble each other more than fraternal twins, differences in genes can be considered to determine differences in the behavior under study.
   b. Adoption studies: Individuals adopted at birth are compared to their biological family members and their adoptive family members. If they resemble their biological family members more than their adoptive parents, the similarity of genes would most reasonably explain this result. If they resembled their adoptive family members more than their biological family members, the logical explanation would be the impact of similar environments. [4, 5, 6, 7, 8, 9] Textbook, Video 4
10. a single; all; two different; about half; identical; fraternal; [4, 5] Textbook, Video 4
11. more; do; [6, 8] Textbook
12. more alike; apart; genes; [5, 6, 11] Textbook
13. all the same; environments; Behavior; environments; genes; [5, 6, 8] Textbook, Video 4
14. similarities; also had; many; firefighters; [6, 8] Video 4
15. similarities; [6, 8] Textbook
16. are not; volunteers who responded to newspaper ads; representative; studies with appropriate comparison groups; [6, 8] Textbook, Video 4
17. identical and fraternal; less similar than; more similar than; significant; [6, 8] Textbook, Video 4
18. some; varies; about 50 percent; [6, 7, 11] Video 4
19. nearly all; adopted; [6, 7] Video 4
20. bathing suits with holes; strengths and limitations; compensate for; much more; [6, 7, 8] Video 4
21. genes; environment; [7, 8] Textbook, Video 4
22. and also; no; permitted; [8] Video 4
23. separation; moderate; confirm; [7, 8] Textbook, Video 4
24. home environment; essentially no; even if; [7, 8] Textbook, Video 4
25. biological; adoptive; no; more; modest; [7, 8, 9] Textbook, Video 4
26. attitudes, manners, beliefs, and values; higher than; lower than; benefit; does; [9] Textbook
27. personality; how we're doing it; with the first few days of life; stable; fairly strong; identical; fraternal; [10] Video 4
28. heritability; [11] Textbook, Video 4
29. groups; cannot; or; [11] Textbook
30. silly; full; and; meaningful; [11, 12] Textbook, Video 4
31. does not mean; high; taller; unlikely; [11, 12] Video 4, Textbook
32. predispose; both genes and environment; two hands clapping; respond to; [12] Video 4
33. a mistake; [12] Textbook, Video 4
34. specific environments; loves; correlated with; [12] Video 4
35. longitudinal; not necessarily; is; [12] Video 4
36. Molecular; several hundred; [13] Video 4
37. promise; prevention before; [13] Video 4
38. evolutionary; behavior; genes; [14] Textbook, Video 4
39. natural selection; Darwin; mutations; most; [14] Textbook, Video 4
40. flexibility; [14] Video 4
41. wrong; psychology; [14] Textbook
42. sweet; high; more; obesity; promoted; retained; [15] Textbook
43. reptile; gun; [15] Video 4
44. altruism; our own; higher; [15] Video 4
45. men; how we evolved; [15, 16] Video 4
46. men; women; men; [15, 16] Textbook

---

1. If your textbook is the older 7th edition of Myers' *Psychology in Modules*, the statistic given there is 95% similarity between humans and chimpanzees.

47. expands; committed; increase; somewhat different; [16] Textbook

48. women; men; older; younger; *Your answer in the lined portion of the item should include the following ideas:* Evolutionary psychologists point out that our ancestors who displayed and acted on these kinds of mate preferences were more likely to survive and pass down their genes to successive generations. Because women's reproductive years end in midlife, natural selection would favor men's attractions to younger women. Because men with resources, or with the capacity to acquire resources, are more able to contribute to the survival of young humans, natural selection would favor women's choice of somewhat older mates with the status and resouces to be a provider to their children. [16, 17] Video 4

49. converge; less; equality; [16, 18] Textbook, Video 4

50. hindsight explanations; backward; responsibility; underestimate; [17] Textbook

ANSWER KEY FOR THE SELF TEST

Item #	Answer	Learning Outcome #	Source	Item #	Answer	Learning Outcome #	Source
1.	c	1	Textbook, Video 4	14.	b	7, 8	Video 4
2.	b	1	Textbook, Video 4	15.	d	10	Textbook, Video 4
3.	a	1	Textbook	16.	a	9, 7	Textbook
4.	d	2	Textbook, Video 4	17.	b	10	Video 4
5.	a	3	Textbook	18.	b	10	Textbook
6.	c	4	Textbook	19.	d	12	Textbook, Video 4
7.	b	4	Textbook	20.	c	12	Video 4
8.	d	4, 5	Textbook, Video 4	21.	a	13	Textbook, Video 4
9.	a	5	Textbook	22.	d	14	Textbook, Video 4
10.	d	5, 6, 8	Textbook	23.	c	14, 15	Video 4
11.	d	8	Textbook	24.	c	16, 15, 14	Textbook, Video 4
12.	d	8	Textbook	25.	a	16, 17	Textbook, Video 4
13.	c	7, 4	Textbook, Video 4				

Lesson 5 (Nurture and Human Diversity)

Different Strokes

Assignments

Reading: The sections "Parents and Peers," "Cultural Influences," "Gender Development," and "Reflections on Nature and Nurture" in Chapter 3; and "Prejudice" in Chapter 18 of *Psychology* by David Myers (Module 7 and the "Prejudice" section of Module 57 in the modular version of *Psychology*)

Video: Episode 5, "Different Strokes"

LEARNING OUTCOMES

Familiarize yourself with the Learning Outcomes for this lesson before you begin the assignments. Return to them to check your learning after completing the Steps to Learning Success. Careful work on these materials should equip you to accomplish the outcomes.

Parent and Peers (Module 7)

1. Discuss what research has revealed about the degree to which parents influence their childrens' personalities.

2. Explain how the prenatal environment can affect the individual's development, and how twins who share the same womb may have differences in their prenatal environment.

3. Recognize the influence of experience on brain development during childhood and throughout life.

4. Compare the influence of parents and peers on childrens' development.

Cultural Influences (Module 7)

5. Define **culture** and describe its contribution to the pattern of our lives.

6. Provide examples of differences in cultural **norms** and practices that influence behavior.

7. Compare **individualism** and **collectivism**, and discuss costs and benefits that come with each of these cultural values.

Gender Development (Module 7)

8. Briefly summarize the similarities and differences between men and women, both biologically and psychologically.

9. Describe some of the distinctions observed in male and female social behavior—connectedness, **aggression**, and dominance.

10. Explain the roles played by chromosomes, genes, and sex hormones in the determination of biological sex.

11. Distinguish among **gender roles**, **gender identity**, and **gender-typing** and discuss the factors that influence each.

12. Be aware of the ways in which children acquire gender identity, and the impact this knowledge has on their emotions, attitudes, and performance.

Diversity and Prejudice (Module 57)

13. Recognize that the differences that help define who we are—our culture, our gender, our race—often separate us in ways that are both cognitive and social.

14. Describe the components of **prejudice**, and distinguish between explicit (conscious) and implicit (unconscious) prejudice.

15. Discuss the social factors that contribute to prejudice, and how social identity issues (**ingroup** vs. **outgroup**) and **scapegoating** come into play.

16. Be aware of the cognitive roots of prejudice and their role in maintaining biases.

17. Briefly summarize the purpose of the Implicit Association Test, recognizing that even if we hold certain prejudices, whether or not we act upon them is under our control.

18. Describe ways in which creating opportunities for groups to cooperate and communicate can help mitigate the distrust and antagonism associated with prejudice.

ACTIVE REVIEW

Each item in this section is based on material presented in the video or the textbook assignment for this lesson, or both. Complete this section, referring as needed to your notes or the source materials themselves. Answers are provided at the end of this lesson.

Parents and Peers

1. The environment is the *(nature / nurture)* portion of the human equation–those factors that further shape the emerging individual. If genetic differences account for about *(one-fourth / one-half / two thirds)* of the variations in personality, what parts of the environment account for the rest? From Freud onward, the assumption has been that it is the

   _____.

2. As Robert Plomin states, genetic data are indicating that children in the same family have *(the same / different)* environments. A direct test is a(n)

   _____ study, in which two children growing up in the same family are not genetically related. How similar are they in personality, learning disabilities, weight? _____

3. What makes brothers and sisters similar is *(nature / nurture)*. What makes them different is the ____-_____ environment, the experiences only they encounter. What percentages does James Jones assign to the influence of each of the following: genes _____ percent; shared family environment _____ percent; non-shared environment _____ percent.

4. If the shared family environment accounts for *(more / fewer)* of our differences than expected, what aspects of the environment–the context–do matter? We start with the _____ environment. Nurture begins in the womb where _____ intake and exposure to _____ agents varies for each embryo. Identical twins who share the same placenta exhibit *(fewer / greater)* differences than those who do not.

5. The AllSpec study in England, a large cohort study of 10,000 families, found that stress, especially in *(early / late)* pregnancy, predicted *(short-term / long-term)* emotional problems for children.

6. Enriched environments encourage the development of _____ connections in the brain. As a child grows, these connections *(increase / decrease)* in areas associated with repetitive activities; unused synapses _____. Researchers have confirmed the importance of _____ for premature babies; early exposure to _____, spoken, written, or signed; and _____ stimulation. The brain's development *(ends / does not end)* with childhood.

7. Psychologists today maintain that parents *(shape / influence)* their childrens' lives. This is most evident, David Myers notes in the text, at the extremes. What are the two extremes he mentions? _____

   _____

   _____

   _____

   _____

8. Like adults, children try to fit into their peer group by _____. Using information from the video and text readings, fill in the following chart comparing the influence of parents and peers.

Parents influence…	Peers influence…

9. If you were to map out susceptibility to peer pressure over time, it increases from childhood through _____ _____, and peaks around the age of _____ before it starts to decline. National surveys indicate that there is *(a significant / not much of a)* generation gap between parents and children. Disagreements tend to be over things like _____ and _____.

Cultural Influences

10. Culture is a set of enduring _____, ideas, _____, values, and _____ shared by a group of people and transmitted from one _____ to the next. James Jones considers it the "fundamental experience of living by the rules and guides, beliefs, and sensibilities, and preferences and tendencies that organize a people." Culture allows us to preserve _____ and pass them to our heirs.

11. Across cultures people differ in many ways— language, monetary system, sports, ideas, traditions. But despite these differences, the capacity for _____ is a common thread among humans. Each culture has its own _____, what Shinobu Kitayama calls explicit rules. Culture is also powerful because imbedded within it are underlying assumptions that define _____ relationships. It is central to understanding human _____.

12. Attitudes, aspirations, and motivations are all created in a context of _____, Angela Ginorio points out. It is the basis for relationships both within the family and in the larger community. She gives an example of how a traditional Latino or Latina, in an attempt to avoid confrontation, will take great care in asking a friend for a _____, expressing it in terms that allow both to save face if the friend cannot respond to the request.

13. When people are exposed to a culture other than their own, they may experience _____ _____, not understanding the norms for behavior. Everything may seem different—what is considered an appropriate personal _____, the way in which people express personal _____, whether the culture tends to be fast- or slow-_____.

14. The way children are raised *(is the same / differs)* from culture to culture. Hazel Markus talks about the contrasting ways American and Japanese mothers teach their toddlers. American mothers concentrate on the _____ of things, like the colors and parts of a bus as they roll the toy vehicle back and forth. Japanese mothers focus on _____ games, relational activities with "please" and "thank you," using the same stimulus.

15. Cultural patterns echo from one generation to the next. Psychologist James Jones uses the acronym TRIOS to describe the characteristics that link black Americans to their _____ roots. What does TRIOS stand for? T_____; R_____; I_____; O_____; S_____. Try to create an acronym for your dominant cultural tradition.

16. Cultures with a strong belief in personal independence and individual achievement are called _____ cultures. Relationships

tend to be *(more temporary / long lasting)*, confrontation is *(acceptable / unacceptable)*, and morality is defined in terms of the *(self / culture)*. Such cultures are primarily found in the United States, _____, and _____ _____.

17. Interdependence, tradition, and harmony are the focus of _____ cultures, found in many parts of _____ and _____. People tend to have *(many / few)* relationships. Those they have are close and enduring. Morality is based on duty to one's *(self / social network)*. They tend to define identity in terms of the _____ _____ and in terms of their _____'s goals and commitments.

Gender Development

18. Males and females are quite *(similar / different)* in their genetic makeup; _____ of the 46 chromosomes are unisex. Physically, they differ in terms of body fat, muscle, height; age at the onset of _____, and life _____. Psychologically, women are more prone to _____ and men to _____ _____ _____.

19. Men tend to behave *(more / less)* aggressively than women across cultures and age groups. In most societies men are socially _____ and occupy *(more / less)* leadership positions, using a _____ management style. Women, however, are *(more / less)* concerned with making connections with others, even at a young age. What *(country/countries)* tend to have the most equality between the sexes? _____

20. The determination of a child's sex is based on the twenty-third pair of _____. The mother's contribution is always *(XX / XY)*; the father's is *(XX / XY)*. The _____ **chromosome** acts as a master switch for the production of the hormone _____, which triggers the growth of external male sex organs in the seventh

week of _____ development. The fourth and fifth prenatal months are also key periods for sexual differentiation.

21. Gender is defined as the set of _____ and _____ influenced characteristics by which people classify male and female. Sex-related genes and _____ influence gender differences in behavior, possibly by affecting _____ development. But many gender differences are _____.

22. The cultural environment that surrounds us shapes our _____ _____ (expectations about how men and women should behave). These learned behaviors *(are the same / vary)* from culture to culture across time. A person's sense of being either male or female is called _____ _____. Some people more than others exhibit these expected behaviors (**gender-_____**).

23. The idea that we learn gender behavior just as we learn other behaviors, through observation, _____, and punishment, is called _____ _____ _____. **Gender schema theory** takes it a step further, adding _____ to the mix. This theory proposes that the cultural "recipe" for being male or female is learned. That knowledge influences the perception of what is appropriate for a gender and behavior follows. Researchers Martin and Ruble call children gender detectives. They build quite rigid stereotypes, which are strongest at ages _____ and _____.

24. Psychological gender differences are *(quite small / larger than most people realize)*. Based on scientific evidence, Janet Shibley Hyde notes, men *(are / are not)* from Mars and women from Venus. Tests of math abilities, thought to be gender linked, and self-esteem issues among adolescent girls show only *(moderate / small)* differences. In his emotion research, Paul Ekman has also found *(differences / no differences)* between males and females.

Diversity and Prejudice

25. Does that mean that the racial divide is greater than the gender divide? James Jones would answer that question *(yes / no)*. He says that African Americans and white Americans live in _____ worlds. And to argue that treating people the same, "as if their race doesn't matter is patently _____." The goal is not to be color _____, comments Janet Helms. "The goal is to notice race and for it _____ ____ _____."

26. The differences that help define who we are—culture, gender, race—often separate us in ways that are both cognitive and social. Dr. Jones says we are _____ misers. Because we can't process all the information that is presented to us, we chunk it and organize it into categories or groups. Gender is one group; _____ is another.

27. Assuming things about another person because of their group is called _____. You wouldn't be human or part of the culture, says Susan Fiske if you didn't absorb some of these associations and the emotional _____ that go with them. "It gets constructed differently depending on who you think of as your _____ and your _____."

28. Prejudice is an attitude encompassing beliefs, emotions, and predispositions to action. The beliefs are frequently _____; the emotions are most often _____; and the action is usually _____.

29. Even research studies in which people are arbitrarily assigned to groups leads to discrimination and _____, as illustrated in the video by the competition between the blue and pink teams. There is a(n) _____ reason for forming alliances and being able to cooperate or compete for limited resources. But this kind of research result, in Dr. Cacippo's terms, "defies logic."

30. In some cases, discrimination and prejudice have distinctly social roots related to _____ within a group—the lack of money, power, and

prestige. In such situations the "_____" develop negative attitudes toward the "_____-_____," in part to justify their more privileged position.

31. As we have learned, we simplify the world by creating _____. When we categorize people we often overgeneralize, resorting to _____. We tend to estimate the frequency of events by remembering the most _____ cases. We justify peoples' less privileged positions by the _____-_____ _____, assuming that the world is just and people get what they _____. Finally, _____ is acute. We believe, after the event, that we would have been able to predict it before it occurred, and thus attribute blame to the _____.

32. Most people would like to believe they are not prejudiced, that they do not hold unjustified _____ attitudes toward _____ and their members. With a technique called the Implicit Association Test, Mahzarin Banaji is helping people become aware that they do harbor attitudes they may not realize. You can try the IAT online at: https://implicit.harvard.edu/implicit/

33. Awareness may be half the battle. Just because people have prejudices doesn't mean they have to engage in _____. As Susan Fiske advises, "Even though you may have these _____ that pop into your head ... you can silence it from the get go if you're thinking about what to serve the person for _____." The situation is malleable by _____.

34. Researchers have also found that creating situations that encourage _____ and _____ among groups can mitigate the distrust and antagonism associated with _____. The basic point, James Jones says, is that people have to want to _____. They have to want to make a better society; they have to talk to each other; they have to care about each other enough so they can have dialogue and ultimately become _____.

SELF TEST

Read each question and circle the letter of the best answer. When you have completed the Self Test, check your answers against the key at the end of this lesson. If you have answered any items incorrectly, review the appropriate materials to correct misunderstandings and cement your knowledge.

1. The environment (those factors that further shape the emerging individual) is the _____ portion of the human equation.
   a. nature
   b. neural
   c. nurture
   d. normative

2. The AllSpec study in England, a large cohort study of 10,000 families, found that
   a. parents' disciplinary styles play a major role in the emotional and physical health of their children.
   b. families with fewer numbers of children have more problems than those with large numbers of offspring.
   c. late pregnancy stress is a precursor for long-term emotional problems for the child.
   d. it is difficult finding replication studies to sustain the research results of any study, especially a large cohort study.

3. Enriched environments in early childhood
   a. often lead to childhood obesity, an increasing problem in the United States.
   b. may help nourish intellectual development, but impede the child's ability to relate to people.
   c. can overwhelm a young child and cause them to withdraw.
   d. encourage the development of neural connections in the brain.

4. Which of the following statements is <u>most</u> accurate?
   a. Today's psychologists maintain that parents shape their children and should be credited with their successes and/or blamed for their failures.
   b. The power of parenting to shape our differences is most apparent at the extremes.
   c. Two children in the same family are more alike than pairs of children selected randomly from the population.
   d. Parents are most important when it comes to the personalities of their children and the values they hold.

5. The enduring behaviors, ideas, attitudes, values, and traditions shared by a group of people and transmitted from one generation to the next is called
   a. culture.
   b. heritage.
   c. ethnicity.
   d. customs.

6. Within the United States we have the opportunity to observe different cultural patterns. Each culture has its own explicit rules called
   a. protocol.
   b. norms.
   c. customs.
   d. standards.

7. Cultural norms are reflected in the behaviors members of that culture exhibit, including
   a. only using the fingers of the right hand for eating as they do in South Asia.
   b. the fact that Scandinavians prefer greater personal space than Arabs.
   c. greater time-consciousness in Japan than in Latin America.
   d. all of the above.

8. According to James Jones, what cultural characteristic of African Americans has been helpful in allowing them to make strategic adaptive responses to changing and unpredictable environments?
   a. Impulsiveness
   b. Soul
   c. Improvisation
   d. Tenacity

9. Allison grew up in an individualist rather than a collectivist culture. As a young aspiring medical student she
   a. gives priority to nurturing and expressing her personal identity.
   b. finds it difficult to move in and out of groups, especially when she's sent into the projects to provide basic health information.
   c. defines morality in terms of her social networks and feels a duty toward them.
   d. has a few close but enduring relationships that she is careful to maintain.

10. In raising their children, many Asians and Africans cultivate
    a. the belief that what brings honor to the family brings honor to the self.
    b. emotional closeness.
    c. the ability of children to think for themselves.
    d. both a and b above.

11. Males and females are quite _____ in their genetic makeup; _____ of the 46 chromosomes are unisex.
    a. different; 18
    b. different; 23
    c. similar; 45
    d. similar; 39

12. Which of the following groups of countries tends to have the most equality between the sexes?
    a. The Scandinavian countries
    b. The United States and Canada
    c. Britain, Scotland, and Ireland
    d. France and Germany

13. In the area of social connectedness, gender differences surface early. When you observe children, you will generally find that
    a. boys typically play in large groups; girls prefer smaller groups, often just one friend.
    b. boys are more open and responsive to feedback than girls. Girls often get their feelings hurt.
    c. boys' play is less competitive than girls'.
    d. when asked a question, girls tend to guess at the answer rather than admit they don't know.

14. The Y chromosome triggers
    a. the development of testes.
    b. the production of the hormone testosterone.
    c. the different brain wiring patterns developed under the influence of testosterone.
    d. all of the above.

15. In the Nigerian village where Abdelahi grew up, it is expected that he, like his father, will be a healer. He is bright, capable, and devoted to the group. This expectation is an example of a culturally-approved
    a. vision.
    b. gender role.
    c. stereotype.
    d. norm.

16. Some people more than others exhibit expected gender behaviors. This characteristic is known as
    a. gender role.
    b. gender-typing.
    c. gender identity.
    d. a cultural norm.

17. Social learning theory suggests that we learn gender behavior, just as we learn other behaviors,
    a. in a group setting.
    b. through careful individual study.
    c. through observation, reinforcement, and punishment.
    d. by trial and error.

18. According to Janet Shibley Hyde, the psychological gender differences between men and women
    a. are non-existent.
    b. are smaller than most people realize.
    c. are larger than people realize.
    d. make no difference in psychology or any other field of study.

19. Tests of math abilities thought to be gender linked
    a. confirmed major differences between men and women.
    b. showed only small gender differences.
    c. illustrated that women actually excel in some areas of math.
    d. both b and c above.

20. Prejudice is an attitude that encompasses
    a. beliefs, often stereotypes.
    b. emotions, generally negative.
    c. predispositions to action, usually discrimination.
    d. all of the above.

21. The "haves" in society often develop negative attitudes toward the "have-nots"
    a. in order to keep them as distant from their lives as possible.
    b. because they deserve their own fate.
    c. to justify their more privileged position.
    d. because they threaten the status the "haves" have attained.

22. Efforts at reducing prejudice and antagonism among unfriendly groups will only be successful if people in the groups
    a. want to change.
    b. have a meaningful dialogue
    c. learn to care about each other enough to become friends.
    d. all of the above.

ANSWER KEY FOR THE ACTIVE REVIEW EXERCISES

1. nurture; one-half; family; [1] Textbook, Video 5
2. different; adoption; not at all; [1 and 4] Textbook, Video 5
3. nature; non-shared; 35-40%; 10%; 40-50%; [1, 4] Textbook, Video 5
4. fewer; prenatal; nutritional; toxic; fewer; [2] Textbook, Video 5
5. late; long-term; [2] Video 5
6. neural; increase; degenerate; touch; language; visual; does not end; [3] Texbook
7. influence; families that abuse and neglect their children; families who love and firmly guide their children; [4] Textbook
8. conforming; [4] Textbook, Video 5

Parents influence...	Peers influence...
religious beliefs	learning to cooperate with others
political attitudes	achieving popularity
manners	how they want to spend their time
selection of neighborhood where they live	finding appropriate styles of communication with peers
education	clothing styles; music trends
discipline	
orderliness	
ways of interacting with authority	

9. early adolescence; 14; not much of a; curfew, friends or television viewing; [4] Video 5
10. behaviors, attitudes, traditions, generation, innovations; [5] Textbook, Video
11. culture; norms; social; behavior; [5] Textbook, Video 5
12. culture; favor; [5] Textbook, Video 5
13. culture shock; space; feelings; paced; [6] Textbook
14. differs; names; social; [6] Textbook, Video 5
15. African; time; rhythm; improvisation; orality; spirituality; [6] Video 5
16. individualistic; more temporary; acceptable; self; Canada; Western Europe; [7] Textbook, Video 5
17. collectivist; Asia, Africa; few; social network; social context, group's; [7] Textbook, Video 5
18. similar; 45; puberty; expectancy; depression; anti-social personality disorder; [8] Textbook, Video 5
19. more; dominant; more; directive; more; countries; Scandinavian; [9] Textbook, Video 5
20. chromosomes; XX; XY; Y; testosterone; prenatal; [10] Textbook
21. biologically, socially; hormones; brain; learned; [10, 11] Textbook, Video 5
22. gender roles; vary; gender identity; typing; [11] Textbook
23. reinforcement; social learning theory; cognition; 5, 6; [11] Textbook
24. quite small; are not; small; no differences; [11] Video 5
25. yes; different; unreasonable; blind; not to matter; [13] Video 5
26. cognitive; race; [13] Textbook, Video 5
27. stereotyping; prejudices; ingroups; outgroups; [14] Textbook, Video 5
28. stereotypes; negative; discrimination; [14] Textbook
29. prejudice; evolutionary; [14] Video 5
30. inequalities; "haves;" "have-nots"; [15] Textbook, Video 5
31. categories; stereotypes, vivid; just-world phenomenon; deserve; hindsight; victim; [16] Textbook
32. negative; outgroups; [17] Video 5
33. discrimination; stereotypes; dinner; context; [17] Video 5
34. cooperation, communication; prejudice; change, friends; [18] Video 5

ANSWER KEY FOR THE SELF TEST

Item #	Answer	Learning Outcome #	Source	Item #	Answer	Learning Outcome #	Source
1.	c	1	Textbook, Video 5	12.	a	9	Video 5
2.	c	2	Video 5	13.	a	9	Textbook
3.	c	3	Textbook	14.	d	10	Textbook
4.	b	4	Textbook, Video 5	15.	b	11	Textbook
5.	a	5	Textbook	16.	b	11	Textbook
6.	b	6	Textbook	17.	c	12	Textbook
7.	d	6	Textbook, Video 5	18.	b	12	Video 5
8.	c	6	Video 5	19.	d	12	Video 5
9.	a	7	Textbook, Video 5	20.	d	14	Textbook
10.	d	7	Textbook, Video 5	21.	c	15	Textbook, Video 5
11.	c	8	Textbook	22.	c	18	Video 5

Lesson 6 (Conception to Childhood)

The Growing Years

Assignments

Reading: "Prenatal Development and the Newborn" and "Infancy and Childhood" in Chapter 4, "The Developing Person," in *Psychology* by David Myers (Modules 8 and 9 in the modular version of *Psychology*)

Video: Episode 6, "The Growing Years"

LEARNING OUTCOMES

Familiarize yourself with the Learning Outcomes for this lesson before you begin the assignments. Return to them to check your learning after completing the Steps to Learning Success. Careful work on these materials should equip you to accomplish the outcomes.

Prenatal Development and the Newborn (Module 8)

1. Explain what **developmental psychologists** study; list and explain the three fundamental issues in developmental psychology.

2. Describe conception and the three stages of prenatal development.

3. State what a **teratogen** is, and identify several teratogens.

4. Specify the sensory and motor capabilities of a newborn infant, and understand what the study of **habituation** reveals about what infants can sense and recognize.

Infancy and Childhood (Module 9)

5. Describe **plasticity** of the brain and identify some of the major developmental changes in the brains of newborns.

6. Understand **maturation** and the typical sequence of motor development in infants.

7. Describe **childhood amnesia**, and present explanations that account for it.

8. Discuss **Piaget**'s ideas of **assimilation** and **accommodation**.

9. Itemize in order Piaget's four **stages of cognitive development** outlined in **Piaget's theory of cognitive development** and realize the major features of each stage.

10. Compare cognitive development in typical children and in children diagnosed with **autism**.

11. Evaluate Piaget's theory of cognitive development in view of findings from more recent research conducted in various parts of the world.

12. Understand the development of language during infancy and early childhood, and recognize influences involved in language development.

13. Describe **secure** and **insecure attachment** relationships, cite factors that influence attachment relationships and **basic trust**, and appreciate the impact of attachment in early life on later outcomes.

14. Review the findings and conclusions from research into the possible effects of day care on children's development.

15. Compare and contrast **authoritarian**, **permissive**, and **authoritative parenting styles** and their relationships to children's outcomes.

ACTIVE REVIEW

Each item in this section is based on material presented in the video or the textbook assignment for this lesson, or both. Complete this section, referring as needed to your notes or the source materials themselves. Answers are provided at the end of this lesson.

Prenatal Development and the Newborn

1. Studying physical, mental, and social changes across the life span is the domain of *(clinical / developmental / counseling)* psychologists.

2. Identify and explain the three major issues in developmental psychology research. _____

   _____

   _____

   _____

   _____

3. The sperm cells of the human male are much *(larger / more numerous)* than women's egg cells. *(Conservation / Conception / Conceptualization)* occurs when after intercourse, one tiny sperm cell, out of a pool of hundreds of millions, makes its way into a single egg cell. Another name for the fertilized egg that is formed at conception is a _____.

4. Within the first two weeks after fertilization, *(about 10% / more than 50% / about 90%)* of zygotes perish. For zygotes that survive, cell division occurs at a *(slow / rapid)* pace during the first two weeks after conception, and the cells within this developing mass begin to _____, specializing for particular functions.

5. Fill in the table below to summarize the features of the three stages of **prenatal development**.

Stage of development	Time span	Processes occurring in this stage
a.	from conception through week ___	
b.	week ___ through week ___	
c.	week ___ through birth	

6. The _____, which forms very early from the zygote's outer layer of cells, attaches to the wall of the uterus and transfers nutrients in. The placenta acts to filter out certain drugs and viruses, but some potentially damaging agents–called _____–may pass through causing problems in development. Some infectious agents such as measles or chicken pox *(can / cannot)* cross the placenta and seriously affect fetal development.

7. In the video, Lawrence Platt tells us that expectant mothers who smoke during pregnancy may have *(smaller / larger)* babies.

8. Alcohol use during pregnancy can cause a child to be born with _____ _____ syndrome, in which the infant is born with a *(smaller / larger)* brain and is likely to be mentally *(retarded / gifted / normal)*.

9. Specify some of the characteristics of **fetal alcohol syndrome**. _____

   _____

   _____

   _____

10. According to comments by Calvin John Hobel in the video, research suggests that psychosocial stress

during pregnancy *(is / is not)* associated with decreased fetal growth, and that low birth weight babies have a *(lower / higher)* risk for various health problems in childhood and beyond. The textbook describes controlled studies of rodents and primates showing that prenatal stress has *(negative / positive / no)* effect on motor development, learning, and brain chemistry.

11. Newborn babies have reflexes that play important roles in survival. For example, finding a nipple and feeding are facilitated by the _____ **reflex**, which causes the infant to open the mouth and turn automatically *(toward / away from)* the direction of a gentle touch.

12. Before the 1960s, it was widely assumed that newborn infants *(could / could not)* see much beyond vague impressions of light and dark. However, laboratory tests have revealed that very young infants *(can / cannot)* make out the shapes of objects, and they spend a longer time gazing at a *(bull's eye pattern / solid disk)* than at a *(bull's eye pattern / solid disk)*, seeming also to prefer looking at *(facelike / inanimate)* objects. They turn their heads *(toward / away from)* the sound of a human voice, and show evidence of being *(able / unable)* to recognize the difference between the voice of their own mother and that of a stranger.

13. Just as adults become bored with samenesss, infants tend to become less attentive when a simple stimulus becomes routine, and this *(decrease / increase)* in responsiveness to a repeated stimulus is termed _____. Researchers, noticing that infants spend more time looking at *(novel / familiar)* displays, have used data from studies of gazing time and habituation to discover that very young infants *(can / cannot)* distinguish between sounds, colors, and shapes and *(can / cannot)* distinguish between different numbers of objects within a collection.

Infancy and Childhood

14. According to Daniel Siegel's comments in the video, an infant's brain at birth has a(n) *(underdeveloped / fully developed)* limbic system and an almost entirely *(underdeveloped / fully developed)* cortex, with a huge number of neurons whose connections are *(already / not yet)* fully established.

15. Michael Merzenich points out in the video that the infant's brain *(is / is not)* ready to absorb input like a sponge, and that during the first six months of life—a so-called "magical period"—learning and genetically-driven changes in brain connections proceed *(only with / even without)* the infant's focused attention, and *(merely / not merely)* as a product of exposure. Researchers estimate that during each second of the first six months of life, a million new neural connections per second are *(formed / broken)*.

16. According to Daniel Siegel's comments in the video, in biology the term _____ is used to mean "open to change due to experience." The brain of an infant has a *(large / limited)* degree of **plasticity**.

17. All humans follow a pattern of biological growth that has been genetically mapped out, called _____, which sets a direction for physiological and psychological development over the life span. The basic process of **maturation** *(is / is not)* greatly influenced by specific experiences.

18. Michael Merzenich mentions in the video that an infant's motor ability depends not just on development of muscle control itself, but also on differentiation and elaboration of _____ feedback to the brain—from the skin, from the muscles and joints, and from the eyes.

19. Motor development in babies shows much more individual variation in the *(sequence / timing)* of the changes than in the *(sequence / timing)*. Most babies, *(except / including)* babies that are blind, acquire the ability to sit unsupported *(before / after)* they crawl,

and to stand *(before/ after)* they walk. Although the age at which children first walk varies, about half of all babies in the U.S. first walk at around age *(one / two)* year(s). The greatest contributor to these rapid physical changes in the control of movement seems to be *(teaching by parents / imitation of siblings / biological maturation)*.

20. According to Janet Shibley Hyde, a moderately large gender difference is found in the fact that boys, as soon as they start moving around, are *(more / less)* active than girls. In the video, Shibley Hyde suggests that this could reflect differences in maturation, with *(boys / girls)* possibly exhibiting an earlier ability to restrain their activity.

21. Research has established that we generally have **childhood amnesia**–an inability to consciously remember events prior to about _____ years of age, possibly because of the large amount of brain reorganization that is occurring during this early period of life. From ages 3 to 6 years, the neural network of the brain undergoes an especially rapid growth of connections in the *(frontal lobes / occipital lobes)*.

22. Research by the famous developmental psychologist Jean Piaget led him to conclude that a child's mind *(is / is not)* merely a scaled-down version of an adult's, and that children think in ways that greatly *(resemble / differ from)* adults' ways of thinking. Piaget viewed all intellectual growth as a(n) *(active / passive)* process of using experience to *(build / receive)* progressively more complete understandings of the world.

23. According to Piaget, our minds mature by building "mental molds" called _____, which allow us to take in and organize information. While experiencing the world, to whatever extent possible, a child incorporates, or *(assimilates / accommodates)*, new information into existing schemas. However, when new information does not fit neatly into existing schemas, the child must alter the schemas to handle the new information, using a process Piaget

called *(transformation / accommodation / operation / schematization)*.

24. The mental processes involved in thinking, knowing, remembering, and communicating are known as _____. Piaget saw children's cognitive development as consisting of a series of *(continuous modifications / distinct stages)*.

25. In the first of Piaget's *(2 / 3 / 4 / 5 / 6)* stages of _____ development, the child gets to know the world through the senses and by moving in relation to objects (in touching, grasping, mouthing, tasting, looking, hearing, and so on). This period, from birth to about _____ years of age, is called the _____ stage. Piaget believed that babies under 8 months of age *(have already / have not yet)* developed _____ _____–the understanding that objects removed from sight continue to exist.

26. Karen Wynn points out in the video that most children utter their first recognizable word at a point a couple of months before or after age *(one / two)* year(s). The word explosion, or "word _____," is a rapid spurt in vocabulary that begins as the child starts combining words, usually at approximately *(10 / 12 / 18 / 36)* months of age. Susie Curtiss suggests that as the brain matures, very young children learn langauge if they are in an environment where they are *(exposed to / intentionally taught)* language. Some children speak earlier than others, although in general, *(girls / boys)* tend to develop language somewhat more rapidly.

27. Present day researchers think that the kinds of tests Piaget used led him to *(underestimate / overestimate)* the cognitive capabilities of children. In addition, as explained in the video by David Myers, "Today's psychologists have come to see the stages as *(more / less)* sharply defined than what Piaget had in mind."

28. The second of Piaget's **stages of cognitive development** is the _____ stage,

which extends from approximately age two years through _____ years. At this stage, Piaget believed that children are *(already / not)* able to carry out mental operations requiring logical thinking. For example, they *(can / cannot)* understand the principle of _____, believing that the amount of liquid in a container has changed when that liquid is transferred to a container of another shape.

29. Piaget thought children in the **preoperational stage** were also _____—unable to show empathy or imagine another person's perspective. It is important to realize that **egocentrism** in preoperational stage children *(is / is not)* equivalent to selfishness, because an egocentric child at this stage is *(aware / unaware)* that others have a different viewpoint. During the preschool age period, however, children typically show the beginnings of a _____ of mind, demonstrating some ability to make inferences about *(their own / other people's)* intentions and thoughts, and the relationship of thoughts to feelings.

30. Children diagnosed with _____ do not show the usual signs of developing a **theory of mind**, having difficulty discerning other people's thoughts *(and also / but not)* their own thoughts, feelings, and intentions.

31. The third stage of cognitive development in Piaget's theory is the _____ _____ stage, extending over the period from approximately _____ to _____ years of age. Children in this stage *(can / cannot)* think logically about *(concrete / abstract)* objects and events, showing an *(ability / inability)* to solve conservation problems and to understand the logic of certain mathematical operations.

32. By around age 12, Piaget said that children enter the _____ _____ stage of cognitive development, when they show an *(inability / ability)* to think in hypothetical terms and to perform mental operations using symbols and abstract concepts.

33. Researchers today believe that children typically show certain signs of cognitive development *(earlier than / later than / about when)* Piaget suggested, that development is more *(gradual / step-like)* than Piaget believed it to be, and that the sequence of the developmental stages is *(different / similar)* for children in various places around the world.

34. Social development can be traced from the very early weeks of life. Newborn babies' responses to voices and faces demonstrate that they are *(attracted to / neutral toward / fearful of)* other human beings, and they quickly come to show preferences for *(familiar / unfamiliar)* faces and voices. Starting at about eight months of age, just *(before / after)* they have developed **object permanence**, infants in most cultures show distress in the close presence of strangers, called _____ _____. By around 12 months, their emotional ties to their caregivers are clear, providing evidence of an infant-parent bond known as *(attachment / stranger anxiety / contact comfort)*.

35. In the video Daniel Siegel mentions English psycho-analyst John Bowlby and his colleague psychologist Mary Ainsworth, who focused their research on *(prenatal growth / attachment relationships / intellectual growth)*, concluding that early experiences form a foundation for an indivdual's developing personality.

36. Monkey studies by Harry Harlow in the 1950s pointed to the critical importance of *(body contact / nourishment)* in the development of attachment. When Harlow reared infant monkeys with two artificial "mothers," one of which was made of wire and the other of terry cloth, the infant monkeys spent more time clinging to the *(wire / cloth)* "mother," *(whether or not / only if)* it included a bottle providing nourishment.

37. Familiarity is another factor in attachment. Newly hatched ducklings or chicks, for example, develop a tendency to follow the first moving object they see during a _____ period of development, providing evidence of a type of attachment called _____.

38. When introduced to a strange laboratory setting, most infants play contentedly and explore the area when the mother is nearby in the room; they show signs of distress when she leaves the room, but calm down when she returns. This particular pattern of behavior in the "strange situation" was classified by Mary Ainsworth as indicating a(n) *(secure / insecure)* attachment relationship. Infants that cling to their mother and fail to explore in this kind of setting, or those that display either extreme distress or indifference when the mother leaves and then returns, were described by Ainsworth as showing *(secure / insecure)* attachment.

39. According to research reviewed in the textbook and comments by Jerome Kagan in the video, the quality of the attachment relationship and an infant's behavior in the "strange situation" may depend on the infant's _____—a general pattern of emotional reactivity, which is thought to be inborn and which contributes to the classification of a baby as "difficult," or "easy." Experimental evidence has confirmed, too, that attachment can be influenced by the parent's *(sensitivity / financial support)* and *(responsiveness / discipline)* in relating to the infant. Parenting involvement of *(mothers / fathers / both mothers and fathers)* contributes to a child's outcomes in life. Erik Erikson theorized that secure attachment relationships early in life foster a sense of basic _____ which could help to shape relationships in adulthood.

40. Of greater importance than the total amount of time the parent spends with the child is the parent's responsiveness to the child. Daniel Siegel comments in the video on the significance of "_____

communication" in the parent-child relationship. This type of communication means that the parent perceives and understands the child's signals, and responds to those signals in a timely and effective way. As a result, Siegel says, the *(parent / child)* "feels felt" by the *(parent / child)*.

41. As compared with children who experience supportive, responsive care early in life, those who are abused or neglected are *(equally / more / less)* likely to grow up to abuse their own children, even though most abused children *(become / do not become)* abusers. Research suggests that trauma early in life may leave *(temporary / lasting)* effects on brain chemistry and hormonal responses. For example, those abused children who later display more aggressive behavior show a delayed pattern of release of the brain neurotransmitter _____.

42. Infants whose attachments are disrupted through early separation show *(no / intial / permanent)* disturbances in eating, sleeping, and relating to their new caregivers, *(but can later / and do not)* recover if placed in loving, stable homes.

43. Early investigations of the impact of maternal employment and day care revealed *(no / significant)* damaging effects on children's development when the day care was of high quality, even though one study found stress hormones in young children *(increased / decreased)* while in day care centers and *(increased / decreased)* at home. While factors such as warmth and responsiveness of the staff, the ratio of children to staff, the mother's sensitivity, and the socioeconomic level of the family affect the outcome of day care, one large U.S. study of 4½-year-old to 6-year-old children found *(more / less)* advanced cognitive abilities but also *(increased / decreased)* aggressiveness when children spent larger amounts of time in day care.

44. Janet Shibley Hyde says in the video that a large-scale research study by the National Institute of Child Health and Human Development on the effects of

day care yielded results that were *(simple / complex)*. But she summarizes the results as showing basically that "kids do just fine as long as the childcare quality is *(average / good to excellent / outstanding)*." She adds the point that generally children *(do well / don't do well)* with poor quality childcare, but that care in the home can also be of poor quality in some cases. When people worry about negative effects of childcare, Shibley Hyde says, they are often thinking in terms of the comparison between an idealized mother and *(good / bad)* child care, overlooking the point that "not all mothers are great mothers."

45. Davd Myers points out that across different cultures, we find children can thrive under a variety of *(minimally adequate / responsive)* caregiving arrangements. For example, in some African cultures, a newborn baby is held by several other women before it is held by its mother, spending all its time during the early weeks of life being held and breast fed, often by other breast-feeding mothers. This pattern leads to *(no / confused / fragile / disrupted / multiple)* attachments. Fundamentally, what children everywhere seem to need is *(consistent / varied)* relationships with warm and responsive people who are *(highly intelligent / financially secure / trustworthy)*.

46. For items a–c below, choose the term from the Key List for the *parenting style* that matches the description, and write the term in the blank provided.

    Key List
    authoritarian
    authoritative
    permissive

    a. _____ Parents set very few guidelines for their children's behavior, allowing the children to decide for themselves; lax or *laissez-faire* parenting.

    b. _____ Parents set and enforce strict rules, insisting on obedience to orders, and often using punishment for failure to comply; one-way, top-down (parent to child) parenting practices.

    c. _____ Parents have standards and expectations that they communicate to the children, generally explaining the reasons for rules, hearing appropriate input from the children, and permitting reasonable exceptions; firm but open parenting practices.

47. Research has established that children with higher self-esteem, self-reliance, and social competence tend to come from homes where the _____ parenting style has been in effect. Of course, this is *(correlational / experimental)* evidence, which *(proves / does not prove)* that the parenting style is the cause of the child's outcomes.

48. Thinking beyond the possibility that the authoritative parenting style may cause an increase in children's competence, suggest at least two other plausible explanations for the correlation between authoritative parenting and children's competence.

SELF-TEST

Read each question and circle the letter of the best answer. When you have completed the Self Test, check your answers against the key at the end of this lesson. If you have answered any items incorrectly, review the appropriate materials to correct misunderstandings and cement your knowledge.

1. Professor Weiss is a research psychologist whose main interest is the changes in vocabulary and thought processes in children from age 6 years through the end of adolescence. His colleague Professor Schwartz focuses her research on the relationship between physical changes in the brain and memory as people over 60 undergo aging. Both Professor Weiss and Professor Schwartz would be classified as _____ psychologists.
   a. social
   b. developmental
   c. clinical
   d. biological

2. During the last few weeks of pregnancy, just before birth, the developing human is called a(n)
   a. embryo.
   b. zygote.
   c. fetus.
   d. preoperational stage infant.

3. The embryonic period of prenatal development extends
   a. from the ninth week after conception until birth.
   b. from the sixteenth week after conception until birth.
   c. from two hours to two weeks after conception.
   d. from the second week to the eighth week after conception.

4. Teratogens ____ during the prenatal period.
   a. damage development
   b. are genes that guide normal processes of development
   c. speed up maturation
   d. do not affect development

5. Babies born with fetal alcohol syndrome
   a. recover fully if given adequate nutrition and megavitamin treatments.
   b. have smaller heads, facial defects, brain abnormalities, and mental retardation.
   c. both of the above.
   d. none of the above.

6. Which of the following is a reaction of the newborn that serves to facilitate feeding?
   a. Conservation
   b. Habituation
   c. Teratogen
   d. Rooting reflex

7. When an infant undergoes habituation to a visual stimulus, he or she
   a. shows signs of excitement when that same visual stimulus is repeatedly presented.
   b. begins to cry and squirm.
   c. spends less time looking at the stimulus when it has become familiar.
   d. becomes quite alert and pays closer attention to the stimulus.

8. When given an opportunity to focus visually on any of the following objects, the typical young infant would be likely to show a preference for gazing at
   a. a bull's-eye pattern.
   b. a solid colored disk.
   c. anything that is familiar to them.
   d. none of the above, since very young infants are unable to see clearly enough to be tested.

9. Karen Wynn, in her comments in the video, makes the point that the newborn human infant
   a. is far from a blank slate, having a variety of tendencies, including a basic readiness to interact socially.
   b. is a blank slate, with essentially no basis for responding to the physical and social world.
   c. is confused and distressed by a jumble of incomprehensible events during the first few weeks of life
   d. understands the world in essentially the same way as adults do.

10. According to experts featured in the video, which of the following is true regarding the development of the brain in newborns?
   a. The cortex is estimated to form an average of a million new connections per second during the first few months of life.
   b. The cortex is fully developed at birth.
   c. Neurons do not begin forming in the brain until after birth.
   d. To form new connections and to learn, newborn infants need to be awake, paying attention, and receiving rewards for their activities.

11. According to information provided in the video episode and in the textbook, which of the following statements is accurate regarding motor development in infancy?
    a. The timing of motor development is more predictable than the sequence.
    b. Not only muscle development, but also sensory feedback from the muscles, joints, and eyes contributes to the infant's increasing control over its movements.
    c. Babies typically learn to crawl before they learn to sit up without support.
    d. Crawling develops significantly earlier in children who are routinely put to sleep on their backs.

12. "Childhood amnesia"
    a. is a term for a normal inability of adults to consciously recall events occurring before they were about 3½ years of age.
    b. occurs when severe child abuse causes repression of early childhood memories.
    c. can be entirely overcome through hypnosis or short-term psychotherapy.
    d. has not been investigated at all by psychologists.

13. Psychologist Jean Piaget suggested that one important element in cognitive development is our tendency to take in new information and add it to our existing schemas using the process of
    a. accommodation.
    b. assimilation.
    c. intellectualization.
    d. conservation.

14. Which of the following alternatives lists Piaget's stages of cognitive development in the correct sequence?
    a. preoperational, concrete operational, sensorimotor, formal operational
    b. sensorimotor, formal operational, preoperational, concrete operational
    c. formal operational, concrete operational, preoperational, sensorimotor
    d. sensorimotor, preoperational, concrete operational, formal operational

15. According to Piaget, children in the early months of the ___ stage of cognitive development do not yet understand object permanence.
    a. formal operational
    b. preoperational
    c. sensorimotor
    d. concrete operational

16. According to developmental psychologist Karen Wynn's comments in the video, most infants utter their first word
    a. between six and nine months of age.
    b. between nine and fourteen months of age.
    c. between fourteen and eighteen months of age.
    d. between eighteen months and 2 years of age.

17. Jean Piaget suggested that children have acquired the ability to understand the concept of conservation by the beginning of the ____ stage of cognitive development.
    a. sensorimotor
    b. formal operational
    c. preoperational
    d. concrete operational

18. According to Piaget's theory, toddlers during the preschool years would typically be in the ___ stage of cognitive development.
    a. preconventional
    b. preoperational
    c. concrete operational
    d. formal operational

19. In Piaget's view, children in the preoperational stage of cognitive development show a tendency to be egocentric, which means that they
    a. cannot understand someone else's point of view.
    b. cannot think logically.
    c. are intentionally selfish and uncaring.
    d. have a complete understanding of the concept of conservation.

20. Piaget concluded that children between the ages of about 2 and 6 years
    a. would be expected to be in the formal operational stage of cognitive development.
    b. can perform mental operations that allow them to think logically about concrete objects and events.
    c. are taken in by appearances, believing that objects that have changed shape must also have changed their quantity.
    d. none of the above.

21. Children with autism
    a. have difficulty communicating and interacting socially.
    b. cannot easily infer the thoughts and feelings of other people.
    c. could be described as having an impaired "theory of mind."
    d. all of the above.

22. Today's psychologists believe that the stages of cognitive development that Piaget proposed
    a. offer a completely accurate description of how children's thinking actually develops.
    b. can be observed in children worldwide, but not in the same order in which Piaget listed them.
    c. can be observed in children in the U.S. and Europe, but not at all in children in other parts of the world.
    d. are not as separate and distinct as Piaget believed.

23. When one-year-old Timothy enters an unfamiliar laboratory playroom with his mother, he stays near her for a while. But soon he ventures out to play with some colorful and interesting toys, looking back at his mother every few minutes and bringing toys to her now and then. Later, when his mother leaves the room for a moment, Timothy cries and seems distressed, but he calms down shortly after she returns. Based on this description, a developmental psychologist would probably see Timothy as having a(n) _____ relationship with his mother.
    a. insecure attachment
    b. secure attachment
    c. overly dependent
    d. unsupportive and unresponsive

24. According to the textbook and the video episode, which of the following conclusions has been supported by results of research into the effects of day care on young children?
    a. Children do poorly even if they are cared for in high quality day care facilities.
    b. A mother's care is always superior to care provided in a day care facility.
    c. Children do poorly if they are cared for in poor quality day care facilities.
    d. All of the above.

25. Fourteen-year-old Erika has parents that are very easy-going and relaxed people. Erika's boyfriend Jeremy is amazed that Erika's parents do not set any rules about how late she can stay out on weekends. In fact, Jeremy's parents impose more rules for him than Erika's parents do for her, even though Jeremy is two years older. Most likely, Erika's parents would be classified as having a(n) _____ style of parenting.
    a. permissive
    b. authoritative
    c. authoritarian
    d. abusive

ANSWER KEY FOR THE ACTIVE REVIEW EXERCISES

1. developmental; [1] Textbook
2. a) <u>nature / nurture</u>: the contribution of genes and experience to development; b) <u>continuity / stages</u>: whether development proceeds gradually, or through distinct separate stages; c) <u>stability / change</u>: whether our personalities later in life resemble what we displayed earlier in life [1] Textbook
3. more numerous; Conception; zygote; [2] Textbook, Video 6
4. more than 50%; rapid; differentiate; [2] Textbook
5. (a) zygote; from conception through week 2; Cell division and differentiation; attachment to the uterine wall and formation of the placenta (b) embryo; week 2 through week 8; Organs begin to form and function; heart begins to beat (c) fetus; week 9 through birth; Continued growth and maturing of organs (with the ability to survive if birth occurs as early as during the sixth prenatal month); [2] Textbook, Video 6
6. placenta; teratogens; can; [2, 3] Textbook, Video 6
7. smaller; [3] Textbook, Video 6
8. fetal alcohol; smaller; retarded; [3] Textbook, Video 6
9. smaller head, facial abnormalities, brain abnormalities, cognitive impairment (mental retardation), behavioral disruptions; [3] Textbook, Video 6
10. is; higher; negative; [3] Video 6
11. rooting; toward; [4] Textbook
12. could not; can; bull's-eye pattern; solid disk; facelike; toward; able; [4] Textbook
13. decrease; habituation; novel; can; can; [4] Textbook, Video 6
14. underdeveloped; underdeveloped; not yet; [4, 5] Video 6
15. is; even without; merely; formed; [5] Video 6
16. plasticity; large; [5] Video 6
17. maturation; is not; [6] Textbook
18. sensory; [6] Video 6
19. timing; sequence; including; before; before; one; biological maturation; [6] Textbook, Video 6
20. more; girls; [6] Video 6
21. 3½; frontal lobes; [5, 6, 7] Textbook
22. is not; differ from; active; build; [8] Textbook, Video 6
23. schemas; assimilates; accommodation; [9] Textbook
24. cognition; distinct stages; [9] Textbook, Video 6
25. 4; cognitive; 2; sensorimotor; have not yet; object permanence; [9] Textbook, Video 6
26. 1 year; spurge; 18; exposed to; girls; [12] Textbook, Video 6
27. underestimate; less; [11] Textbook, Video 6
28. preoperational; 6 or 7; not; cannot; conservation; [9] Textbook, Video 6
29. egocentric; is not; unaware; theory; other people's; [10] Textbook
30. autism; and also; [10] Textbook
31. concrete operational; 6 or 7; 11; can; concrete; ability; [9] Textbook, Video 6
32. formal operational; ability; [9] Textbook, Video 6
33. earlier than; gradual; similar; [11] Textbook, Video 6
34. attracted to; familiar; after; stranger anxiety; attachment; [13] Textbook, Video 6
35. attachment relationships; [13] Textbook, Video 6
36. body contact; cloth; whether or not; [13] Textbook
37. critical; imprinting; [13] Textbook
38. secure; insecure; [13] Textbook, Video 6
39. temperament; sensitivity; responsiveness; both mothers and fathers; trust; [13] Textbook, Video 6
40. contingent; child; parent; [13] Video 6
41. more; do not become; lasting; serotonin; [13] Textbook
42. initial; but can later; [13] Textbook
43. no; increased; decreased; more; increased; [14] Textbook, Video 6
44. complex; good to excellent; don't do well; bad; [14] Video 6
45. responsive; multiple; consistent; trustworthy; [13, 14] Textbook
46. permissive; authoritarian; authoritative; [15] Textbook, Video 6
47. authoritative; correlational; does not prove; [15] Textbook, Video 6
48. *Your answer should reflect these general ideas:* 1) The child's behavior could be a cause of the parenting style. Children who already tend to be cooperative and competent may bring out authoritative parenting practices in their parents. More difficult, aggressive children may "push their parents' buttons," causing the parent to "lay down the law," more often setting strict rules and applying harsher punishment. 2) Both the parent's style and the child's behavior may be a product of a third variable. For example, genes that influence aggressiveness or social competence could exert an effect on the parent's choice of parenting styles and could independently influence the child's social competence. Mild-mannered, relaxed parents might have mild-mannered, docile children, independent of any impact from parenting practices. Aggressive and controlling parents, who may tend to be more punitive, may lean toward an authoritarian style of parenting, but might have children who tend to be more aggressive, headstrong, and unruly, whether or not the parenting style contributed to this; [15] Textbook

ANSWER KEY FOR THE SELF TEST

Item #	Answer	Learning Outcome #	Source	Item #	Answer	Learning Outcome #	Source
1.	b	1	Textbook	14.	d	9	Textbook, Video 6
2.	c	2	Textbook, Video 6	15.	c	9	Textbook, Video 6
3.	d	2	Textbook	16.	b	12	Video 6
4.	a	3	Textbook, Video 6	17.	d	9	Textbook, Video 6
5.	b	3	Textbook, Video 6	18.	b	9	Textbook, Video 6
6.	d	4	Textbook	19.	a	9	Textbook
7.	c	4	Textbook	20.	c	9	Textbook, Video 6
8.	a	4	Textbook	21.	d	10	Textbook
9.	a	4	Video 6	22.	d	11	Textbook, Video 6
10.	a	5	Video 6	23.	b	13	Textbook, Video 6
11.	b	6	Video 6, Textbook	24.	c	14	Textbook, Video 6
12.	a	7	Textbook	25.	a	15	Textbook
13.	b	8	Textbook				

Lesson 7 (Adolescence to Older Adults)

The Becoming Years

Assignments

Reading: "Adolescence," "Adulthood," and "Reflections on Two Major Developmental Issues" in Chapter 4 of *Psychology* by David Myers (Modules 10 and 11 in the modular version of *Psychology*)

Video: Episode 7, "The Becoming Years"

LEARNING OUTCOMES

Familiarize yourself with the Learning Outcomes for this lesson before you begin the assignments. Return to them to check your learning after completing the Steps to Learning Success. Careful work on these materials should equip you to accomplish the outcomes.

Adolescence (Module 10)

1. Explain what is meant by the statement that psychologists today view development as a lifelong process.

2. Define **adolescence** and describe some of the major changes and challenges that are a part of this period of human development.

3. List and describe physical changes in growth patterns and in **primary** and **secondary sex characteristics** that occur around the time of **puberty**, and discuss differences in the timing of physical maturation in boys and girls, including the effects of individual variations.

4. Describe physical changes that occur in the brain during adolescence, and relate these to changes in adolescents' thinking capacities and patterns of emotional expression.

5. Identify which of **Piaget's stages of cognitive development** is attained by the typical adolescent, and describe the new modes of adolescent thinking and behavior that accompany this stage.

6. Explain how the **imaginary audience** and the **personal fable** are related to aspects of adolescents' behavior, emotions, and social relationships.

7. List and explain the distinction between the three levels of moral reasoning proposed by **Lawrence Kohlberg**, and discuss issues surrounding the relationship among moral reasoning, feeling, and actions.

8. Explain **Erikson's theory of psychosocial development**, focusing on research into the developmental tasks that Erikson cited as important during adolescence and at various points during adulthood.

9. Describe changes in parent-child relationships and peer relationships during adolescence.

10. Discuss what research has revealed about risk-taking during adolescence, and how adolescent risk-taking relates to changes in the brain.

11. Describe historical changes in the duration of adolescence in the Western world, noting changes in the timing of sexual maturity and achievement of independence.

Adulthood (Module 11)

12. Describe the physical changes that occur in young adulthood, middle adulthood, and old age, and list some of the factors that can influence these changes.

13. Describe the events associated with **menopause** and their timing, and summarize research findings that have helped to distinguish the facts from some of the widely circulated myths about menopause.

14. Describe the changes in behavior and the brain that accompany **Alzheimer's disease**.

15. Summarize the findings of research on changes in memory and intellect with age, and explain why researchers have come to varying conclusions about the nature of these age-related changes.

16. Summarize what the textbook author and experts interviewed in the video episode say about whether there are stages in adult social development, and whether adults typically experience a **midlife crisis**.

17. Discuss the concept of the **social clock**, comparing it with the idea of developmental stages.

18. List several factors that are related to the success and longevity of marriages, and the level of life satisfaction experienced by adults in general.

19. Summarize the results of research investigating people's reactions to the prospect of their own death or the death of a loved one.

20. Describe Erikson's views on the major developmental task of the elder years.

Reflections on Two Major Developmental Issues (Module 11)

21. Summarize the main points made by the textbook author about the developmental issues of **continuity and stages**, and **stability and change**, and compare the ideas of major developmental theorists on these issues.

ACTIVE REVIEW

Each item in this section is based on material presented in the video or the textbook assignment for this lesson, or both. Complete this section, referring as needed to your notes or the source materials themselves. Answers are provided at the end of this lesson.

Adolescence

1. **Developmental psychologists** emphasize the idea that development occurs *(early in / late in / throughout)* life. "From womb to tomb," David Myers points out in the video, "life is *(a struggle / development / unchanging)*," and "we are always in the process of *(becoming / conflict / constancy / decline)*".

2. According to Laurence Steinberg's comments in the video, the transitional period of development that includes the teen years, extending roughly from ages 10 to 20, is termed *(the prenatal period / childhood / adolescence / senescence)*. **Adolescence** begins with a set of dramatic physical changes, including a *(spurt / stabilization)* of growth, followed soon by profound changes in the maturity of the reproductive system known as _____, and ending roughly at the time when individuals are no longer *(growing in height / rebelling against authority / dependent on parents)*.

3. **Puberty** occurs about ___ years *(earlier / later)* in girls than in boys. List some of the physical changes that define puberty. _____
_____

4. *(Primary / Secondary)* sex characteristics are those that are directly involved in reproduction, whereas *(primary / secondary)* sex characteristics are those that are not directly involved. Changes in the ovaries and testes in adolescence, then, would qualify as *(primary / secondary)* sex characteristics, whereas beard growth in males, breast enlargement in females, and the appearance of underarm and pubic hair would be classified as changes in *(primary / secondary)* **sex characteristics**. Puberty involves changes in *(primary / secondary / primary and secondary)* **sex characteristics**.

5. Important events of puberty include, in girls, the onset of the first menstrual period, called _____, and in boys, the occurrence of the first _____, which is generally a nocturnal emission. On an individual basis, the timing of the various changes of puberty is quite *(variable / predictable)*, whereas the sequence of these changes is more *(variable / predictable)*.

6. Earlier physical maturation seems to be associated with social advantages, such as increased popularity

and greater self-assurance for *(boys / girls / both boys and girls)*, but early maturation also *(raises / lowers)* their risk for involvement with alcohol use and sexual activity. Girls who mature *(earlier / later)* than their peers are more likely to feel self-conscious and to be subjected to teasing.

7. In the video, Daniel Siegel comments on the role of experience in the *(massive / minor)* restructuring of the brain that occurs during adolescence, and says that a teen who plays lots of sports or music will have brain circuits specific to those activities that are very *(well / poorly)* developed. During adolescence, unused neural connections in the brain are selectively *(reduced / enhanced)* through a process of pruning, and the presence of the fatty insulating material known as myelin is *(increased / decreased)*, all of which makes the brain *(more / less)* efficient.

8. Maturation of the *(frontal lobes / limbic system)* moves ahead more quickly than does the growth and development of the *(frontal lobes / limbic system)*, and this pattern provides insight into teenagers' limitations in judgment and their tendency to be *(more / less)* emotional, impulsive, and risk-prone until the brain has matured more fully.

9. During the last of Piaget's *(three / four / five)* stages of cognitive development, individuals demonstrate an *(ability / inability)* to think symbolically, to see alteratives to what exists, and to note flaws in others' reasoning. This final stage, which Piaget called the _____ _____ **stage**, is achieved by *(very few / most / all)* adolescents. The newfound cognitive abilities of this stage may help to explain why many adolescents demonstrate idealism, sensitivity to others' hypocrisy, an ability to think systematically about *(concrete / abstract)* topics, and a freshly expanded capacity to envision and perhaps worry about various alternatives for the future.

10. Adolescents become increasingly self-focused or **egocentric**, and may have a sense that everyone else is noticing them and looking at them—a phenomenon called the *(imaginary audience / personal fable)*. Adolescents may also believe that their own feelings are

unlike anyone else's, therefore thinking that no one else could possibly understand them. An adolescent's typical belief in his or her own uniqueness is called the *(imaginary audience / personal fable)*.

11. Psychologist Lawrence _____ developed a stage theory of moral reasoning involving a sequence of *(three / four / five / eight)* levels of thinking about right and wrong.

12. Match the descriptions given below with the appropriate level of moral development from the Key List, based on *Kohlberg's theory.* Write your answer in the blank provided.

Key List
conventional morality
postconventional morality
preconventional morality

a. _____ This type of self-interested moral reasoning is typical of children younger than age 9 years, with the child judging morality according to which choices bring tangible rewards or prevent punishment.

b. _____ The individual operating at this level of moral reasoning can understand social rules and laws, and decides what is moral according to those rules and laws.

c. _____ Those who reach this level of moral reasoning base their choices about what is moral not simply on concrete rewards and punishments or on adherence to social rules and laws, but instead on a recognition of broader ethical principles, ideals, and agreed-upon rights.

13. According to research findings, the three levels of moral development Kohlberg proposed are observed to unfold according to a strict *(sequence / timeline)*, although the _____ level does not seem to be equally common among all cultures and groups of people. For example, in certain Asian societies, as well as among *(men / women)* in Western societies, morality may be built around *(genetic / caring / competitive)* relationships, rather than being based on abstract principles.

14. Psychologists are interested not just in our moral reasoning abilities, but also in our moral feelings and actions. The social intuitionist explanation holds that moral reasoning *(follows / precedes)* moral feelings, suggesting that our rapidly evoked "gut feelings" about a situation have an important impact on the moral judgments we make. Research has suggested that learning to *(achieve / delay)* gratification may equip us to act in ways that are consistent with our moral judgments.

15. Erik Erikson proposed *(three / four / five / eight / ten)* stages of *(cognitive / emotional / moral / psychosocial)* development, with these stages spanning the period from *(infancy / toddlerhood / childhood / adolescence)* through (*adolescence / young adutlhood / middle adulthood / late adulthood)*.

16. In Erikson's view, the major psychosocial issue to be tackled and resolved during adolescence is *(trust vs. mistrust / initiative vs. guilt / identity vs. role confusion / intimacy vs. isolation)*. While working on this issue, Western adolescents typically explore and try out various roles before settling on a coherent sense of self—their_____, which incorporates a sense their personal beliefs, values, goals, and direction. Laurence Steinberg mentions in the video that adolescents may remain for a time in a state of psychosocial *(moratorium / potentiation / disconnection)* while they experiment with various roles and try on different identities. Adolescents who do not successfully form an identity fall into a state of role *(confusion / dependency / rebellion)*, according to Erikson.

17. As teenagers gradually become more independent of parents, conflicts with their parents are observed to *(increase / decrease)* in intensity as these conflicts *(increase / decrease)* in frequency, and peer relationships become increasingly *(important / irrelevant)*. Laurence Steinberg says the typical conflict between adolescents and their parents *(is / is not)* about big things, but that it is part of the process by which kids develop *(closeness / autonomy)* and a sense of *(connection to / independence from)* their parents.

18. The tendency toward risk-taking is another feature that tends to *(increase /decrease)* in prominence during the teen years. According to Keith Humphreys' comments in the video, those adolescents who do absolutely no risk-taking tend to have *(better / worse)* outcomes than those who take some moderate risks.

19. Laurence Steinberg's experiments have demonstrated that in a driving simulator, teens took *(more / fewer)* risks when friends were nearby than when there were no friends present. Teens raised in permissive households are *(more / less)* susceptible to peer influence than those raised in *(authoritarian / authoritative)* households. Steinberg comments that susceptibility to peer influence tends to be *(lower / higher)* in 8th or 9th graders than in 4th graders or 12th graders, following a pattern of rising from childhood until the *(beginning / middle / end)* of the teens, and droppings off somewhat after that point.

20. The textbook points out that in Western societies today, adolescence has become a *(shorter / longer)* period of development because of *(earlier / later)* sexual maturity and *(earlier / later)* independence.

Adulthood

21. According to David Myers, psychologists *(now / no longer)* regard adulthood as one long plateau spanning the period between adolescence and old age. Development *(pauses / continues)* during adulthood. Yet in comparison with what is true during childhood, age during adulthood is a(n) *(equally / less / more)* precise indicator of capacities, abilities, and life changes.

22. Various physical indicators, such as cardiac output, keenness of the senses, muscle strength, and speed of reactions, generally *(reach a peak / remain stable / continue to increase)* as people reach their mid-twenties. In middle adulthood, reductions in vigor occur at a *(faster / slower / constant)* rate, and the rate of decline is *(related / unrelated)* to the individual's exercise patterns and health habits.

23. In comparison to men, peak physical abilities for women tend to be attained at *(an earlier / a later / the same)* age. Occurring at an average age of *(40 / 50 /*

60), *(puberty / menarche / menopause)* brings women's menstrual cycles and their fertility to a natural end, as the production of the hormone _____ declines. Hot flashes are a(n) *(common / uncommon)* occurrence during **menopause** for women in the U.S. and Canada, and a *(more / less)* common symptom of menopause in Japan. Research on American and Australian women has revealed that middle-aged women experiencing menopause are *(more / no more / less)* likely to be depressed than middle-aged women not experiencing menopause.

24. Men in middle age experience a reduction in reproductive hormones that is *(more abrupt than / more gradual than / very similar to)* that of women, suggesting that the idea of a male menopause is a *(myth / reality)*.

25. Research studies support the conclusion that older people are *(less / more)* susceptible to short-term illnesses, and that a *(minority / majority)* of people over the age of 65 live in nursing homes and other institutional care facilities. Most adults who live to the age of 90 *(do / do not)* suffer from senile dementia, and the life satisfaction ratings of older adults is *(higher than / lower than / similar to)* that of other age groups.

26. As we advance toward older ages, neural processing in the brain *(slows down / speeds up)*, especially for *(simple / complex)* tasks. As compared with younger adults, people who live to age 80 typically undergo a *(small / huge)* overall *(loss / gain)* in brain weight and number of brain cells. Such changes tend to be more minor, however, in those who keep up their levels of *(physical / mental / physical and mental)* activity.

27. About three percent of people over age 75 succumb to the significant mental deterioration that occur with _____ disease, a type of dementia that causes a progressive and extreme decline in cognitive ability over time. Neurons that produce the neurotransmitter _____ degenerate as this disease progresses.

28. As people age, the ability to *(recall / recognize)* words declines more than the ability to *(recall / recognize)* them. Also, for older adults, a decline in memory is more obvious in tasks requiring memory for *(meaningful / meaningless)* information than for *(meaningful / meaningless)* information. Even though individual variations in this and other cognitive abilities can be quite significant, remembering to do something in the future, called _____ memory, can be especially difficult for older adults. Time management strategies and reminder cues *(are / are not)* helpful ways to compensate for age-related prospective memory difficulties.

29. Early research findings on the relationship between aging and intellectual ability came primarily from *(cross-sectional / longitudinal)* studies, which compare the performance of people of differing ages. These studies showed that older adults tended to perform *(the same as / better than / worse than)* younger adults. But later _____ studies, based on testing and retesting of the same individuals as they age, provided evidence that intellectual ability *(declines / does not decline)*. But there are limitations in both kinds of studies. Cross-sectional studies compare individuals who were raised in *(the same / different)* eras and circumstances, making it *(easy / difficult)* to identify the exact reasons for the differences in performance. But longitudinal studies may mask actual age-related declines in intellect if *(less / more)* competent people happen to die before the end of the study.

30. David Myers points out that intelligence *(is / is not)* a simple, unitary charateristic, and that various elements of intelligence may change in different ways as we age. For example, the speed of processing information, an important component of *(crystallized / fluid)* intelligence, diminishes with age. On the other hand, _____ intelligence, which draws more on one's resevoir of knowledge and verbal skills, seems to rise as adults approach old age.

31. According to Henry Roediger's comments in the video, when compared with younger people, older adults have *(slower / faster)* retrieval of memories, and show an *(increased / decreased)* tendency to have false memories. People who are involved in intellectually challenging activities tend to demonstrate *(inferior /*

average / superior) cognitive ability. Based on this research finding, it *(is / is not)* clear *(whether / that)* cognitive exercise maintains and perhaps even boosts intellectual ability. Another possibility, Roediger points out, is that people who already have *(better / poorer)* memories are those who choose to engage in these kinds of intellectual activities.

32. Research has revealed that the idea of a midlife crisis occurring during middle adulthood is largely a *(myth / reality)*. In fact, researchers *(have / have not)* found evidence for a noticeable rise in rates of divorce, suicide, marital and job satisfaction, and general unhappiness during the early forties. According to the comments of Ginger Osborne in the video, crises may be more common for women when they are in their *(twenties /sixties)* than in their forties, and such crises tend to be *(related / unrelated)* to undesired events such as a divorce, loss of a job, or death of a loved one.

33. The _____ **clock**, which is the cultural expectation about the "right time" in life for events such as completing one's education, getting a job, getting married, having children, and retiring, is *(the same / different)* from one culture to the next, and major life events such as those prescribed by the social clock are occurring these days at increasingly *(predictable / unpredictable)* ages.

34. Couples who cohabitate prior to marriage are *(more / less)* likely than others to divorce, *(particularly if / unless)* they have lived together prior to engagement.

35. In Europe and in North America, married people report *(higher / lower)* levels of happiness than do unmarried people. Although having children can bring tremendous satisfaction to people, research evidence supports the idea that the empty nest period, when children leave home, is associated with *(a drop / an increase)* in parents' happiness and marital satisfaction.

36. For women, satisfaction and fulfillment appears to depend more on the *(number of hours / quality of experience)* at home or at work than on the specific role chosen.

37. Grief over the death of a loved one is often *(more / less)* intense, prolonged, and complicated when death claims a loved one before the expected time on the social clock. Stronger grief reactions *(always / do not always)* resolve grief more quickly, and there are *(no / three / four / five)* predictable stages of reactions in facing a terminal illness or bereavement.

38. Erik Erikson's theory of psychosocial development holds that the major developmental task of old age is to reflect on one's life and *(develop trust / form an identify / forge intimate relationships / achieve ego integrity)*. Gerontologist James Birren's guided auto-biography workshops *(support / undermine)* this process by encouraging participants to write about their experiences, read aloud what they have written in the presence of other participants, and in so doing, take time to reflect on, integrate, and find meaning in the strands of their lives.

Reflections on Two Major Developmental Issues

39. Developmental theorists such as Jean Piaget, Lawrence Kohlberg, and Erik Erikson each focused their work on different aspects of human development, but each proposed that development involves *(gradual, cumulative processes / a series of distinct stages)*. As such, they all would be classified as favoring the *(continuity / stages)* side of the continuity-stages issue.

40. David Myers points out that ideas of these stage theorists *(have / have never)* been criticized. For example, younger children apparently understand somewhat *(more / less)* than Piaget believed they could, casting some doubt on the details of his stage theory of *(cognitive / moral / psychosocial)* development.

41. Critics of Kohlberg have focused on the possibility that the theory appears to be centered around values that are more common among educated *(males / females)* in *(individualistic / collectivistic)* societies, and places a higher degree of emphasis on moral *(feeling / thinking)* than on moral *(actions / thinking)*.

42. Erikson's work has been criticized on the basis of *(research evidence / logic / opinion)* suggesting that a

fixed sequence series of predictable stages *(does in fact / does not)* take place as adults develop.

43. With all of this in mind, David Myers goes on to suggest that the idea of stages of development has *(remained useful / outlived its usefulness)* as a means of emphasizing the differences in people's thoughts and behavior at different ages.

44. In regard to the issue of stability versus change, David Myers finds that the weight of the evidence supports the existence of *(stability / change / both stability and change)* in our personalities as we develop over the life span. We *(can / cannot)* predict a great deal about an individual's traits in adulthood from knowing about them during the first two years of life. Still, as people age, there is a(n) *(abrupt / gradual)* increase in the degree of *(stability / change)* in many aspects of their personalities.

45. For each item listed below, select from the Key List the name of the *developmental theorist* whose theory is described in the item. Note that any item may be used more than once.

    Key List
    Erik Erikson
    Lawrence Kohlberg
    Jean Piaget

    a. _____ He formulated a theory with four stages in the development of thinking, ending with the formal operational stage.

    b. _____ He attempted in his theory to describe psychosocial development throughout the life span.

    c. _____ This theorist formulated the idea of three different levels of moral development, proposed to unfold in a specific order.

    d. _____ This theorist has been viewed by some of his critics as having formulated a theory that is biased toward individualistic cultural values and values that are more characteristic of males than of females.

    e. _____ This theorist proposed eight stages, unfolding over the period from birth to advanced old age.

    f. _____ Contemporary critics of this theorist claim that the types of tests he used led him to see greater limitations than are in fact present in what young children know and understand at a given age.

    g. _____ Regarding this theorist's work, today's researchers have found that not all adults face the same psychosocial issues at the same points in life, so that the stages are not as neat and sequential as his theory seemed to suggest.

    h. _____ According to this theorist, trust versus mistrust is the issue that is resolved one way or another during infancy, depending on the responsiveness and sensitivity of the infant's caregivers.

    i. _____ All children, according to this theorist, go through a period when that which is considered moral is judged on the basis of rewards and punishments.

    j. _____ According to this theorist's view of cognitive development, infants are in the sensorimotor stage and at first do not understand object permanence.

SELF TEST

Read each question and circle the letter of the best answer. When you have completed the Self Test, check your answers against the key at the end of this lesson. If you have answered any items incorrectly, review the appropriate materials to correct misunderstandings and cement your knowledge.

1. Based on the comments of David Myers in the video, which of the following accurately depicts human development from adolescence through adulthood?
   a. The steps of life move upward until the age of about 50, and downward throughout the rest of life.
   b. From womb to tomb, life is development and we are always in the process of becoming.
   c. All major developmental transformations are complete about two years before the onset of

adolescence, and the rest of life brings very few changes.

   d. Adolescence is a time of turmoil and confusion, and old age is a time of inevitable deterioration, but there is a relatively long quiescent period of adulthood in between.

2. Laurence Steinberg states in the video that _____ begins at the point when a surge of hormones triggers changes associated with sexual maturation, and it ends when an individual becomes financially and residentially independent.
   a. childhood.
   b. adulthood.
   c. puberty.
   d. adolescence.

3. Puberty
   a. is associated with hormonal changes.
   b. ends with an adolescent growth spurt.
   c. occurs about two years earlier in boys than in girls.
   d. all of the above.

4. All of the following items are secondary sex characteristics except
   a. increase in body hair, especially of the underarm and pubic areas.
   b. changes in boys' voices.
   c. enlargement of breasts in girls.
   d. development of the ovaries, testes, and external genitalia that allow sexual reproduction.

5. "Menarche" is the term for
   a. any physical change during puberty in girls.
   b. any physical change during puberty in boys.
   c. the first menstrual period in girls.
   d. the first ejaculation of semen in boys.

6. Extremes in emotional expression and emotional experience during adolescence most likely relate to the relatively rapid growth and development of the _____ of the brain that occurs during adolescence.
   a. cerebellum
   b. corpus callosum
   c. limbic system
   d. medulla oblongata

7. Measurable increases in adolescents' display of executive functions such as the cognitive capability for planning, logical problem solving, and thinking ahead to anticipate the consequences of one's actions, are probably based mainly on growth of the

_____ lobes of the brain, which continues at least into early adulthood.
   a. frontal
   b. parietal
   c. occipital
   d. temporal

8. When puberty begins, research has revealed that there is a genetically preprogrammed _____ of the synaptic connections between neurons in the brain.
   a. destruction or "pruning"
   b. increase or expansion
   c. stabilization
   d. slowing

9. What are some of the characteristics associated with adolescence, according to experts in the video?
   a. A surge of the reproductive hormones estrogen and testosterone
   b. More intense emotional arousal and expression, and a tendency toward greater risk-taking
   c. Greater sensitivity to the reactions of other people
   d. All of the above

10. Piaget's theory of cognitive development holds that the fourth and last stage of cognitive development, reached by most adolescents, is the _____ stage.
   a. postconventional
   b. formal operational
   c. germinal
   d. genital

11. Marco, age 13, is at home getting ready to leave with friends to watch his junior high basketball playoffs. Just before leaving, he quickly glances in the mirror and is horrified to notice a pimple on his chin. He immediately becomes preoccupied with the thought that throughout the game, all of his friends will be focused on that blemish on his face. Developmental psychologists would view Marco's unrealistic concern that others will be paying special attention to him as an example of:
   a. the preoperational stage of cognitive development.
   b. a hallucination.
   c. the personal fable.
   d. the imaginary audience.

12. Amanda has just reached the age of 14 and is interested in boys but does not have a boyfriend. Lately, she has become increasingly worried that she is the only girl that none of the boys at school seem to notice. Her belief that she is different, and that

nobody else her age is experiencing any of the same thoughts, worries, and concerns, exemplifies
a. the turmoil of youth.
b. the imaginary audience.
c. the teenage doldrums.
d. the personal fable.

13. According to Kohlberg's theory, an individual at the preconventional level of moral development makes judgments about what is moral by considering which course of action would
a. conform to social rules and laws.
b. adhere to broader ethical principles and promote agreed-upon rights.
c. maximize rewards and prevent punishment.
d. feel good at the moment.

14. In the video, Laurence Steinberg describes psychologist Erik Erikson's concept of the psychosocial moratorium as a time when adolescents
a. rebel, reject their parents' values and beliefs, and identify with the counter-culture.
b. experiment with different roles and try on various personalities before settling on a coherent personal identity.
c. opt out of the process of self-exploration and self-discovery, and decide to become whatever their parents expect them to become.
d. base their important life decisions on a strict code of moral values, instead of on what would give them personal satisfaction and enjoyment.

15. Which of the following descriptions best characterizes influences on adolescents' behavior during the teenage years?
a. Parents lose all their influence and peer influence becomes dominant.
b. Parents become somewhat less influential while peer influence increases.
c. Parents continue to have just as strong an influence while peers gain a little influence.
d. The idea that peers become more influential and parents less influential is a widely accepted myth with no evidence to support it.

16. According to Laurence Steinberg's comments in the video, susceptibility to peer influence reaches a peak at about age ___, and then declines thereafter.
a. 10
b. 14
c. 18
d. 24

17. In the video, Laurence Steinberg makes comments suggesting that there is a link between increases in risk-taking in adolescence and the earlier development of areas of the brain that regulate _____, while the areas that help us to _____ are not fully mature until the mid-twenties.
a. thinking ahead and planning … seek out new experiences and sensations
b. problem-solving and worrying … become sexually aroused
c. body movement … process sensory input
d. sensation-seeking and arousal … think ahead and plan

18. Which of the following is true regarding historical changes in the timing of adolescence in Western societies?
a. Sexual maturity occurs later now than it did 100 years ago, and independence from parents is achieved earlier.
b. Sexual maturity occurs earlier now than it did 100 years ago, and independence from parents is achieved later.
c. Adolescence has become shorter only in recent decades, primarily because young people marry earlier than they did in the 1950s.
d. None of the above.

19. As adults reach their mid-twenties,
a. physical capacities crest and then begin to decline.
b. developmental stages and life events begin to become more obvious and more consistent from one individual to the next.
c. fitness begins to decrease at a rate that is unrelated to exercise habits.
d. psychological responses to the physical changes of adulthood are quite similar, regardless of culture.

20. All of the following have been found to be specifically associated with menopause, except
a. occasional hot flashes.
b. cessation of menstrual cycles.
c. a decline in the body's production of estrogen.
d. emotional depression.

21. Which of the following is a disease that causes progressive impairment of memory and cognition as acetylcholine-containing neurons in the brain undergo degeneration?
a. Alzheimer's disease
b. Parkinson's disease
c. Multiple sclerosis
d. Myasthenia gravis

22. Which of the following is true regarding memory in older adults?
    a. Older adults show greater reductions in their ability to recall information than in their ability to recognize information.
    b. Most people over the age of 65 have Alzheimer's disease.
    c. Older adults do better than younger people in prospective memory tasks.
    d. Older adults are more likely to remember meaningless material than meaningful material.

23. Which type of research study is performed by testing the same individuals repeatedly over years, and comparing them at different ages?
    a. Longitudinal
    b. Cross-sectional
    c. Cohort comparison
    d. Successional

24. Martin, a 44-year-old mid-level corporate manager who lives in New York City, finds himself in a financial position that allows him to retire from his job and spend all his time traveling with his family, golfing, and doing major volunteer projects for two of his favorite charitable organizations. Based on David Myers' points about adult development, which of the following conclusions would be appropriate regarding Martin's choice to retire from work at this point in his life?
    a. According to Kohlberg's theory of moral development, Martin has apparently not developed beyond the conventional level.
    b. The transitions Martin has made at this point do not entirely conform to the social clock, which in Western cultures would normally place retirement at a later age.
    c. Martin's choices are strong evidence that he is having a midlife crisis, which research suggests is quite common for men at this age.
    d. All of the above

25. Which of the following is accurate regarding adult development?
    a. Cultures vary in their traditions and expectations for behavior, but the social clock is constant, regardless of culture.
    b. As compared with children and adolescents, the development of adults can be much more neatly divided into distinguishable stages.
    c. Chronological age is only a rough indicator of the developmental processes during the adult years, and our development is much more continuous than stage theories would suggest.
    d. Surveys of representative samples of adults show that from adolescence onward, people's ratings of their satisfaction with their lives drop significantly with each successive decade of life.

ANSWER KEY FOR THE ACTIVE REVIEW EXERCISES

1. throughout; development; becoming; [1]; Video 7
2. adolescence; spurt; puberty; dependent on parents; [1, 2, 3]; Video 7, Textbook
3. 2; earlier; *Your answer in the lined area should include many of the following ideas:* Biological, sexual maturation: rapid growth in height and weight (adolescent growth spurt), surges of the sex hormones (estrogen and testosterone), development of primary sex characteristics (ovaries and testes and external genitalia), and secondary sex characteristics (breasts in girls, lower voice in boys, appearance of underarm and pubic hair in both boys and girls), changes in the brain (development of the limbic areas and frontal lobes, and a restructuring of the brain due to pruning of connections); [2, 3]; Video 7, Textbook
4. Primary; secondary; primary; secondary; primary and secondary; [3]; Textbook, Video 7
5. menarche; ejaculation; variable; predictable; [3]; Textbook
6. boys; raises; earlier; [3]; Textbook
7. massive; well; reduced; increased; more; [4]; Video 7, Textbook
8. limbic system; frontal lobes; more; [4]; Textbook, Video 7
9. four; ability; formal operational; most; abstract; [5]; Textbook
10. imaginary audience; personal fable; [6]; Video 7, Textbook
11. Kohlberg; three; [7]; Textbook
12. a) preconventional morality; b) conventional morality; c) postconventional morality; [7]; Textbook
13. sequence; postconventional; women; caring; [7]; Textbook
14. follows; delay; [7]; Textbook
15. eight; psychosocial; infancy; late adulthood; [8]; Textbook
16. identity vs. role confusion; identity; moratorium; confusion; [8]; Textbook, Video 7
17. increase; decrease; important; is not; autonomy; independence from; [9]; Textbook, Video 7
18. increase; worse; [10]; Video 7
19. more; more; authoritative; higher; middle; [10]; Video 7, Textbook
20. longer; earlier; later; [11]; Textbook
21. no longer; continues; less; [1, 12, 16]; Textbook
22. reach a peak; faster; related; [12]; Textbook, Video 7
23. an earlier; 50; menopause; estrogen; common; less; no more; [12]; Textbook
24. more gradual than; myth; [13]; Textbook
25. less; minority; do not; similar to; [12, 14, 15]; Textbook
26. slows down; complex; small; loss; physical and mental; [14, 15]; Textbook, Video 7
27. Alzheimer's; acetylcholine [14]; Textbook, Video 7
28. recall; recognize; meaningless; meaningful; prospective; are; [15]; Textbook, Video 7
29. cross-sectional; worse than; longitudinal; does not decline; different; difficult; less; [15]; Textbook
30. is not; fluid; crystallized; [15]; Textbook
31. slower; increased; superior; is not; whether; better; [15]; Textbook
32. myth; have not; twenties; related; [16]; Video 7, Textbook
33. social; different; unpredictable; [17]; Textbook
34. more; particularly if; [18]; Textbook
35. higher; an increase; [18]; Textbook
36. quality of experience; [18]; Textbook
37. more; do not always; no; [19]; Textbook
38. achieve ego integrity; support; [20]; Textbook, Video 7
39. a series of distinct stages; stages; [21]; Textbook, Video 7
40. have; more; cognitive; [21]; Textbook, Video 7
41. males; individualistic; thinking; actions; [21]; Textbook
42. research evidence; does not; [21]; Textbook
43. remained useful; [21]; Textbook
44. both stability and change; cannot; gradual; stability; [21]; Textbook
45. a) Jean Piaget; b) Erik Erikson; c) Lawrence Kohlberg; d) Lawrence Kohlberg; e) Erik Erikson; f) Jean Piaget; g) Erik Erikson; h) Erik Erikson; i) Lawrence Kohlberg; j) Jean Piaget; [5, 7, 8, 20, 21]; Textbook, Video 7, Video 6

ANSWER KEY FOR THE SELF TEST

Item #	Answer	Learning Outcome #	Source	Item #	Answer	Learning Outcome #	Source
1.	b	1	Video 7	14.	b	8	Video 7
2.	d	2	Video 7	15.	b	9	Textbook
3.	a	3	Video 7, Textbook	16.	b	9	Video 7
4.	d	3	Textbook, Video 7	17.	d	10, 4	Video 7
5.	c	3	Textbook	18.	b	11	Textbook
6.	c	4	Video 7, Textbook	19.	a	12, 16	Textbook
7.	a	4	Video 7, Textbook	20.	d	13	Textbook
8.	a	4	Textbook, Video 7	21.	a	14	Textbook, Video 7
9.	d	2, 3, 4, 6	Video 7	22.	a	14, 15	Textbook
10.	b	5	Textbook	23.	a	15	Textbook
11.	d	6	Video 7	24.	b	16, 17, 7	Textbook, Video 7
12.	d	6	Video 7	25.	c	17, 18, 19, 21	Textbook, Video 7
13.	c	7	Textbook				

Lesson 8 (Sensation)

Connections

Assignments

Reading: Chapter 5, "Sensation," in *Psychology* by David Myers (Modules 12, 13, 14, and 15 in the modular version of *Psychology*)

Video: Episode 8, "Connections"

LEARNING OUTCOMES

Familiarize yourself with the Learning Outcomes for this lesson before you begin the assignments. Return to them to check your learning after completing the Steps to Learning Success. Careful work on these materials should equip you to accomplish the outcomes.

Introduction (Module 12)

1. Define and distinguish between **sensation** and **perception** and **bottom-up** and **top-down processing**.

2. Compare the **human senses** with the sensory systems of other animals.

Sensing the World: Some Basic Principles (Module 12)

3. Distinguish between **absolute** and **difference thresholds**, and describe how **sensory adaptation** and various other factors can affect **attention** and **signal detection** abilities.

4. Summarize the controversy over claims that **subliminal stimulation** can influence behavior, describing the findings of scientific investigations.

Vision (Module 13)

5. Specify the physical characteristics of **light** that correspond to our perceptual experiences of brightness and color in vision.

6. List the major **structures of the eye** and explain their functions.

7. Compare and contrast **rods** and **cones**, and explain the process of **transduction**.

8. Describe the structure of the **retina** and compare and contrast the **fovea** and the **blind spot**. Name the cells in the three layers of the **retina** and describe their connections to one another, specifying which of these cells form the **optic nerve**. Then describe the basic pathway from the optic nerve to the **primary visual cortex**.

9. Describe research with **microelectrode recording** suggesting that visual cortex neurons serve as **feature detectors**, and discuss **parallel processing** in the visual system.

10. Discuss **blindsight**, and explain what investigations into this and other conditions that affect awareness of ongoing visual processing have revealed about visual information processing.

11. List and compare the two basic **color vision theories** presented in the textbook, and discuss evidence supporting each theory.

12. Explain **color constancy** and provide examples of this phenomenon.

Hearing (Module 14)

13. Specify the physical characteristics of **sound** that determine the auditory experiences of **loudness** and **pitch**.

14. List the main components of the **auditory system** (structures of **outer**, **middle**, and **inner ear**, and the

brain areas related to hearing), and explain the role played by each of these structures.

15. Explain the major **theories of pitch perception** and discuss the interrelationship between these theories.

16. List and explain the cues we use to locate the source of a sound.

17. Compare the various types of **hearing loss**, explaining their causes and treatments, and discuss various adaptations to deafness.

The Other Senses (Module 15)

18. Discuss **tactile sensitivity** and the receptors involved in the various dimensions of touch.

19. Describe **phantom limb** sensations, and relate these to the functioning of the brain.

20. Discuss a variety of factors that influence the experience of **pain**, and summarize the basic ideas of the **gate control theory of pain**, citing supporting examples and evidence.

21. List the basic taste sensations, and discuss the structural properties and activities of our **taste receptors**.

22. Give examples illustrating **sensory interaction**, and discuss **plasticity** of the brain in regard to sensory processing.

23. Describe the **olfactory receptors**, discussing their role in odor sensations and flavor and the relationship among odors, emotions, and memories.

24. Explain how we sense body position and movement, distinguishing between **kinesthesis** and the **vestibular sense** and identifying the location of the receptors for each of these systems.

ACTIVE REVIEW

Each item in this section is based on material presented in the video or the textbook assignment for this lesson, or both. Complete this section, referring as needed to your notes or the source materials themselves. Answers are provided at the end of this lesson.

Introduction

1. The process of taking in physical energy from the environment and encoding it in the form of neural signals is called _____, whereas the more complex and varied processes of organizing, interpreting, and assigning meaning to sensory input is known as _____.

2. Viewing sensation as beginning at sensory receptors and moving up to what goes on at the higher levels of sensory systems provides us with an understanding of _____-_____ **processing**, while an emphasis on _____-_____ _____ stresses how our expectations and past experiences influence how we interpret our incoming sensations.

3. Gilles Laurent points out in the video that if we examine the animal world, we find evidence for *(five / more than five / more than a thousand)* senses, and that some animals have sensitivities that humans do not

share, such as _____

_____

_____

_____.

Sensing the World: Some Basic Principles

4. Our **attention** is most likely to be seized by stimuli that are *(changing / unchanging)*, because these are often critical to our survival.

5. One way to gauge our sensitivity to input is to measure the minimum level of a stimulus required for reliable detection, called the _____ _____. In this case, "reliable" is defined as detection of the stimulus on _____ percent of the occasions when it is presented. Factors such as motivation, past experience, and level of fatigue *(can / cannot)* alter the absolute threshold.

6. The minimum change in a stimulus, or the difference between two stimuli that is required for reliable detection of the change or difference, is known as the _____ _____. The psychophysical law known as _____ law

holds that the size of the difference threshold is proportional to the magnitude of the starting stimulus. So if we begin with a very dim light, a very small change in the brightness of that light will be noticeable; but beginning with a much brighter light, a much greater change is required for a j.n.d., which stands for "(j)____ (n) _____ (d)_____ ", another term for the difference threshold.

7. With sustained exposure to a particular stimulus, our sensitivity to that stimulus is diminished through a process known as _____ _____, which serves to limit distractions and focus our attention on potential opportunities and threats in the environment. Tiny movements of the eyes (**microsaccades**) in humans, and the constant movement of the whiskers (**vibrissae**) of a rat have in common the fact that they increase variations in input, thereby *(increasing / reducing)* sensory adaptation and maintaining sensitivity to current input.

8. One controversial issue is whether stimuli that fall below the absolute threshold, referred to as _____ stimuli, can affect us. Based on the definition of the absolute threshold, we should expect that sounds and sights too weak to be detected 50% of the time would *(always / sometimes / never)* be registered at a conscious level.

9. Experiments on **priming** *(support / do not support)* the idea that subliminal stimuli can influence our responses to other stimuli. Research has shown that any such influences are typically *(nonexistent / weak / strong)* and *(brief / prolonged)* enough to make it highly *(likely / unlikely)* that advertisers could use subliminal stimuli to manipulate people. Furthermore, careful research has shown that subliminal self-help tapes *(are / are not)* more effective than placebo tapes that contain no relevant self-help messages.

Vision

10. Sensory **receptors** not only take in certain types of energy, they also convert that raw stimulus energy into signals that travel along sensory pathways in the nervous system. The receptors' conversion of raw stimulus energy into electrochemical signals that can travel along nerves is called _____.

11. Light is the visible portion of the _____ _____ energy spectrum. The **hue** of light we experience is determined by the _____ of light within this spectrum. Light appearing to have a red hue comes from the *(shorter / longer)* wavelength range of this spectrum, and blue-violet light comes from the *(shorter / longer)* range. The **intensity** or amplitude of light determines our perceptions of _____.

12. After light enters the eye, it passes through the opening known as the *(iris / pupil / cornea)*, and is focused by the **lens** onto the light-sensitive lining at the back of the eyeball, the _____.

13. The **photoreceptors** for vision include the _____ and _____, located in the back layer within the **retina**. Fill in the blanks on the table below to compare the properties of the two general types of photoreceptors in the visual system.

	Cones	Rods
Shape		
Approximate number in the retina of each human eye		
Location of the largest number		
Specialized roles in vision		
Types (how many?)		

14. After the rods and cones have transduced light into neural signals that can be passed along nervous system pathways, these signals with the retina next reach the _____ **cells**, which in turn pass them on to the _____ cells whose axons form the _____ **nerve**. Ganglion cells, according to Thomas Albright's comments in the video, have **center-surround selectivity**, which means that they are sensitive not only to light but to contrast between adjacent areas.

15. There are *(no / few / many)* receptors at the point where the optic nerve originates and passes through the back of the eyeball, which explains why we have a *(fovea / blind spot)* located in that area of the retina.

16. Most of the neural signals from the optic nerve travel to the _____ _____ **nucleus** (a region within the relay area of the brain known as the _____) before being projected on toward the **primary** _____ _____, the outer wrinkled covering of the _____ **lobe** at the back of the brain. A midbrain area involved in visual-motor control, the _____ _____ also receives some input from the optic nerve. Projections from the optic nerve also reach the **hypothalamus**, where information about light levels can serve to synchronize the body's _____ _____.

17. Researchers can monitor the activity of an individual neuron in one of the visual areas of the brain, using a tiny recording probe called a _____, to discover the features that these individual visual neurons detect. Semir Zeki placed microelectrodes in areas anterior to the primary visual cortex and discovered each tiny region within this area had neurons that reacted quite *(specifically / generally)* to *(one / many)* dimension(s) of the visual stimulus presented to the retina, such as motion, color, or distance. David Hubel and Torsten Wiesel found that within the primary visual cortex, individual neurons

could be shown to react, for example, to vertical lines *(and also / but not)* horizontal lines, or vice versa.

18. The primary visual cortex sends information to further visual processing areas in the _____ and _____ lobes, where certain regions handle a variety of specialized functions, such as the ability to detect movement or recognize faces or other categories of complex objects. Much of the work of the visual system involves *(parallel / serial)* **processing**, with the brain using separate pathways to analyze simultaneously such aspects as color, form, movement, and depth.

19. In discussing the issue of how much sensory information is recorded by the brain without conscious awareness, David Myers comments in the video that unconscious information processing is evidenced by split-brain patients in whom the *(right / left)* **hemisphere** of the brain may be able to carry out activities which the more verbal _____ **hemisphere** cannot report.

20. Other striking cases involve people with damage to the primary visual cortex, who are surprisingly *(accurate / inaccurate)* in detecting and reporting on certain limited features of a visual stimulus (such as its location, angle of orientation, or direction of movement), while at the same time being quite *(aware / unaware)* of seeing the stimulus. This surprising phenomenon is known as _____.

21. Cases of blindsight demonstrate what Christof Koch points out in the video: we see with the _____, not with the eyes, meaning that the mere processing of light by the eyes *(is / is not)* enough to make us consciously aware of the visual world.

22. All the colors we see result from coded signals arising in _____ *[how many?]* different ranges of light wavelengths. The visual receptors begin the process of color vision, as certain cones respond mostly to light that our visual systems detect as *(red / yellow / purple)*; other cones react strongly to *(green / orange / indigo)*

light, and still others respond more to light in the *(blue / white / black)* wavelength range of the visible spectrum. The existence of the three types of cones lends support to the _____ **theory of color vision**, first formulated by _____ and _____.

23. After staring at a patch of red for a minute or so and then shifting the gaze to a white surface, the typical individual reports seeing a patch of *(green / blue / yellow)*. Sensory aftereffects such as these are called _____. Christof Koch comments in the video that these sorts of aftereffects demonstrate that there *(is / is not)* a simple one-to-one relationship between the outside stimulus and the corresponding perceptual experience.

24. The finding that viewing a red stimulus consistently yields an afterimage of the complementary hue green, and a blue stimulus yields an afterimage of the complementary hue _____ led to the development of **Hering's** _____ _____ **theory of color vision**, which suggests that there is some linkage in the nervous system between the processes that underlie the perception of red and green, and likewise for blue and yellow. Modern research involving recording from cells beyond the receptors *(has / has not)* supported this theory. For example, some individual visual neurons are turned "on" by red light and turned ("on" / "off") by green light, whereas others show the reverse pattern of response, or they react in a differential manner to blue versus yellow.

Hearing

25. **Sound**, the stimulus for **audition**, involves vibrations –waves of increasing and decreasing air pressure. The **strength** of these sound waves determines our perceptions of the *(loudness / pitch)* of the sound, whereas the **frequency** of the air pressure variations– rapid variations producing short waves, or slow

variations producing long waves–determines whether we hear a high or low *(loudness / pitch)*.

26. Sound waves enter the outer ear, first causing vibrations of the membrane called the _____, which sets into motion the little bones (the _____, _____, and _____) of the *(inner / middle)* ear. These tiny bones press against the oval window of inner ear's bony fluid-filled coiled tube, the _____, causing the bending of the receptors for hearing, the _____ _____, that rest on the **basilar membrane**. The hair cells serve as the transducers that convert sound energy into neural signals that travel along the _____ **nerve** toward the **auditory cortex** in the _____ lobe of the brain.

27. We detect loudness according to the *(number / location)* of hair cells that respond to a sound. Exposure to loud noise over time can lead to pain, ringing in the ears, and damaged hearing. Excessively loud noise also contributes to stress, particularly if the noise is *(predictable / unpredictable)*.

28. How do we distinguish pitch? The _____ **theory** bases pitch perception on having one movement of the basilar membrane with each wave of the sound, so that the auditory hair cells trigger *(one / two / ten)* impulse(s) per second for each peak of the sound wave–for example, 400 impulses per second for a sound wave with a frequency of _____ waves per second, and _____ impulses per second for a sound wave with a frequency of 800 waves per second. Of course, since neurons *(can / cannot)* fire at rates above about 1000 impulses per second, this frequency theory of pitch perception *(can / cannot)* account for our ability to distinguish between the pitch of sound frequencies above 1000 per second.

29. To explain how we distinguish sounds with higher pitch, **von Helmholtz** proposed the _____ **theory**, which holds that sounds of different frequencies lead to activity at differing locations

along the basilar membrane, with *(high / low)* frequencies producing greater stimulation near the base of the cochlea (closest to the middle ear), and *(high / low)* frequencies producing greater activity of hair cells near the top turn of the cochlea, farthest from the oval window. This theory best explains how we detect the pitch of sounds in the *(higher / lower)* range of audible frequencies, since low frequencies stimulate the entire basilar membrane.

30. Our best understanding of pitch perception across the entire audible range of frequencies, then, results when we draw upon *(place theory / frequency theory / both theories)*.

31. To locate a sound source, the brain is able to detect even extremely tiny differences in *(pitch / time of arrival)* of the sound at each ear. Not only does the ear that is closer to the sound source receive the sound first, but that ear also receives a somewhat *(more / less)* intense sound input. The brain can compare the inputs to the two ears and, based on these time and intensity differences, identify the direction from which the sound came.

32. **Hearing loss** can stem from a variety of causes. Loud noise exposure or diseases that damage the hair cells or the auditory nerve can induce _____ _____ **hearing loss**. When mechanical problems with the outer or middle ear reduce the passage of vibration to the inner ear, the resulting problem is classified as _____ **hearing loss**. **Cochlear implants** are electronic devices that can help restore hearing in people with *(sensorineural / conduction)* hearing loss.

The Other Senses

33. The skin has receptors that can provide at least four different kinds of basic sensations: _____, _____, _____, and _____. Other sensations result from combinations and variations of these four primary skin sensations. A sensation of heat, for example, can

be induced by simultaneously stimulating _____ and _____ spots on the skin. Researchers have found that, except in the case of pressure receptors, there *(is / is not)* a simple one-to-one correspondence between the type of specialized receptors found in the skin and the type of sensations that result from their stimulation.

34. Michael Merzenich states in the video that when a finger has been amputated, the area of the brain that formerly registered sensory input from that finger now can be shown to respond to input from adjacent fingers. Yet in such cases, the individual *(does / does not)* demonstrate confusion about the location of tactile stimulus contacting the adjacent fingers. Chronically blind people, when reading Braille, show activation not just of tactile areas but also of some areas of the cerebral cortex that would normally have been devoted to *(vision / hearing / smell)*. Jenny Singleton points out that deaf signers have regions of the *(visual / auditory / olfactory)* cortex that are activated to handle the heavier visual processing load experienced in communicating with sign language. All these findings attest to the remarkable adjustability, known as _____, of sensory areas of the cerebral cortex.

35. **Pain** can result from a variety of stimuli—often from *(high / low)* intensities of the same stimuli that cause other sensations, such as cold, warmth, or roughness. Although pain can be adaptive in alerting us to danger and motivating us to take corrective action, amputees can often experience pain or other sensations that feel as though they are originating in a missing limb. These are called _____ _____ **sensations**.

36. Melzack and Wall's _____-_____ **theory of pain** holds that activity in large-diameter nerve fibers that carry signals about *(pain / other sensations)* can *(open / close)* the "gates" that allows the passage of pain signals to the brain. This theory *(can / cannot)* help us to understand the pain-relieving

effects of ice packs, heating pads, massage, or electrical stimulation.

37. Basic taste sensations include _____, _____, _____, _____, and a more recently discovered _____ taste sensation. The taste receptors, which sense chemical properties of substances that contact the tongue, *(can / cannot)* regenerate when damaged.

38. Much of the flavor of food arises from the interaction between taste and another chemical sense, *(audition / olfaction / gustation / kinesthesis)*, which is another term for the sense of _____.

39. For the sense of **smell**, we have a much *(greater / smaller)* variety of receptor types than we do for vision. Gilles Laurent states in the video that depending on the species, there may be an estimated one or perhaps even two *(hundred / thousand / million)* different types of olfactory receptors, with each type specialized to respond to a certain set of chemical molecules. According to the textbook, humans have at least *(a dozen / several dozen / several hundred)* different types of olfactory receptors.

40. Even though we *(have / do not have)* a distinctly different receptor for each separate odor we can distinguish, odorous molecules fit into specialized olfactory receptors. Recent research has revealed that our olfactory receptors come in a far *(greater / smaller)* range of types than do our visual receptors.

41. People have a(n) *(easy / difficult)* time naming odors they recognize. Nonetheless, memories and emotions *(are / are not)* easily evoked by scents.

42. Our ability to detect our own **body position and movement** using sensors located in our muscles, tendons, and joints, is called _____. We also sense our position and movement through the use of hair-like receptors in the fluid-filled chambers near the cochlea, the _____ **canals** and the _____ **sacs**, which together form the _____ **sense**. These inner ear structures can send off a barrage of signals to the cerebellum to register a change in the position or pattern of movement of the *(head / limbs / torso)*.

43. In the video, David Myers, who has experienced progressive **hearing loss** over several years, states his personal opinion that *(vision / hearing)* is the primary sense and the one he would most miss if he lost both vision and hearing. In speaking of her experience with being both blind and deaf, Helen Keller is quoted as having said that her *(blindness / deafness)* was more bothersome than her *(blindness / deafness)*, based on the tremendous role hearing plays in forming and maintaining social relationships.

SELF TEST

Read each question and circle the letter of the best answer. When you have completed the Self Test, check your answers against the key at the end of this lesson. If you have answered any items incorrectly, review the appropriate materials to correct misunderstandings and cement your knowledge.

1. Sensation
   a. involves organizing and interpreting stimulus inputs.
   b. is defined as an awareness of touch stimuli applied to the skin.
   c. depends primarily on top-down processing.
   d. consists of receiving inputs and encoding them as neural signals.

2. When Janet calls out from an upstairs bedroom to Lyle in the basement laundry room of their large old house, Lyle often cannot hear her voice at all, even if the house is completely quiet. In this situation, we could say that any sound waves arriving in the laundry room from Janet's vibrating vocal cords are
   a. transmitted through top-down processing.
   b. causing sensory adaptation.
   c. below Lyle's absolute threshold.
   d. sensed but not perceived.

3. Angela volunteered for a research study in which she was placed in a soundproof chamber and periodically presented with a variety of very soft tones through headphones. She was instructed to press a button every fifteen seconds to indicate whether or not she heard any tone during that interval. At the conclusion of the study, she was informed that she had shown typical overall performance, detecting only 28% of the very weak sounds that were presented to her, and that this had been a test of her
   a. sensory adaptation.
   b. extrasensory perception.
   c. difference threshold.
   d. absolute threshold.

4. Leah dips her feet into a very hot tub of water, which after just a few seconds feels comfortably warm rather than very hot. Most likely, this reduction in the sensation of heat after a period of continued exposure represents a change known as
   a. transduction.
   b. receptor saturation.
   c. sensory adaptation.
   d. the absolute threshold.

5. Subliminal stimuli
   a. fall above the absolute threshold.
   b. have been shown through priming experiments to have weak and brief effects under certain conditions.
   c. are too weak to be detected under any circumstances.
   d. are powerfully persuasive in affecting the subconscious mind, and can manipulate consumers without their awareness.

6. Light consists of certain wavelengths within the spectrum of _____ energy.
   a. electromagnetic
   b. photochemical
   c. mechanical
   d. nuclear

7. Rods and cones are located in the
   a. retina.
   b. cochlea.
   c. cornea.
   d. optic nerve.

8. The retina
   a. lines the inner surface at the back of the eyeball.
   b. contains the rods and cones.
   c. is the area where light rays come into focus for a person with normal visual acuity.
   d. all of the above.

9. Transduction in sensory systems
   a. is carried out by receptors.
   b. is a process by which stimulus energy is converted into signals that can be processed by the nervous system.
   c. both of the above.
   d. none of the above.

10. At the fovea, humans have
    a. rods, but no cones.
    b. cones, but no rods.
    c. a high concentration of rods and cones.
    d. ganglion cells, but no rods and no cones.

11. The cones of the retina
    a. are less sensitive to dim light than are rods.
    b. are less sensitive to detail than are rods.
    c. are more numerous than rods.
    d. play little or no role in color vision.

12. Ganglion cells in the retina
    a. have axons that form the optic nerve.
    b. receive information from the bipolar cells that have been stimulated by visual receptors.
    c. are sensitive not just to light affecting the receptors that feed signals to them, but to contrast.
    d. all of the above.

13. Most of the neurons that form the optic nerve send their signals on to
    a. the secondary visual cortex and then to the primary visual cortex.
    b. the inferior colliculus and then directly to the cerebellum.
    c. areas of the thalamus and then to the primary visual cortex.
    d. the amygdala and then to the parietal lobe.

14. Individual neurons in the primary visual cortex can be viewed as "feature detectors," meaning that each of these neurons
    a. responds when there is any sort of light input to the retina, regardless of its characteristics.
    b. responds only when the retina is stimulated with a dot of light against a dark background.
    c. responds selectively to one particular aspect of the visual stimulus, such as a specific shape, angle of orientation, or direction of movement.
    d. reacts only to faces or other equally complex visual stimuli.

15. Blindsight involves
    a. an ability to navigate through unfamiliar areas with the use of a special cane or a guide dog.
    b. no awareness of seeing, but an astonishing ability to detect certain aspects of a visual stimulus presented in the blind portions of the visual field.
    c. every normal person's lack of awareness of a blind spot existing in a small area of each retina.
    d. psychic powers similar to telepathy.

16. Which of the following provides specific support for the trichromatic theory of color vision?
    a. The existence of three different types of cones in the retina, each responding to a different range of visible wavelengths.
    b. The fact that green afterimages appear after viewing a patch of red, and yellow afterimages appear after seeing a blue patch.
    c. Both of the above
    d. None of the above

17. The major difference between a high-pitched tone and a low-pitched tone is the ___ of the sound waves.
    a. amplitude
    b. decibel level
    c. strength
    d. frequency

18. The cochlea of the inner ear
    a. is an air-filled chamber that contains the hammer, anvil, and stirrup.
    b. funnels sound waves toward the middle ear.
    c. is a fluid-filled chamber containing the basilar membrane and auditory receptors, the hair cells.
    d. contains the eardrum, hammer, anvil, and stirrup.

19. The most complete explanation as to why we hear various frequencies as differing in pitch comes from
    a. trichromatic theory.
    b. place theory.
    c. frequency theory.
    d. a combination of place and frequency theories.

20. To know that a sound originated off to the left side of the body, our brains generally
    a. use only the information from the left ear.
    b. use only the information from the right ear.
    c. compare the differences in intensity and time of arrival of the sound at each ear.
    d. ignore the auditory information altogether and search for visual cues.

21. Which kind of hearing loss is diagnosed when there is damage to the eardrum or when the middle ear bones lose their ability to convey vibrations from the eardrum to the cochlea?
    a. Cochlear hearing loss
    b. Tympanic hearing loss
    c. Sensorineural hearing loss
    d. Conduction hearing loss

22. Sensorineural hearing loss is most often caused by
    a. calcium deposits or tumors in the middle ear.
    b. infections that cause temporary swelling or fluid accumulation in the middle ear.
    c. aging or exposure to loud noise.
    d. wax in the auditory canal that blocks out sound or limits movements of the eardrum.

23. Melzack and Wall's gate-control theory of pain
    a. fits well with the observation that a person can experience reduction of pain with massage or with application of a heating pad or an ice pack.
    b. suggests that the amount of pain experienced is always directly proportional to the amount of damage to the tissues.
    c. holds that the pain receptors of the skin and muscles have a simple uninterrupted pathway to a definable pain processing area of the brain.
    d. provides the only explanation of how we can suffer from headaches even though the brain has no pain receptors.

24. The basic taste sensations are thought to be
    a. pungent, salty, putrid, and sweet.
    b. sweet, salty, sour, bitter, and umami.
    c. salty, sweet, and sour
    d. too numerous to list, given the hundreds of types of receptors that equip our tongues to sense thousands of dimensions of flavor in food.

25. The sensory system that specifically reacts to changes in the position and movement of the head is
    a. the vestibular sense.
    b. kinesthesis.
    c. olfaction
    d. gustation.

ANSWER KEY FOR THE ACTIVE REVIEW EXERCISES

1. sensation; perception; [1] Textbook, Video 8
2. bottom-up; top-down processing; [1] Textbook
3. more than five; electric sense in the platypus and in some fish, responsiveness to certain vibrations in spiders, magnetic field sensitivity in birds, male silkworm moth's ability to detect the female moth's sex attractant (or other examples from the video or text); [2] Textbook, Video 8
4. changing; [3] Textbook, Video 8
5. absolute threshold; 50; can; [3] Textbook, Video 8
6. difference threshold; Weber's; just noticeable difference; [3] Textbook, Video 8
7. sensory adaptation; reducing; [3] Textbook, Video 8
8. subliminal; sometimes; [4] Textbook
9. support; weak; brief; unlikely; are not; [4] Textbook, Video 8
10. transduction; [5] Textbook, Video 8
11. electromagnetic; wavelength; longer; shorter; brightness; [5] Textbook
12. pupil; retina; [6] Textbook, Video 8
13. rods; cones; [7] Textbook, Video 8

	Cones	Rods	Source
Shape	Shorter, pointed (cone shaped)	Elongated, thinner (rod shaped)	Textbook
Approximate number in the retina of each human eye	6 million	120 million	Textbook, Video 8
Location of the largest number	Near the fovea, the point of clearest vision	Outside of the fovea	Textbook
Specialized roles in vision	"Daylight" vision (in bright light conditions)	"Night" vision (in dim light conditions)	Textbook
	Color vision	Black-and-white vision	Textbook, Video 8
	Higher acuity (detailed vision)	Lower visual acuity	Textbook
Types	Three types (R, G, B)	One type only	Textbook, Video 8

14. bipolar; ganglion; optic; [6, 8] Textbook, Video 8
15. no; blind spot; [8] Textbook
16. lateral geniculate; thalamus; visual cortex; occipital; superior colliculus; circadian rhythms; [8] Textbook, Video 8
17. microelectrode; specifically; one; but not; [9] Textbook, Video 8
18. parietal, temporal; parallel; [8, 9] Textbook, Video 8
19. right; left; [10] Video 8
20. accurate; unaware; blindsight; [10] Textbook, Video 8
21. brain; is not; [10] Video 8
22. three; cones; red; green; blue; trichromatic; Young, von Helmholtz; [11] Textbook, Video 8
23. green; afterimages; is not; [11] Textbook, Video 8
24. yellow; opponent process; has; "off"; [11] Textbook
25. loudness; pitch; [13] Textbook
26. eardrum; hammer, anvil, stirrup; middle; cochlea; hair cells; auditory; temporal; [14] Textbook
27. number; unpredictable; [13] Textbook
28. frequency; one; 400; 800; cannot; cannot; [15] Textbook
29. place; high; low; higher; [15] Textbook
30. both theories; [15] Textbook
31. time of arrival; more; [16] Textbook
32. sensorineural (or nerve deafness); conduction; sensorineural; [17] Textbook
33. pressure, warmth, cold, pain; warmth, cold; is not; [18] Textbook
34. does not; vision; auditory; plasticity; [19, 22] Video 8
35. high; phantom limb; [20] Textbook
36. gate-control; other sensations; close; can; [20] Textbook
37. sweet, salty, sour, bitter, umami (or meaty); can; [21] Textbook
38. olfaction; smell; [21, 22, 23] Textbook
39. greater; thousand; several hundred; [23] Textbook, Video 8
40. do not have; greater; [23] Textbook, Video 8
41. difficult; are; [23] Textbook,
42. kinesthesis; semicircular; vestibular; vestibular; head; [24] Textbook
43. vision; deafness; blindness; Video 8

ANSWER KEY FOR THE SELF TEST

Item #	Answer	Learning Outcome #	Source	Item #	Answer	Learning Outcome #	Source
1.	d	1	Textbook, Video 8	14.	c	9	Textbook, Video 8
2.	c	1, 2	Textbook, Video 8	15.	b	10	Textbook, Video 8
3.	d	3	Textbook, Video 8	16.	a	11	Textbook, Video 8
4.	c	3	Textbook, Video 8	17.	d	13	Textbook
5.	b	4	Textbook	18.	c	14	Textbook
6.	a	5	Textbook	19.	d	15	Textbook
7.	a	6	Textbook, Video 8	20.	c	16	Textbook
8.	d	6, 7, 8	Textbook, Video 8	21.	d	17	Textbook
9.	c	7, 8	Textbook, Video 8	22.	c	17	Textbook
10.	b	8	Textbook, Video 8	23.	a	20	Textbook
11.	a	7	Textbook, Video 8	24.	b	21	Textbook
12.	d	8	Textbook, Video 8	25.	a	24	Textbook
13.	c	8	Textbook, Video 8				

Lesson 9 (Perception)

Interpretations

Assignments

Read: Chapter 6, "Perception," in *Psychology* by David Myers ("Introduction" and "Selective Attention" sections in Module 12 and Modules 16 and 17 in the modular version of *Psychology*)

Video: Episode 9, "Eye of the Beholder"

LEARNING OUTCOMES

Familiarize yourself with the Learning Outcomes for this lesson before you begin the assignments. Return to them to check your learning after completing the Steps to Learning Success. Careful work on these materials should equip you to accomplish the outcomes.

Introduction (Module 12)

1. Distinguish between **sensation** and **perception**.

Selective Attention (Module 12)

2. Describe research findings and examples showing that **selective attention** greatly influences what we perceive, and that we may at times be influenced by stimuli we fail to notice.

Perceptual Organization (Module 16)

3. Explain why psychologists have been interested in **perceptual illusions**, and describe the phenomenon of **visual capture**.

4. Discuss the work of **Gestalt psychologists** in the early twentieth century, explaining the distinction between **figure** and **ground** and the importance of figure-ground distinctions.

5. List, describe, and provide examples of the five Gestalt perceptual **principles of grouping**.

6. Identify the focus of the **binding problem** and comment on its current status according to experts interviewed in the video.

7. Describe research illuminating the contribution of biological predispositions and experience to **depth perception**.

8. Distinguish between the **binocular** and **monocular cues** for visual depth perception, listing and explaining each of the eight major monocular and binocular depth cues.

9. Discuss the **motion perception** and illusions involving apparent motion.

10. Explain **perceptual constancy**, providing examples, and discuss the relationship between perceptual constancy and certain types of illusions.

Perceptual Interpretation (Module 17)

11. Summarize the long-standing **nature-nurture debate** in relation to perception, and provide an overview of human and laboratory animal research pertaining to **critical periods** for perceptual development.

12. Describe research on **perceptual adaptation** to special lenses that significantly alter visual input.

13. Explain and provide examples of the effects of **perceptual set** and **context** on perception, and list factors that contribute to perceptual set or perceptual **schemas**.

14. Cite examples illustrating how **human factors psychologists** work to design devices that are safer and more convenient to use.

Is There Extrasensory Perception? (Module 17)

15. Define **parapsychology**, and distinguish between claims of **telepathy**, **clairvoyance**, and **precognition**. Summarize the findings from research investigating claims of extrasensory perception, and provide an overview of the textbook author's points in discussing such claims.

ACTIVE REVIEW

Each item in this section is based on material presented in the video or the textbook assignment for this lesson, or both. Complete this section, referring as needed to your notes or the source materials themselves. Answers are provided at the end of this lesson.

Introduction

1. The process of **sensation** involves receiving raw physical energy from the environment and converting it into coded neural signals, whereas the process of _____ goes beyond sensation to include selecting, interpreting, and organizing the sensory input to create meaning.

2. Perceptions are not just a matter of **bottom-up processing**, but are greatly influenced by expectations, through what is termed _____ processing.

Selective Attention

3. Out of the many millions of bits of information our sensory systems take in every second, our **selective attention** focuses on *(all / most / only a very few)* of these.

4. In the video, Thomas Albright and Anne Treisman both describe **attention** as a filter of sorts, and they make the point that we can pay attention to *(only one thing / many things)* at a time. The failure to notice something because of focusing attention elsewhere has been called _____ _____.

5. The **cocktail party effect** is a term that is used to describe selective attention in certain kinds of settings —our *(ability / inability)* to pick out one conversation from many in a crowded room. But the fact that our attention shifts quickly if we hear someone say our name suggests that we *(are / are not)* processing the stimuli we are filtering out.

6. In the video, Daniel Simons states that people are quite *(underconfident / realistic / overconfident)* in estimating how much they are aware of in the visual environment. Careful measurements under controlled conditions show that when asked to count the number of passes made on a basketball court by players wearing a certain color of uniform, about ____% of viewers miss seeing events that would seem to be blatantly obvious, such as a person in a gorilla suit or a woman with an umbrella strolling across the screen in the midst of the game.

7. Another name for **inattentional blindness** is _____ _____, demonstrated in experiments with face-to-face interactions in which research participants frequently *(notice / fail to notice)* the substitution of a new person for the stranger with whom they were conversing moments before. Results such as these *(are / are not)* limited to visual attention alone. In the auditory realm, people may fail to notice a shift from one speaker to another when listening intently to a taped list of challenging words—a phenomenon known as _____ _____.

8. Research into attention in perception has especially important practical implications for automobile drivers and airplane pilots. In driving simulations comparing drivers listening to the radio with drivers talking on a cell phone, those on a cell phone missed *(half / twice)* as many traffic signals.

Perceptual Organization

9. **Perceptual illusions** have long fascinated psychologists because they often *(obscure / provide clues about)* the ways we normally organize and interpret sensations. For example, in the classic *(Ames room / Ponzo / Müller-Lyer)* **illusion**, we judge two equal line segments as being of *(equal / unequal)* length when those line segments each end with arrow tips that point in opposite directions. These distorted judgments may result when encounter cues that are normally associated with differences in visual depth encourage us to perceive differences in size.

10. Objects that are less sharply visible (for example, cars or trucks whose outlines are blurred by snowfall or fog) are generally judged to be *(closer / farther away)* than when more clearly visible. Predictable errors in perceiving distance may account for some of the risks encountered while driving in inclement weather.

11. Illusions *(are / are not)* limited to vision. For example, a steady series of clicks is often perceived as though the clicks are *(separate and equal / grouped or accented)*.

12. When the information we get from our vision and from another sense do not match, the *(visual / other)* sense is likely to dominate in our perception—a phenomenon called _____ _____.

13. In the early 1900s, a group of German researchers known as the _____ **psychologists** began to study the principles by which we organize our sensations of separate elements into integrated and meaningful patterns. The German word "gestalt" means *(part or element / form or whole)*.

14. An important idea in Gestalt psychology is that "whole is *(less than / equal to / greater than)* the sum of its parts," meaning that a specific combination of elements has properties that *(are / are not)* found within each separate element.

15. To recognize any object, we must distinguish it from its background. Gestalt psychologists referred to the object of attention as the _____, and the surrounding area beyond as the _____.

16. Figure-ground relationships are *(always / sometimes / never)* reversible, demonstrating that a given stimulus can be the basis for *(only one / more than one)* perception. Cultural factors may also determine what is figure and what is ground. In the video, Shinobu Kitayama describes research showing that in cases where a typical *(American / Japanese)* person would begin by describing a big fish with various patterns on its body swimming in a watery environment and surrounded by bubbles, stones, and clams, a more typical pattern of description for a(n) *(American / Japanese)* person would begin by focusing on a description of the context (water currents, bubbles, seaweed, etc.), and then mentioning a big fish swimming in that scene.

17. Match examples a–d below with the appropriate term from the Key List to indicate which *Gestalt principle of grouping* it illustrates.

    Key List
    similarity
    continuity
    proximity
    closure

    a. _____ As you sit working on your term paper, the display screen on your laptop computer is positioned so that it obstructs your view of a small part of one corner of the window in the room. Yet you don't really notice the "missing" corner, and you continue to perceive the window frame as a complete rectangle.

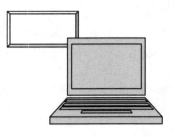

b. _____ As you scan across the line of symbols below, each series of three matching letters (e.g., <u>XXX</u>, and <u>mmm</u>) can easily be perceived as a unit, appearing to be somewhat distinct from the other nearby letters. It is less likely that you would organize this series into units with mixtures of symbols (such as <u>XXXm</u>, <u>mmOO</u>, <u>Oi</u>, <u>iiB</u>, and so on).

<u>XXXmmmOOOiiiBBBxxxTTTuuu</u>

c. _____ We naturally tend to group together items that are nearer to one another, and that principle helps to explain the difference in our perceptions of the two lines of print shown below.

CA NYOURE A<u>DTH IS</u>S EN TENCEMO REQUI CKLY?

or

CAN YOU READ <u>THIS</u> SENTENCE MORE QUICKLY?

d. _____ We more readily perceive the display shown below as one curved line intersecting a straight line, instead of two shorter straight lines and two shorter curved lines that meet in the center of the display.

18. Gestalt principles such as figure-ground relationship, proximity, continuity, and closure *(apply / do not apply)* to auditory as well as visual perception. For example, the ability to perceive where one word ends and the next word begins—called

_____ —is a far easier task

when hearing a familiar language than in hearing an unfamiliar language, suggesting an important role for *(bottom-up / top-down)* processing in understanding spoken language.

19. In 1960, Gibson and Walk studied the development of visual depth perception using the _____ _____ apparatus, which included a bold checkerboard-patterned surface with a shallow side next to a visible drop-off, all covered for safety with a strong sheet of glass. In testing the behavior of infants as their mothers called to them, Gibson and Walk found that the infants were *(eager / reluctant)* to cross over into the "deep" side, suggesting that by the *(crawling / walking)* stage, they *(had / had not)* developed the ability to perceive depth.

20. Similar tests with kittens, baby goats, and newly hatched chicks showed *(similar / different)* results—that at the time they become mobile, they *(already / do not)* possess depth perception ability.

21. We can classify visual cues to depth as either _____ cues (requiring two-eye vision) or _____ cues (available even with one-eye vision). A person who is blind in one eye is *(able / unable)* to judge depth, and would be able to use *(binocular / monocular / none of the)* depth cues that are normally available to a person whose two eyes function normally.

22. The two major **binocular depth cues** are _____ _____ —a difference between the images the two eyes receive before the brain merges these into a single three-dimensional perception, and _____ —based on information the brain receives about the tension in various eye muscles when the eyes turn inward to focus on a nearby object or outward to focus on a distant object.

23. If there is only a small difference between the images received by the two eyes, the brain *(can / cannot)* merge the two images into a single three-dimensional

view. When there is a large disparity, as when the image of a key is projected to one eye and an image of a dog is projected to the other eye, the brain *(can / cannot)* fuse the two disparate images, and we experience a continuing alternation between one of the images and the other, called _____

_____ .

24. **Monocular depth cues** *(are / are not)* available as clues to visual distance when viewing a scene with one-eye vision.

25. Match the description given in each item below with the name of the specific *monocular depth cue* listed in the Key List, writing your answer in the blank provided.

Key List
interposition
linear perspective
relative clarity
relative height
relative motion (motion parallax)
relative size
texture gradient

a. _____ As you look out your car window while riding along a main road in the business district of a small town, the shops next to the street appear and disappear quickly, but houses located on the hills above town seem to move less quickly across your visual field. You judge the objects that sweep across your visual field quickly as being closer, and those that move across more slowly as being farther away.

b. _____ As the drummers in a large marching band pass by your vantage point and continue down the street in the holiday parade, they cast a smaller and smaller image on your retina. Instead of seeing the members of the band as shrinking, you judge them to be moving away from you.

c. _____ On your daily brisk walk along a straight stretch of sidewalk near your home, you notice that the parallel edges of the sidewalk appear to become progressively closer together in the distance, even though you know the width of the sidewalk does not change.

d. _____ On a hazy day, you can barely see the mountains above the town, and they look very far away; but when the weather clears, the same mountains appear to be not at all far away.

e. _____ While lying on the lush green grass at the park, you notice that nearby blades of grass appear coarse and distinct, whereas the blades that are farther away look progressively less coarse until they seem to merge into an indistinct carpet of solid green.

f. _____ As you sit in your seat at the movie theater, the people sitting in the row just ahead of you are partially blocking your view of others in the audience; so it is an easy matter to know that those who are covered over are farther away from you, and those whose bodies block out the view are closer to you.

g. _____ Your photographs of friends playing volleyball at the beach show the people across the net on the opposing team as higher up from the bottom of the picture than your teammates who are closer to the camera, even though everyone is standing on the same flat stretch of sand.

26. To portray depth and distance in a realistic looking sketch or painting, artists must have a good working knowledge of *(binocular / monocular / both classes of)* visual cues for depth and distance.

27. When each light in a series of lights is quickly illuminated and then turned off before the next one is illuminated, the result is a type of illusory *(color / depth / movement)* known as the _____ **phenomenon**.

28. In the video episode, Christof Koch mentions that researchers *(have / have never)* identified cases of people who could not perceive motion.

29. A familiar object's characteristics (color, brightness, shape, and size) tend to be perceived as stable, despite frequent changes in the actual input from the object to our sensory systems. For example, _____ **constancy** is the basis for our tendency to judge a white dinner plate as white, whether it is viewed under dim candlelight or bright sunlight. _____ **constancy** is exemplified

in our tendency to perceive the dinner plate as round, even though the edges of the plate cast an elliptical image on the retina when viewed from an angle. Furthermore, the dinner plate casts a larger image on the retina when viewed from a close range than when it is viewed from a distance; _____ _____ is the term that describes that tendency to judge the dimensions of an object as the same, despite changes in the actual size of the image on our retina as we view that object at close range or from farther away.

30. There is an especially close relationship between our visual judgments of distance and the perception of the *(size / color / brightness)* of an object. For familiar solid objects, such as the dinner plate used in the previous examples, a decrease in the size of the image on the retina is normally interpreted as a(n) *(increase / decrease)* in the distance from the viewer.

31. There is some evidence that this **size-distance relationship** might help to explain the **moon illusion**—the tendency for the full moon to appear *(smaller / larger)* when near the horizon than when seen high in the sky.

32. The **Müller-Lyer illusion** is another illusion that relates to the size-distance relationship. As compared with people from rural environments, people who have lived in urban environments containing many straight lines and sharp angled corners make *(larger / smaller)* errors in estimating the lengths of the line segments, suggesting that susceptibility to the **Müller-Lyer illusion** *(is / is not)* dependent on experience and perceptual learning.

Perceptual Interpretation

33. Philosophers have adopted various positions on the relative importance of inborn tendencies and experience in shaping our perceptions, taking sides in the so-called _____-_____ debate. Immanuel _____, a German philosopher, suggested that we have innate modes of organizing sensory input, whereas John _____, a British philosopher, put greater weight on the role of _____, suggesting that learning most strongly affects how we perceive.

34. Scientific evidence relevant to the **nature-nurture debate** has emerged from case studies of people born with cataracts, and from laboratory animals reared with restricted sensory input. When cataracts are surgically removed, allowing clear vision for the first time in adulthood, people *(can / cannot)* sense colors and *(can / cannot)* see the distinctions between **figure** and _____. When presented with objects that are familiar through touch, they *(can / cannot)* visually recognize these objects. Studies of kittens and monkeys reared with the opportunity to see light but no patterns yield *(similar / opposite)* results.

35. Kittens allowed to see only vertical stripes during the first few weeks of life are later able to distinguish and react normally to *(only horizontal / only vertical / all)* orientations of lines. The same visual restriction later in life produces *(serious / moderate / no)* lasting impairment of visual perception. This research suggests that there is an early _____ **period** during which visual experience has *(lasting / temporary)* effects on nervous system organization and perceptual capacities.

36. When people are fitted with distorting lenses that displace objects 40 degrees off to one side, they *(immediately / quickly / eventually / never)* adjust their movements to compensate for the displaced visual input. Adjustment to lenses that cause everything to appear upside down takes several *(minutes / days / weeks)*, demonstrating our capacity for _____ _____.

37. Our past experiences and expectations can exert a strong *(top-down / bottom-up)* influence on how we organize sensory inputs. For example, to someone who has just been hearing a sports report on the news, the word "bat" may evoke images of an object used to hit baseballs. Yet to someone who has been hearing

about mammals that can fly, the same word may evoke images of a winged creature gliding across the night sky. In this case, the differing interpretations of the same stimulus may stem from a **schema** or _____ _____ established before hearing the word "bat."

38. One area of applied research in psychology is the design of work environments and equipment (household appliances, control panels for vehicles, machinery in factories, etc.) to increase ease of use and minimize errors people make in using these products. For _____ _____ **psychologists**, the emphasis is on *(training people to use products / designing products to fit people)*. In their research, for example, they might assess what difficulties people face when attempting to connect the various components of an entertainment system, contributing to a safer and more convenient design.

Is There Extrasensory Perception?

39. Claims about **ESP**, or _____ _____, range from the idea that knowledge of ongoing events can be sensed from afar (_____), to the notion that events can be perceived before they have occurred (_____), to the idea that people can communicate mind-to-mind (_____).

40. People who study paranormal events are known as _____.

41. Magician James Randi pointed out many years ago that the task of convincing skeptics that a claimed psychic phenomenon is real would require *(a large number of / several / only one)* reproducible demonstration(s) of the paranormal phenomenon under conditions allowing authentication–that is, in a *(controlled experiment / demonstration on stage)*.

42. An extensive research study (Sweat & Dunn, 1993) has revealed that the majority of police departments in large cities *(have / have not)* used psychics to help them solve crimes. Furthermore, of those police departments that had used psychics, *(all / most / some / none)* reported finding it to be useful in solving the crime in question.

43. One controlled experiment on ESP (Bem & Honorton, 1994) led to *(positive / negative)* findings on telepathy, using tests of sending and receiving with the "ganzfeld" procedure. Considerable debate followed the publication of that experiment, and dozens of more recent efforts to replicate the original finding *(have / have not)* succeeded in demonstrating the existence of psychic abilities.

44. In regard to ESP, a report of the National Research Council concluded that "the best available evidence *(does / does not)* support the contention that these phenomena exist." David Myers points out in the textbook that people's predisposition to *(believe in / question / reject)* claims of ESP may be an expression of "an unsatisfied hunger for wonderment, an itch to experience the magical." Myers goes on to point out that if we look carefully enough, we can find evidence of the extraordinary, the profound, and the mysterious *(within / outside)* the bounds of our own perceptual experiences.

45. The opinion of several experts interviewed in the video *(clash with / echo)* Myers' view that there is plenty of mystery and room for wonder as we contemplate our own sensory and perceptual systems. Gilles Laurent points out that we know *(very little / a lot)* about which neurons in the brain react to specific kinds of sensory input, and yet we *(have / have not)* answered the question of how the brain merges the various kinds of inputs it is processing into a unitary experience–the so-called _____ **problem**.

SELF TEST

Read each question and circle the letter of the best answer. When you have completed the Self Test, check your answers against the key at the end of this lesson. If you have answered any items incorrectly, review the appropriate materials to correct misunderstandings and cement your knowledge.

1. Sensation is to perception as
   a. touching is to seeing.
   b. detecting physical energy is to creating meaning.
   c. being aware is to having knowledge.
   d. top-down processing is to bottom-up processing.

2. While at a large social gathering, with many conversations going on at the same time, we have the ability to focus attention on one conversation while filtering out other conversations around us. This is called the _____, and it serves as a good example of _____.
   a. "cocktail party effect" . . . selective attention
   b. "cocktail party effect" . . . change blindness
   c. "change blindness" . . . bottom-up processing
   d. "change blindness" . . . selective attention

3. Which of the following could be cited as an example of our selective attention to features of our surroundings?
   a. Cocktail party effect
   b. Inattentional blindness
   c. Change deafness
   d. All of the above

4. Which of the following illustrates "visual capture"?
   a. Attention shifts away from your original conversational partner when a person off to your left says your name.
   b. Motorists are less attentive to their driving when they are paying attention to a conversation on a cell phone.
   c. When sound emanates from a movie projector located behind us, we typically perceive the sound as coming from the mouths of actors on the screen.
   d. We hear a steady series of clicks as though they are occurring in pairs.

5. The German word "gestalt" means
   a. "form" or "organized whole."
   b. "expectation" or "bias."
   c. "understanding" or "comprehension."
   d. "randomness" or "chaos."

6. As we perceive the world, which of the following most strongly contributes to our tendency to recognize patterns or organized wholes instead of collections of separate and unrelated elements?
   a. Precognition, psychokinesis, and subliminal perception
   b. A blend of bottom-up and top-down processing
   c. Binocular cues
   d. Visual capture

7. Which of the following examples illustrates the perceptual principle of *proximity*?
   a. Despite a tiny break of the line in a quick sketch of a circle, we still perceive the sketch as a circle.
   b. We tend to perceive this display:
      □□□•••□□□•••
      as groups of alternating squares and dots, rather than as an array of twelve separate and distinct geometric shapes.
   c. When we see separate beads on a long string, we perceive the string as whole and unbroken, even though the beads cover portions of the string.
   d. We tend to perceive this display:
      □□□ □□□ □□□
      as having a pattern consisting of three groups of squares, rather than as simply nine separate and distinct squares.

8. Kim calls Alex on her cell phone from an area where the signal quality is poor. Even though Alex cannot hear each word clearly ("Can you mee_ me and Sarah at 4 o'cl___ for coff__ at the __arbucks over by your hou__ –the one at the cor___ of Lake and Ca_fornia?"), Alex has no trouble understanding what Kim is saying, thanks to the perceptual principle of
   a. proximity.
   b. figure-ground distinction.
   c. closure.
   d. similarity.

9. Gestalt principles of grouping help us to understand
   a. the mechanisms that allow us to perceive depth in two-dimensional stimuli.
   b. the basis for our tendency to perceive certain kinds of patterns when we see an array of objects.
   c. the basis for all visual illusions.
   d. how cultural experience helps us to develop our visual abilities.

10. The question of how the brain forms a unified experience out of various separate elements that impinge upon the senses is known as
    a. the segmentation question.
    b. the binding problem.
    c. the nature-nurture debate.
    d. the visual cliff problem.

11. When placed on the visual cliff apparatus, the most typical response of a human infant, a kitten, or a newborn goat is to
    a. avoid the "deep" side, suggesting that they already perceive depth at this early point in development.
    b. cross over onto the "deep" side, suggesting that depth perception has not yet developed.
    c. move wherever their mothers coax them to go, whether toward the "deep" or the "shallow" side of the apparatus.
    d. fall off the edge of the apparatus.

12. Binocular cues for depth perception
    a. are useful only for nearsighted people.
    b. function primarily when objects are viewed from a great distance, but not when objects are close to the viewer.
    c. require the use of the two eyes together.
    d. can be utilized just as well with one-eye vision as with two-eye vision.

13. Retinal disparity
    a. is a type of blindness that occurs when the visual receptors degenerate in old age.
    b. is one of the major binocular cues for depth perception.
    c. supplies important monocular cues for depth perception.
    d. ordinarily interferes with depth perception.

14. As Brenda looks off into the distance while waiting for her train to arrive, the tracks give the appearance of becoming progressively closer to one another as the distance increases. This is known as _____, an important _____ cue for depth.
    a. convergence . . .binocular
    b. interposition . . . binocular
    c. linear perspective . . .monocular
    d. retinal disparity . . . monocular

15. As Marcie approaches her psychology classroom door and sees the door swing open toward her, the rectangular image of the door changes to a trapezoidal image on her retina, yet Marcie still recognizes the door, perceiving a change in its

position, not its shape. This example illustrates the perceptual phenomenon known as
    a. linear perspective.
    b. size constancy.
    c. shape constancy.
    d. the phi phenomenon.

16. One explanation that has been given for the famous Müller-Lyer illusion suggests that the two lines between the arrow tips appear to be unequal because
    a. size constancy leads to an abnormality in shape constancy.
    b. cues similar to those associated with distance have an impact on size judgments.
    c. the horizontal-vertical illusion takes over.
    d. binocular cues overcome our reliance on monocular cues.

17. Which of the following philosophers argued strongly that our ways of organizing sensory inputs are based primarily on *experience* (rather than on innate mechanisms)?
    a. John Locke
    b. Immanuel Kant
    c. both of the above
    d. neither of the above

18. Surgery sometimes has been successful in correcting visual problems in adults who were born blind because of cataracts. After recovery from the surgery, these patients
    a. show no visual deficits whatsoever, demonstrating that all visual functioning is innate.
    b. can almost immediately distinguish figure from ground and sense colors, suggesting that these basic visual functions are innate.
    c. can immediately recognize shapes and faces they previously knew by touch, but gradually lose this ability as the accumulating visual input leads to profound confusion.
    d. must spend many years learning to sense colors and to distinguish figure from ground, showing that all perceptual functions are acquired through experience.

19. Research by Blakemore and Cooper has demonstrated that kittens deprived of early visual exposure to horizontal lines later show evidence of
    a. normal responsiveness to lines of all orientations.
    b. unresponsiveness to vertical lines.
    c. unresponsiveness to all lines.
    d. unresponsiveness to horizontal lines.

20. Perceptual set
    a. is a predisposition to interpret sensory input in a particular way, based on past experience, emotion, or motivation.
    b. is described by David Myers as the idea that "to believe is to see."
    c. is involved when we see only one of several possible perceptual interpretations of an ambiguous stimulus, such as seeing a bunny when the same line drawing could be viewed as a duck.
    d. all of the above.

21. Research has demonstrated that an actual photograph of a familiar face, such as Arnold Schwarzenegger, is often harder to recognize than a computer-created caricature that emphasizes the distinctive facial features of that same person. These findings demonstrate the importance of
    a. visual capture.
    b. monocular cues.
    c. perceptual schemas.
    d. Gestalt principles of grouping.

22. Human factors psychologists investigate
    a. how appliances, machines, and jobs can be designed to make human tasks easier to do and less likely to lead to errors and accidents.
    b. how people from diverse backgrounds can relate more effectively to one another and perceive each other in a more positive and respectful way.
    c. how people can be retrained to work more efficiently with the technology they already have available to them.
    d. how to make products more attractive to the consumer, so that sales of those products will increase.

23. Diana believes that she can read her friend Lucy's thoughts, even when Diana is at home in Chicago and Lucy is off on vacation in Boston. Diana would be classified as someone who believes in the existence of
    a. telepathy.
    b. context effects.
    c. precognition.
    d. binocular cues.

24. Which of the following is true of tips given to police crime investigators by people claiming to be psychics?
    a. Many such tips and predictions are offered to police departments each year.
    b. Surveys reveal that the majority of police departments do not use psychics in their efforts to solve crimes.
    c. Among police departments that have followed up on tips given to them by psychics, such tips have been found not to be useful.
    d. All of the above.

25. Regarding claims of ESP, psychologists
    a. have produced and replicated hundreds of well-designed research studies that support a variety of claims for the existence of ESP.
    b. do not bother to conduct research into such claims.
    c. believe that there is ample evidence for precognition, but not for clairvoyance or telepathy.
    d. none of the above

ANSWER KEY FOR THE ACTIVE REVIEW EXERCISES

1. perception; [1] Textbook, Video 9
2. top-down; [1] Textbook, Video 9
3. only a very few; [2] Textbook, Video 9
4. only one thing; inattentional blindness; [2] Textbook, Video 9
5. ability; are; [2] Textbook
6. overconfident; 50; [2] Video 9
7. change blindness; fail to notice; are not; change deafness; [2] Textbook, Video 9
8. twice; [2] Textbook
9. provide clues about; Müller-Lyer; equal; [3] Textbook
10. farther away; [3] Textbook
11. are not; grouped or accented; [3] Textbook
12. visual; visual capture; [3] Textbook
13. Gestalt; form or whole; [4] Textbook, Video 9
14. greater than; are not; [4] Textbook
15. figure; ground; [4] Textbook, Video 9
16. sometimes; more than one; American; Japanese; [4] Video 9
17. (a) closure; (b) similarity; (c) proximity; (d) continuity; [5] Textbook, Video 9
18. apply; segmentation; top-down; [4, 5] Textbook, Video 9
19. visual cliff; reluctant; crawling; had; [7] Textbook
20. similar; already; [7] Textbook
21. binocular; monocular; able; monocular; [8] Textbook, Video 9
22. retinal disparity; convergence; [8] Textbook, Video 9
23. can; cannot; binocular rivalry; [8] Video 9
24. are; [8] Textbook, Video 9
25. (a) relative motion (motion parallax); (b) relative size; (c) linear perspective; (d) relative clarity; (e) texture gradient; (f) interposition; (g) relative height; [8] Textbook, Video 9
26. monocular; [8] Textbook
27. movement; phi; [9] Textbook
28. have; [9] Video 9
29. lightness (*or* brightness); Shape; size constancy; [10] Textbook, Video 9
30. size; increase; [10] Textbook
31. larger; [10] Textbook
32. larger; is; [10] Textbook
33. nature-nurture; Kant; Locke; experience; [11] Textbook
34. can; can; ground; cannot; similar; [11] Textbook
35. only vertical; no; critical; lasting; [11] Textbook
36. quickly; days; perceptual adaptation; [12] Textbook
37. top-down; perceptual set; [13] Textbook, Video 9
38. human factors; designing products to fit people; [14] Textbook
39. extrasensory perception; clairvoyance; precognition; telepathy; [15] Textbook
40. parapsychologists; [15] Textbook
41. only one; controlled experiment; [15] Textbook
42. have not; none; [15] Textbook
43. positive; have not; [15] Textbook
44. does not; believe in; within; [15] Textbook
45. echo; a lot; have not; binding; [15] Video 9

ANSWER KEY FOR THE SELF TEST

Item #	Answer	Learning Outcomes	Source	Item #	Answer	Learning Outcomes	Source
1.	b	1	Textbook, Video 9	14.	c	8	Textbook
2.	a	2	Textbook, Video 9	15.	c	9, 10	Textbook, Video 9
3.	d	2	Textbook, Video 9	16.	b	10	Textbook
4.	c	3	Textbook	17.	a	11	Textbook
5.	a	4	Textbook	18.	b	11	Textbook
6.	b	4	Textbook, Video 9	19.	d	11	Textbook
7.	d	5	Textbook, Video 9	20.	d	13	Textbook
8.	c	5	Textbook, Video 9	21.	c	13	Textbook
9.	b	5	Textbook, Video 9	22.	b	14	Textbook
10.	b	6	Video 9	23.	a	15	Textbook
11.	a	7	Textbook	24.	d	15	Textbook
12.	c	8	Textbook, Video 9	25.	d	15	Textbook
13.	b	8	Textbook, Video 9				

Lesson 10 (States of Consciousness)

A Great Mystery

Assignments

Reading: Chapter 7, "States of Consciousness," in *Psychology* by David Myers (Modules 18, 19, and 20 in the modular version of *Psychology*)

Video: Episode 10, "A Great Mystery"

LEARNING OUTCOMES

Familiarize yourself with the Learning Outcomes for this lesson before you begin the assignments. Return to them to check your learning after completing the Steps to Learning Success. Careful work on these materials should equip you to accomplish the outcomes.

Consciousness and Information Processing (Module 18)

1. Discuss the definition of **consciousness** and the changes in the way consciousness has generally been regarded by psychologists over the history of the field.

2. Summarize the main ideas in the debate about what consciousness is, who has consciousness, and how consciousness can be studied.

3. Explain what split-brain research, as described in the video by Michael Gazzaniga, has contributed to our understanding of consciousness.

4. Compare and contrast the characteristics of **sub-conscious** and **conscious information processing.**

Sleep and Dreams (Module 18)

5. Identify and give examples of **circadian rhythms** and other biological rhythms with cycle lengths shorter and longer than circadian rhythms.

6. Describe research on brain mechanisms, hormones, and environmental signals involved in regulating circadian rhythms, and discuss practical applications of this knowledge.

7. Explain how sleep is studied in a sleep lab.

8. Distinguish between relaxed wakefulness, **REM sleep,** and the four different **stages of nonREM sleep**, and describe how these sleep states and stages are distributed across a normal night of sleep

9. Explain the relationship between REM sleep and **dreaming**.

10. Indicate how much sleep a typical adult needs. Discuss the prevalence and consequences of **sleep deprivation**, and summarize the results of research into the benefits of getting adequate sleep.

11. Explain the effects of alcohol and sleeping pills on **insomnia,** and suggest positive steps people can take to get a better night of sleep.

12. List and describe several **sleep disorders,** and summarize what is known about causes and treatments for each disorder.

13. List and compare various theories on why we sleep.

14. Summarize what researchers have discovered about the **manifest content** of people's dreams.

15. Discuss several theories that have been put forth to explain the functions of REM sleep. Include a summary of the fundamental ideas of the **activation synthesis theory of dreaming**, and compare and contrast this theory with **Freud**'s ideas on the significance of dream content.

16. Describe the effects of **REM sleep deprivation**.

Hypnosis (Module 19)

17. Define **hypnosis**, discuss hypnotic susceptibility, and compare and contrast the behavior of hypnotized and nonhypnotized people.

18. Review the evidence about what hypnosis can and cannot do, and distinguish between claims about hypnosis that have been supported in carefully conducted research and those that have not been supported.

19. Compare the **social influence theory** and **divided consciousness theory** of hypnosis, reviewing the evidence pertaining to each and indicating how these theories are regarded by today's hypnosis researchers.

Drugs and Consciousness (Module 20)

20. Explain what a **psychoactive drug** is, and identify and distinguish between drug **tolerance**, **withdrawal**, **dependence**, and **addiction**.

21. List the three categories of psychoactive drugs discussed in the textbook, and give examples of each.

22. Describe in a general way how psychoactive drugs exert their effects, and cite specifics on the effects of **opiates** and **cocaine** on transmission at synapses in the brain.

23. Discuss some of the biological, psychological, social, and cultural influences on drug use.

Near-Death Experiences (Module 20)

24. Compare **near-death experiences** with other altered states of consciousness, and contrast mind-body **dualists'** and **monists'** interpretations of near-death experience.

ACTIVE REVIEW

Each item in this section is based on material presented in the video or the textbook assignment for this lesson, or both. Complete this section, referring as needed to your notes or the source materials themselves. Answers are provided at the end of this lesson.

Consciousness and Information Processing

1. In its earliest days, the field of psychology *(was defined as / excluded)* the study of **consciousness**. However, when **behaviorism** emerged as a dominant influence, behaviorists promoted a swing toward defining psychology as the science of _____. After about 1960, as new research tools were developed in the neurosciences and cognitive science, psychologists increasingly *(embraced / disregarded)* consciousness as a topic for research.

2. **Aristotle** believed that consciousness was a property of the *(brain / heart / stomach)*. Today's prominent neuroscientists and philosophers, including several interviewed in the video, seem to *(agree / disagree)* about the idea that consciousness is tied to the functions of the **brain**, even though questions about the specific brain mechanisms involved in consciousness have *(just recently / not yet)* been resolved.

3. In the video, various experts highlighted some of today's unsettled issues about consciousness. One such issue is whether consciousness involves the whole brain. Christof Koch states that he thinks certain specific neural elements will be found to be *(just as / more)* important to consciousness *(than / as)* others, even though he considers this topic to be a(n) *(open research question / purely philosophical debate)*.

4. Michael Gazzaniga has studied **split-brain patients**, who have had the two hemispheres of the brain surgically *(joined together / split apart)* as a treatment for severe _____. After surgery, these patients *(are / are not)* aware of things to the left of their visual fixation point. Yet rather surprisingly, they *(always / fail to)* comment on this lack of awareness. Gazzaniga expresses the opinion that probably about *(50 / 75 / 90 / 99)* percent of what we do is ordinarily handled unconsciously.

5. *(All / Not all)* experts agree on whether it is useful to view consciousness as a spotlight, illuminating first one thing and then another. In commenting in the video on whether consciousness is an all-or-none phenomenon and whether animals have consciousness, Susan Greenfield explains that she prefers to view it as a(n) *(dimmer / on-off)* switch with *(only one / many)* possible setting(s). According to this conceptualization, a *(more / less)* sophisticated brain would be capable of a greater degree of consciousness.

6. Various examples are cited in the textbook to illustrate our *(ability / inability)* to respond to stimuli we do not perceive consciously, such as when a person skilled at keyboarding quickly and automatically selects letters to tap. When we are conscious of our body movements, our awareness generally *(precedes / coincides with / follows)* the brain processes that trigger the movements.

7. **Subconscious** information processing occurs in multiple *(parallel / serial)* pathways in the brain, but **conscious** processing takes place in a *(parallel / serial)* fashion, making it a *(slower and more limited / faster and less limited)* kind of information processing *(capable / incapable)* of solving new problems.

Sleep and Dreams

8. Periodic fluctuations in body processes over time are called **biological** *(rhythms / clocks)*, and these variations seem to be controlled by internal body mechanisms called **biological** *(rhythms / clocks)*. List examples of processes that ebb and flow according to cycles of the following lengths:

    a. Annual cycles: _____
    _____

    b. 28-day cycles: _____
    _____

    c. 24-hour cycles: _____
    _____

    d. 90-minute cycles: _____
    _____

9. Our bodies' 24-hour daily cycles are called _____ **rhythms**, and these rhythms serve to keep our body processes (such as temperature, sleep and alertness, and variations in hormone secretions) coordinated with the earth's cycles of day and night. According to Sonia Ancoli-Israel, a researcher interviewed in the video, the word "circadian" is derived from the Greek word roots "circa" and "diem," which together mean literally *(cycle or die / about a day / exercise and diet)*

10. Sonia Ancoli-Israel explains that adequate exposure to _____ during the day is a very important way to keep our **circadian rhythms** regular. She states that we need about _____ hours of bright light per day (sunlight, ideally) to maintain good, strong circadian rhythms. For people who cannot fall asleep until very late at night, bright light exposure in the *(morning / afternoon / evening)* can help them to feel sleepy earlier in the evening and to awaken *(earlier / later)* in the morning.

11. A long airline flight across time zones initially *(enhances / does not affect / disturbs)* the coordination between our body's **circadian rhythms** and the time of day at our destination, causing the condition known as _____ _____. However, exposure to intense _____ at the proper time of the day can reset our **biological clock** so that it becomes synchronized with the new time zone.

12. Bright light exposure prompts the **retina** of the eye to send signals to the _____ _____ **(SCN)**, a tiny cluster of brain cells that in turn signals the _____ **gland** to alter its release of the hormone _____. The effect of **melatonin** is to promote *(sleepiness / alertness)*. Secretion of melatonin by the **pineal gland** is *(increased / decreased)* in the dark, and *(suppressed / enhanced)* by light, which explains why exposure to bright artificial lights in the evening hours may delay sleep and can shift our circadian rhythms, potentially contributing to sleep deprivation.

13. The brain *(continues / stops)* being active during sleep. We exhibit a biological rhythm during sleep in the

form of repeated *(30-minute / 60-minute / 90-minute / 2-hour)* cycles of sleep that include two general states: a) _____ _____ _____ **(REM) sleep** and b) **nonREM sleep,** which is further broken down into *(2 / 3 / 4 / 5)* different stages or depths. The very lightest sleep during which one is barely dozing off is called **Stage ___** , and the very deepest sleep is called **Stage ___.**

14. To detect the various states and stages of sleep, researchers connect a sleep lab volunteer to an array of electrodes: one set placed on the chin to detect _____ _____, another set near the eyes to measure _____ _____, and another set against the scalp to monitor variations in _____ _____. Sleep researchers *(may also / do not)* use additional devices to check on other physiological changes, such as respiration, body temperature, heart rate, and blood flow to the genitals.

15. For each item listed below, select from the Key List the name of the *sleep stage* described in the item, and write your choice in the blank provided. Many of the alternatives may be used more than once.

    Key List
    relaxed wakefulness
    Stage 1
    Stage 2
    Stages 3 and 4
    REM sleep

    a. _____ A night of sleep typically begins with this stage of sleep.

    b. _____ When awakened from this kind of sleep, the person will most likely report a vivid, story-like **dream,** rich in sensory detail.

    c. _____ A light stage in which we spend about half of a normal night of sleep.

    d. _____ The period of sleep when **hypnagogic hallucinations,** such as the sensation of falling or floating, are most likely to be experienced.

    e. _____ Our deepest sleep.

    f. _____ Successive bouts of this type of sleep get longer as the night progresses.

    g. _____ Most of this kind of sleep occurs in the first three or four hours of a normal night of sleep.

    h. _____ **Sleepwalking, sleeptalking** and **night terrors** are most likely to occur during this kind of sleep.

    i. _____ Sometimes called **paradoxical sleep,** because the brain waves resemble those during a a wakeful state, but the large muscles of the body are extremely relaxed.

    j. _____ **Alpha waves** dominate the **EEG** record in this state.

    k. _____ **Sleep spindles** occur on the EEG record during this stage.

    l. _____ The sleeper exhibits slow, large **delta waves** on the EEG during this kind of sleep.

    m. _____ The term **slow-wave sleep** is often used to describe this kind of sleep.

    n. _____ Rapid saw-toothed waves on the **EEG,** resembling the brain waves seen in a wakeful state, occur along with increased heart rate, rapid breathing, genital arousal, and relaxation of most muscles to the point of immobility, except for occasional brief twitches.

    o. _____ When deprived of **REM sleep,** people compensate by exhibiting more of this during the next undisturbed night.

16. Although sleep needs vary widely, Sonia Ancoli-Israel states in the video that as we grow into adulthood, the majority of adults need about ____ hours of sleep per night. The textbook reports that if left to sleep without restrictions, most adults will sleep at least ____ hours per night, and will awaken *(refreshed / sluggish)* and perform *(better / more poorly)* than if they were limited to a shorter night of sleep. In fact, an extra hour of sleep per night, the textbook author claims, can be shown to *(lift / depress)* one's mood, *(impair / improve)* memory, *(strengthen / weaken)* the immune system, and *(reduce / increase)* risk of death due to accidents.

17. Research volunteers paid to participate in a week-long experiment requiring them to stay in bed for 14 hours a day averaged *(6 / 8 / 10 / 12)* hours of sleep a day, and felt a(n) *(increase / drop)* in their mood and energy levels after paying off their "sleep debt" in this way. When deprived of sleep, people show *(faster / slower)* reaction times and *(increased / decreased)* errors on visual performance tasks.

18. The results of sleep deprivation studies clearly confirm our need to sleep. But why are humans built to sleep? Summarize the basic ideas of the four major theories on why we sleep._____

    _____

    _____

    _____

    _____

    _____

    _____

    _____

    _____

    _____

19. **Insomnia**, a very *(rare / common)* complaint among adults today, is described by Sonia Ancoli-Israel as usually being a *(primary / secondary)* disorder stemming from other medical conditions, such as those involving pain or discomfort, or from psychiatric conditions such as depression or anxiety. Insomnia can be made *(better / worse)* by the use of alcohol or sleeping pills, because of sluggishness the next day and the possible need to *(decrease / maintain / increase)* the dose to sustain its effects over time.

20. List several suggestions the textbook author gives for getting a better night of sleep without resorting to sleeping pills or alcohol. _____

    _____

    _____

    _____

    _____

    _____

21. For each item listed below, select from the Key List the name of the *sleep disorder* described in the item, and write your choice in the blank provided. Some alternatives may be used more than once.

    Key List
    cataplexy
    insomnia
    narcolepsy
    night terrors
    sleep apnea

    a. _____ Involves an inability to continue breathing normally during certain stages of sleep.

    b. _____ Complaints of this problem are made by about 10 to 15 percent of adults, even though the complainers often overestimate how long it takes for them to fall asleep and underestimate how long they have slept.

    c. _____ Short periods of extreme sleepiness that can be accompanied by involuntary "sleep attacks," with **cataplexy** in some cases; these problems may occur even when the person has had plenty of sleep the night before.

    d. _____ Occurring in people with **narcolepsy**, a type of muscular weakness or paralysis that can be triggered by very strong emotions. This sudden loss of muscle tone, resembling what occurs in REM sleep, may cause the individual to collapse.

    e. _____ Occurs more commonly in older, overweight men who are snorers.

    f. _____ Understanding of the biochemical basis of this sleep disorder has been advanced because of in-depth research on dogs that have the same disorder.

    g. _____ People with this sleep disorder may be unaware that they are waking up hundreds of times per night to resume breathing. If left untreated, this disorder elevates the risk of heart attack and stroke.

    h. _____ Researchers have linked this disorder to an absence of specific cells in the **hypothalamus** that would normally produce the neurotransmitter **hypocretin**.

i. _____ Although this is not a nightmare, the child appears to wake abruptly from deep stage of sleep looking terrified, with rapid breathing and a high heart rate, but the next morning will often remember little or nothing of the experience.

22. **Night terrors, sleepwalking,** and **sleeptalking,** which are most common in *(children / adults),* happen during Stage ____ sleep, and not in REM. This makes sense when we consider that our muscles are effectively paralyzed during *(REM / nonREM)* sleep, making major movements impossible. Such a physiological arrangement protects us by assuring that we *(will / will not)* get up and act on the hallucinated images we experience when we dream.

23. Jerome Siegel mentions in the video that the occurrence of *(apnea / cataplexy)* in **narcolepsy** provides a rare opportunity to study the unusual combination of loss of muscle tone unaccompanied by a loss of consciousness. The loss of muscle tone in narcolepsy is the same kind of paralysis we normally experience during *(Stage 1 / Stage 2 / Stage 3 / Stage 4 / REM)* sleep.

24. People who say they do not dream, when awakened in the midst of a REM sleep period, in fact *(do / do not)* report dreams. About 80 percent of dreams are reported to contain *(positive / negative / no)* emotions, and most dreams *(contain / do not contain)* sexual imagery. Surveys show that we most often dream of *(common / bizarre)* settings and events.

25. **Freud** theorized that dreams *(fulfill wishes / consolidate memories),* and that the content of our dreams has *(no / questionable / deep)* significance, expressing in a symbolic way our hidden desires and conflicts, often of a sexual nature. In Freud's theory, the elements of the dream that are obvious on the surface, called the _____ **content,** are merely the outward symbols representing the deeper underlying meaning–the _____ **content.** Other psychologists have contended that Freud's theory of dreaming is *(scientific / unscientific)* because it provides *(ample / no)* basis for determining the validity of any of the many possible dream interpretations.

26. An **information processing** view of dreaming holds that REM sleep may allow the brain to sort and file away remnants of waking mental activity. Research has shown that sleep following learning *(impairs / enhances)* memory, and that being deprived of sleep seems to *(interfere with / boost)* memory consolidation.

27. Dreams and/or REM sleep may have a **physiological function,** triggering periodic states of *(activity / rest)* in the brain, thereby fostering the maintenance and development of brain pathways; or alternatively, dreams may mirror **cognitive development.**

28. In the video, Allan Hobson states the opinion that REM sleep supports brain development. Newborn babies sleep about *(10 / 12 / 14/ 16)* hours per day, with about *(one-quarter / one-third / half)* of these hours spent in REM sleep. Jerome Siegel agrees, saying that the constant activation of sensory and motor systems of the brain during REM may promote *(normal / abnormal)* development.

29. Allan Hobson has proposed a neurological explanation of dreams, which he discusses in the video. Hobson's _____-_____ **theory of dreaming** suggests that the emotional content of dreams is strong because during REM sleep the brain stem activates the *(limbic system / cerebellum).* From there, signals are fed to the cortex, and it is the job of the *(cortex / limbic system / brain stem)* to make sense out of these unusual patterns of brain activity by somehow weaving together (synthesizing) the fragments. Because the **prefrontal cortex** is *(activated / deactivated)* while the rest of the brain is turned on during REM sleep, logical thinking is *(limited / enhanced),* giving rise to dream themes that can be bizarre and disjointed.

30. Whatever its function may be, researchers agree that REM sleep is *(clearly / not)* necessary. When people are deprived of REM by being awakened each time they begin REM sleep, they exhibit *(greater / the same / smaller)* amounts of REM sleep when allowed to sleep undisturbed. This pattern of compensation for lost REM sleep is called _____ _____.

Hypnosis

31. Interest in hypnotic techniques can be traced back as far as several *(decades / centuries)* ago. In **hypnosis**, one person presents to another certain *(commands / suggestions)* about behaviors, perceptions, thoughts, or feelings that will be experienced. Psychologists can agree that hypnosis involves a state of *(heightened / diminished)* suggestibility, and their research in recent decades has revealed that many of the claims made about hypnosis have been *(verified / exaggerated)*.

32. Based on the information presented in the textbook, identify the following items as true or false by writing the correct answer in the blank. After each item, provide further explanation to justify your answer.

    a. _____ Everyone is equally hypnotizable.
    _____
    _____

    b. _____ Hypnosis can make people perform dangerous or unethical things they would not do without hypnosis. _____
    _____
    _____

    c. _____ Hypnosis can help people experience lower levels of discomfort with procedures normally experienced as painful. _____
    _____
    _____

    d. _____ Hypnotized people can demonstrate superhuman physical strength. _____
    _____
    _____

    e. _____ Hypnosis can increase accurate and detailed recall of events from the scene of a crime. _____
    _____
    _____

    f. _____ Hypnosis can be used to induce age regression, allowing people to go back in time to re-experience a forgotten event from an earlier point in life. _____

_____
_____

    g. _____ Hypnosis has been reported to be of some use in treating certain problems, but it does not improve chances for success in breaking addictions to drugs, smoking, and alcohol.
    _____
    _____
    _____

    h. _____ People who are hypnotized and instructed to remember events they have presumably forgotten will often be motivated to report details that are not accurate, and may as a result be vulnerable to the formation of pseudomemories. _____
    _____
    _____

    i. _____ In their efforts to explain hypnosis, researchers have rejected the social influence theory in favor of the dissociation theory of hypnosis. _____
    _____
    _____

Drugs and Consciousness

33. **Psychoactive drugs** are distinguished from other drugs by the fact that they *(are highly addictive / are hallucinogenic / alter perceptions or mood)*.

34. Use of psychoactive drugs *(always / does not always)* lead(s) to **addiction**. But repeated use of some kinds of psychoactive drugs can lead to the development of _____, which means that a larger dose is required to bring about the same effect that a smaller dose initially produced. In some cases, when people stop using certain psychoactive drugs, they may experience uncomfortable side effects known as _____, which might include cravings and discomfort.

35. The three categories of psychoactive drugs listed in the textbook are _____, _____, and _____.

36. **Alcohol** is classified as a *(stimulant / depressant)*. List some of the important effects of alcohol on body systems, behavior, and mental processes. _____
_____
_____
_____
_____

37. The effects of most psychoactive drugs can be traced to their ability to affect _____, which serve as chemical messengers at synapses in the brain. Psychoactive drugs can work as they do because they generally **stimulate**, **inhibit**, or _____ the activity of the brain's naturally occurring neurotransmitters.

38. **Opium, morphine**, and **heroin** are all _____ drugs classified as **depressants**. Opiates have effects that mimic our brain's own naturally occurring opiate-like neurotransmitters, called the *(endorphins / dopamines / serotonins)*, which normally cause euphoria and block the perception of pain. With introduction of opiates into the body, the brain *(reduces / increases)* its production of endorphins. Then, if the person discontinues use of the opiate drugs, the shortage of both the naturally occurring and externally introduced opiates can trigger extremely uncomfortable **withdrawal** effects.

39. **Cocaine**, which acts in the brain as a *(stimulant / depressant)*, also changes events at brain synapses, *(enhancing / blocking)* the process of reabsorption (reuptake) of certain neurotransmitter molecules after their release from the sending neuron, and in this way amplifying the effects these neurotransmitters would normally have.

40. Review drug categories by matching each specific *drug* with a category in the Key List. Write your choice in the blank provided. Some alternatives may be used more than once.

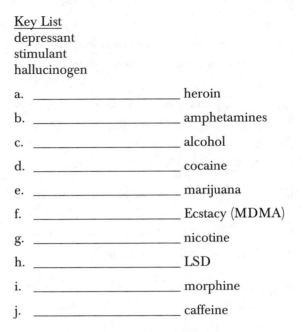

Key List
depressant
stimulant
hallucinogen

a. _____ heroin

b. _____ amphetamines

c. _____ alcohol

d. _____ cocaine

e. _____ marijuana

f. _____ Ecstacy (MDMA)

g. _____ nicotine

h. _____ LSD

i. _____ morphine

j. _____ caffeine

Near-Death Experiences

41. Ronald Siegel has argued that **near-death experiences** share *(little / much)* in common with hallucinogenic drug effects, *(frontal / temporal)* lobe seizures, and oxygen deprivation effect. Others disagree, claiming there is not much similarity in the experience or the impact of these experiences.

42. Mind-body **dualists**, who believe that mind and body are *(distinctly different and separable entities / two aspects of the same fundamental thing)*, prefer to see near-death experiences as an indication that humans have the capacity for immortality. **Monists**, on the other hand, are *(more / less)* likely than dualists to interpet near-death experiences as a reflection of how brain activity changes in highly stressful circumstances. David Myers suggests that this debate highlights issues whose answers affect how we humans view ourselves, while also emphasizing that there are questions that fall *(within / beyond)* the scope of what science can answer.

SELF TEST

Read each question and circle the letter of the best answer. When you have completed the Self Test, check your answers against the key at the end of this lesson. If you have answered any items incorrectly, review the appropriate materials to correct misunderstandings and cement your knowledge.

1. Over the period from the early 1900s to about 1960, the movement known as _____ influenced psychologists to abandon the definition of psychology as the science of consciousness, and redefine it as the science of _____.
   a. behaviorism ... behavior
   b. psychoanalysis ... subconscious information processing
   c. cognitive psychology ... automatic information processing
   d. emotionalism ... emotion

2. According to Christof Koch and other experts in the video, one of today's continuing scientific debates about consciousness concerns whether
   a. the brain has anything at all to do with consciousness.
   b. the heart is the center of consciousness.
   c. consciousness is a property of the whole brain or of a particular set of neurons in the brain.
   d. anesthetics can affect conscious awareness at all.

3. According to Michael Gazzaniga, patients who have had split-brain surgery
   a. feel as though they have two conscious minds.
   b. are not aware of things to the left of where their eyes are fixating, but do not comment on their lack of awareness.
   c. complain constantly about a lack of awareness of portions of the visual environment.
   d. do not seem to experience consciousness of any sort.

4. Which characteristics listed below apply more to <u>conscious</u> information processing than to subconscious information processing?
   a. It is faster than subconscious information processing
   b. At any give time, it can be busy processing many streams of information simultaneously.
   c. Its operation resembles that of a chief executive, not getting involved in routine business.
   d. It is unable to solve novel problems.

5. As examples of processes that follow a circadian rhythm, in the video Sonia Ancoli-Israel cites
   a. annual migration in birds and winter hibernation in bears.
   b. sleep-wake cycles, fluctuations of core body temperature, and secretion of hormones such as cortisol, prolactin, and melatonin.
   c. the human female menstrual cycle and ovulation.
   d. all of the above.

6. Melatonin
   a. is secreted under darker conditions and inhibited by light.
   b. is secreted under brighter light conditions and inhibited in the dark.
   c. maintains its constant level regardless of light exposure.
   d. is a serious form of skin cancer that can be fatal.

7. What leads to stimulation of the retinohypothalamic tract to the suprachiasmatic nucleus, helping to keep circadian rhythms regular?
   a. Bright light to the eyes
   b. Adrenalin from the bloodstream
   c. Melatonin
   d. Caffeine

8. In studying sleep, the electroencephalograph (EEG) is used to detect
   a. rapid eye movements.
   b. brain waves.
   c. muscle tone.
   d. respiration.

9. Alpha waves on the EEG occur during
   a. all stages of nonREM sleep.
   b. deep sleep.
   c. relaxed states of wakefulness.
   d. REM sleep.

10. The slowest, largest brain waves (having the lowest frequency and largest amplitude) occur during
    a. REM sleep.
    b. Stage 1 sleep.
    c. Stage 2 sleep.
    d. Stages 3 and 4 sleep.

11. During REM sleep, we show
    a. greatly increased muscle tone.
    b. slow, large brain waves.
    c. a lack of temperature regulation.
    d. all of the above.

12. REM sleep
    a. occurs only in people who remember their dreams in the morning.
    b. occurs in mature adults, but not in infants or young children.
    c. is the sleep stage during which people have night terrors.
    d. occurs about every 90 minutes throughout a normal night of sleep.

13. About half a normal night of sleep is spent in
    a. REM sleep.
    b. Stage 1.
    c. Stage 2.
    d. Stage 4.

14. Which of the following would not be typical during REM sleep?
    a. Increased tension in most large postural muscles of the body
    b. Vaginal lubrication and clitoral engorgement in women, or penile erection in men
    c. Elevated heart rate
    d. Irregular breathing

15. After being deprived of sleep, people show evidence of
    a. memory impairment.
    b. difficulties with attention and concentration.
    c. REM rebound.
    d. all of the above.

16. To overcome insomnia, the author of the textbook advises practicing each of the following habits, except:
    a. exercising vigorously in an effort to induce fatigue just before bed.
    b. avoiding caffeine after the late afternoon hours.
    c. relaxing in the evening with dimmer lighting.
    d. keeping a regular sleep schedule, going to bed at the same hour and getting up at the same hour each day.

17. Night terrors
    a. are most closely associated with Stage 4 sleep, and occur most often within a few hours after falling asleep.
    b. occur primarily during REM sleep.
    c. are the same as nightmares.
    d. are more common in adults than in children.

18. People with sleep apnea
    a. are keenly aware of their multiple awakenings during the night.
    b. may not know their sleep quality is poor because their awakenings during the night are so brief.
    c. may feel tired in the daytime, but do not encounter any other health problems.
    d. have cataplexy as part of the disorder.

19. Cataplexy
    a. can be cured with exposure to very bright lights.
    b. involves paralysis of the muscles while the individual remains aware of what is going on.
    c. is found in cats but not in humans.
    d. can be successfully treated with a special high-protein diet.

20. Individuals with narcolepsy show evidence of
    a. a bacterial infection that has been transmitted to them from household pets.
    b. damage to the centers in the medulla that control breathing.
    c. a psychological disorder that can be treated with psychotherapy.
    d. loss of cells in the hypothalamus that would ordinarily produce the neurotransmitter hypocretin.

21. Freud referred to the most obviously apparent elements we report when we describe the story line of a dream as the _____ content, and the deeper meaning as the_____ content.
    a. manifest … latent
    b. latent … manifest
    c. REM … nonREM
    d. aggressive … sexual

22. Newborn humans sleep about 16 hours a day, and studies of their sleep indicate that they spend
    a. about 90% of their sleep time in REM sleep.
    b. about half of their sleep time in REM sleep.
    c. about one-quarter of their sleep time in REM sleep, just as adults do.
    d. none of their sleep time in REM sleep; they are too young to have anything to dream about.

23. Which of the following has been offered as a possible explanation for the occurrence of REM sleep?
    a. REM sleep helps us to convert memories into long-term learning.
    b. REM sleep has physiological functions in maintaining neural connections, and in balancing

out body systems, especially the temperature regulation system.

c. REM sleep is associated with brain growth and cognitive development.

d. All of the above

24. Which of the following claims about hypnosis has been supported by research data?

a. With hypnotic suggestion, people are more successful in their attempts to rid themselves of serious drug addictions.

b. Hypnosis can be effectively used as an age regression tool to bring out accurate memories of long-forgotten childhood experiences.

c. People who are hypnotized become capable of physical feats that cannot be accomplished by

even the most highly motivated non-hypnotized people.

d. With hypnotic suggestion, some people can more comfortably tolerate dental and medical procedures that would otherwise be quite painful and uncomfortable.

25. The psychoactive drugs discussed in the textbook are categorized as

a. neurotransmitters and reuptake inhibitors.

b. antibiotics and psychedelics.

c. stimulants, depressants, and hallucinogens.

d. opiates, hallucinogens, and stimulants.

ANSWER KEY FOR THE ACTIVE REVIEW EXERCISES

1. was defined as; behavior; embraced; [1, 2] Textbook
2. heart; agree; not yet; [2] Video 10
3. more; than; open research question; [2] Video 10
4. split apart; epilepsy; are not; fail to; 99; [3] Video 10
5. Not all; dimmer; many; more; [2, 4] Video 10
6. ability; follows; [4] Textbook
7. parallel; serial; slower and more limited; capable; [4] Textbook
8. rhythms; clocks; *The answers for the lined portion of this item should include a reasonable selection from the following lists of examples:* a) migration in birds; hibernation in certain mammals; and appetite, sleep, and mood changes in some humans. b) the menstrual cycle in human females. c) sleep-wake cycles, core body temperature fluctuations, and secretion of hormones such as growth hormones, cortisol, prolactin, and melatonin. d) fluctuations of the various stages of sleep (REM and nonREM sleep) in humans. [5] Textbook, Video 10
9. circadian; about a day; [5] Textbook Video 10
10. light; two; morning; earlier; [5, 6] Video 10
11. disturbs; jet lag; light; [6] Textbook Video 10
12. suprachiasmatic nucleus; pineal; melatonin; sleepiness; increased; suppressed; [6] Textbook, Video 10
13. continues; 90-minute; rapid eye movement; 4; 1; 4; [5, 6, 8] Video 10
14. muscle tension [or muscle tone] eye movements; brain waves [or EEG activity]; may also; [7] Textbook, Video 10
15. a) Stage 1; b) REM sleep; c) Stage 2; d) Stage 1; e) Stages 3 and 4; f) REM sleep; g) Stages 3 and 4; h) Stages 3 and 4; i) REM sleep; j) relaxed wakefulness; k) Stage 2; l) Stages 3 and 4; m) Stages

3 and 4; n) REM sleep; o) REM sleep. [8, 9] Textbook, Video 10
16. 8; 9; refreshed; better; lift; improve; strengthen; reduce; [10] Textbook, Video 10
17. 12; increase; slower; increased; [10] Textbook
18. *Your answer should touch on the following ideas:*
a) Protection: Sleep at night protected our ancestors from predators and other dangers in the dark.
b) Repair and restoration: Sleep promotes healing, facilitates thermoregulation (balancing out of the temperature system), and allows new enzymes to be synthesized to repair neurons and weaken unused brain pathways. c) Remembering: Sleep promotes recall of recent experiences, boosts creativity, and improves problem solving. d) Growth: Pituitary growth hormones are secreted during the deeper stages of sleep, and brain development may be fostered by REM sleep. [13] Textbook, Video 10
19. common; secondary; worse; increase; [10, 11, 12] Textbook, Video 10
20. *Your list should include the following ideas:* 1) Relax with dimmer light before bedtime. 2) Avoid caffeine, especially later in the day. 3) Maintain a consistent sleep schedule, getting up at the same time each day. 4) Get regular exercise, but not in the late evening. 5) Don't fret unduly over a temporary loss of sleep. 6) If all else fails, shorten your sleep time to improve the quality of your sleep. [11] Textbook
21. a) sleep apnea; b) insomnia; c) narcolepsy; d) cataplexy; e) sleep apnea; f) narcolepsy; g) sleep apnea; h) narcolepsy; i) night terrors; [11, 12] Textbook, Video 10
22. children; 4; REM; will not; [12] Textbook, Video 10
23. cataplexy; REM; [12] Video 10

24. do; negative; do not contain; common; [9, 14] Textbook
25. fulfill wishes; deep; manifest; latent; unscientific; no; [15] Textbook
26. enhances; interfere with; [15] Textbook
27. Activity; [15] Textbook
28. 16; half; normal; [15] Video 10
29. activation-synthesis; limbic system; cortex; deactivated; limited; [15] Textbook, Video 10
30. clearly; greater; REM rebound; [15, 16] Textbook
31. centuries; suggestions; heightened; exaggerated; [17] Textbook
32. a) False. People vary in their suggestibility and their ability to become absorbed in fantasy, and therefore in their responsiveness to hypnotic induction.
    b) False. This is not unique to hypnosis. Suggestions from an authoritative person in a legitimate context may encourage unlikely acts in many people, whether hypnotized or not.
    c) True. For many people, hypnosis can reduce discomfort that would otherwise be experienced from submersion of the hand in ice water, dental procedures, certain kinds of surgery, or childbirth.
    d) False. Non-hypnotized people can perform at an equal level if given appropriate instructions and preparation.
    e) False. Hypnosis may encourage the formation of pseudomemories (false memories) that, once reported become, difficult to distinguish from memories of actual past experiences.
    f) False. The information hypnotized people report when given an age regression suggestion is not accurate, and it seems to stem from an active imagination about what the past events would have been like.
    g) True. There have been some reports of greater improvement with hypnosis, but not with serious addictions. Whether hypnosis is therapeutic depends in part on the condition being treated.
    h) True. This is why in many countries, courts have prohibited the use of testimony from witnesses who have undergone hypnosis.
    i) False. Researchers have started to see both dissociation and social influence as ingredients in hypnosis. [17, 18, 19] Textbook
33. alter perceptions or mood; [20] Textbook
34. does not always; tolerance; withdrawal; [20] Textbook
35. depressants, stimulants, hallucinogens; [21] Textbook
36. depressant; *Your answer should include many of the following concepts:* Reduction of inhibitions, including those for sexual and aggressive behavior; slowing of the sympathetic nervous system; slowed motor reactions and reduced coordination; disruption of memory and judgment; [21] Textbook
37. neurotransmitters; mimic; [22] Textbook
38. opiate; endorphins; reduces; [22] Textbook
39. stimulant; blocking; [22] Textbook
40. a) depressant; b) stimulant; c) depressant; d) stimulant; e) hallucinogen; f) stimulant; g) stimulant; h) hallucinogen; i) depressant; j) stimulant; [22] Textbook
41. much; temporal; [24] Textbook
42. distinctly different and separable entities; more; beyond; [24] Textbook

ANSWER KEY FOR THE SELF TEST

Item #	Answer	Learning Outcome #	Source	Item #	Answer	Learning Outcome #	Source
1.	a	1, 2	Textbook	14.	a	8	Textbook, Video 10
2.	c	2	Video 10	15.	d	10, 15, 16	Textbook, Video 10
3.	b	3	Video 10	16.	a	11	Textbook
4.	c	4	Textbook	17.	a	12	Textbook
5.	b	5, 6	Textbook, Video 10	18.	b	12	Textbook, Video 10
6.	a	6	Textbook, Video 10	19.	b	12	Video 10
7.	a	6	Textbook, Video 10	20.	d	12	Textbook, Video 10
8.	b	7	Textbook	21.	a	14, 15	Textbook
9.	c	7, 8	Textbook	22.	b	15, 8	Textbook, Video 10
10.	d	8	Textbook, Video 10	23.	d	15	Textbook, Video 10
11.	c	8	Textbook, Video 10	24.	d	17, 18	Textbook
12.	d	8, 9	Textbook, Video 10	25.	c	20, 21, 22	Textbook
13.	c	8	Textbook				

Lesson 11 (Learning)

The Learning Machine

Assignments

Read: Chapter 8, "Learning," in *Psychology* by David Myers (Modules 21, 22, and 23 in the modular version of *Psychology*)

Video: Episode 11, "The Learning Machine"

LEARNING OUTCOMES

Familiarize yourself with the Learning Outcomes for this lesson before you begin the assignments. Return to them to check your learning after completing the Steps to Learning Success. Careful work on these materials should equip you to accomplish the outcomes.

Introduction (Module 21)

1. Define **learning** and list the names and contributions of the historically important researchers whose pioneering efforts laid the groundwork for our understanding of various types of learning.

2. Compare and contrast **classical** and **operant conditioning**, and observational learning.

Classical Conditioning (Module 21)

3. Explain how classically conditioned responses are acquired, maintained, and modified by experience, providing examples of **extinction**, **spontaneous recovery**, **generalization**, and **discrimination**.

4. Discuss practical applications of **classical conditioning**.

5. Understand the issues surrounding the role of **cognitive processes** and **biological predispositions** in classical conditioning, and summarize pertinent research evidence.

6. Describe research findings showing that certain fears and aversions are subject to very rapid and persistent classical conditioning effects, and provide an evolutionary explanation.

Operant Conditioning (Module 22)

7. Distinguish between **operant** and **respondent behavior** and describe how operant behaviors are conditioned.

8. Describe the processes and explain the effects of **shaping**, **continuous reinforcement**, and **schedules of partial (intermittent) reinforcement**.

9. Compare and contrast **positive** and **negative reinforcement** and give examples of each.

10. Distinguish between **primary** and **conditioned reinforcers** and give examples.

11. Define **punishment** and explain how punishment differs from negative reinforcement. Explain the disadvantages of relying on punishment as a major means of disciplining children, and list some alternatives to the use of physical punishment.

12. Compare the cognitive view of **operant conditioning** with the strict behaviorist view, and review arguments and evidence pertaining to the controversy between these views.

13. Summarize evidence on the role of biological predispositions in operant conditioning.

14. Explain how operant conditioning principles have been applied in school, work, and home settings.

Learning by Observation (Module 23)

15. Explain the basic ideas of **observational learning**, and summarize what is known about the neural basis for such learning.

16. Provide a description of **Bandura**'s classic studies on observational learning, and discuss the conditions that influence whether people tend to imitate a model.

17. Provide an overview of the research into the influence of media violence on aggressive behavior, and discuss the potential of observational learning for encouraging **prosocial behavior**.

ACTIVE REVIEW

Each item in this section is based on material presented in the video or the textbook assignment for this lesson, or both. Complete this section, referring as needed to your notes or the source materials themselves. Answers are provided at the end of this lesson.

Introduction

1. Psychologists define **learning** as a *(permanent / relatively permanent / temporary)* change in *(behavior / emotion / motivation / thinking)* that is based on _____. The term for the most basic types of **associative learning**, in which an association is formed between one event and another, is _____.

Classical Conditioning

2. The earliest systematic investigations of **conditioning** occurred in the laboratory of Russian physiologist **Ivan** _____, beginning in *(1789 / 1898 / 1928 / 1956)*. His studies of learning in *(dogs / cats / monkeys)* focused on _____ responses to food, revealing that a stimulus closely associated with presentation of food came to induce the same response as did presentation of the food itself. This general principle came to be called _____ **conditioning** because it was the first type of simple associative learning to be researched.

3. Both Pavlov and **John B.** _____ were prime figures in the development of the viewpoint in psychology known as *(behaviorism / mentalism / psychoanalysis)*, which regarded mentalistic concepts, such as thoughts and feelings, as *(essential / unnecessary)* in explaining learning.

4. Pavlov's work was of special importance because it demonstrated that learning *(could / could not)* be studied scientifically, and it suggested that the principles of conditioning *(are / are not)* relevant to the human realm. For example, people's fears and prejudices are examples of emotions that *(can / cannot)* be viewed as classically conditioned responses.

5. A child who receives an immunization from a doctor who is wearing a white coat may respond with distress—crying and increased muscle tension—which constitute the _____ **response** to the sharp jab of a hypodermic needle. The jab of the needle serves as the _____ **stimulus** for the distress response. After this experience, the sight of the child's doctor in a white coat may become a(n) _____ _____ for the **conditioned response** (CR) of fear and distress. This sequence exemplifies the *(acquisition / extinction)* of a classically conditioned fear response.

6. Once a conditioned response has been acquired, stimuli that are similar to the original **conditioned stimulus** (CS) *(can / cannot)* elicit the conditioned response. For example, the child in the previous example may react with distress upon seeing any adult in a white coat similar to her doctor's white coat—an example of _____.

7. If the **CS** is presented repeatedly over time without the **unconditioned stimulus** (UCS), the process of _____ occurs, resulting in a reduction in the strength of the **conditioned** *(stimulus / response)* when the CS is presented. If the doctor in

the previous example appears repeatedly in his white coat, but does not give the child a shot, then the **conditioned fear** response might diminish through the process of _____. This procedure reverses the conditioning process, essentially turning the *(conditioned / neutral)* stimulus into a *(conditioned / neutral)* stimulus again because it no longer elicits the conditioned response.

8. Among the many practical applications of classical conditioning principles is the work of researcher John Garcia, who devised a method to discourage coyotes from attacking ranchers' _____ in California. Garcia laced sheep meat with _____ **chloride** (a tasteless and odorless substance that causes nausea and vomiting), and placed these packets of meat where coyotes could eat them. After becoming ill, the coyotes associated the taste and smell of sheep with nausea. In this case, the lithium chloride served as the *(conditioned / unconditioned)* **stimulus**, which was paired with the taste and smell of sheep. The taste and smell of sheep meat functioned originally as a **neutral stimulus** with regard to the response of nausea and vomiting. But after the researchers presented these stimuli in combination with the nausea-inducing lithium, the taste and smell of sheep became a *(conditioned / unconditioned)* **stimulus**, which by itself (even without lithium) could elicit the *(conditioned / unconditioned)* *(stimulus / response)* of nausea.

9. Garcia's efforts to establish a **conditioned taste aversion** required *(only one or two / multiple)* pairings of the sheep meat and the lithium, after which the coyotes avoided attacking the sheep. The ease with which taste aversions can be established in humans and other animals suggests the possibility that the process of **natural selection** over the course of *(individual development / evolution)* has endowed us with a **biological** _____ that encourages us to quickly learn to dislike foods associated with becoming ill.

10. **Biological** *(perversions / predispositions / instincts / incentives)* brought out by **natural selection** as humans evolved may also explain why we more

quickly acquire fear of *(flowers and mushrooms / snakes and spiders)* than of other stimuli that were less likely to pose threats to our ancestors.

Operant Conditioning

11. The psychologist who became famous for his studies of **operant conditioning** was *(Ivan Pavlov / John B. Watson / B. F. Skinner / Albert Bandura)*.

12. **Operant conditioning** occurs with behaviors that operate on the environment and are followed by a specific _____. The two main types of consequences in operant conditioning are **reinforcement**, which *(strengthens / weakens)* the behavior it follows, and **punishment**, which acts to *(strengthen / weaken)* the behavior it follows when used effectively.

13. Operant conditioning occurs with operant behavior, whereas classical conditioning typically involves an automatic response to a stimulus, termed _____ behavior.

14. In the blank next to each behavior listed below, write the word **operant** or **respondent** to indicate which kind of behavior is being described. <u>HINT</u>: Remember that a respondent behavior is one that occurs as an automatic, reflexive response brought about by a specific stimulus. An operant behavior may occur in the presence of a particular stimulus (a **discriminative stimulus**), but certain consequences follow only if the operant behavior has first occurred, and the likelihood of repeating the operant behavior depends on these consequences.

a. _____ Moving your steering wheel to make a left turn when you see the intersection near your home

b. _____ Crying when in severe pain after being kicked by another player in a soccer game

c. _____ Blinking when a gust of wind hits your face

d. _____ Saying "No, thanks" when offered more food after eating enough to feel stuffed

e. _____ Salivating after placing a morsel of food in your mouth

f. _____ Answering the telephone when it rings

g. _____ Salivating when you enter the kitchen and hear the clattering sound of dinner plates with food being dished up

h. _____ Reaching across your desk to pick up a coffee cup

15. When using reinforcement, for example in obedience training of dogs, one way to get a particular operant behavior to occur when that behavior is unlikely to occur on its own, is to use the technique of _____. This technique involves reinforcing **successive** _____ to the desired behavior. For example, in teaching a dog to come toward the handler when called from across the yard, the handler could begin by first presenting an effective **reinforcer** (such as praise with a pat on the back, or "Good boy!" with morsel of food) when the dog has responded by approaching from a very *(short / long)* distance, even if the response occurs very slowly. Next, the reinforcement would be withheld until the dog successfully follows the command a little more quickly and/or from a somewhat longer distance. Step-by-step over time, slightly *(faster / slower)* approaches from somewhat *(shorter / longer)* distances would be required for each additional reinforcement, until the dog is finally able to follow the command immediately and fully.

16. A schedule of **continuous reinforcement** involves reinforcement presented on *(all / some / none)* of the occasions when a particular operant behavior has occurred. After shaping, a period of continuous reinforcement helps to promote rapid learning of the operant behavior. But if reinforcement is suddenly discontinued, the operant behavior begins to occur less often—a process known as _____.

17. Dogs that have been obedience trained using shaping and continuous reinforcement procedures often *(will / will not)* continue to perform the correct operant behaviors if reinforcement begins to be presented after only some of the responses—a schedule called _____ _____.

18. A mother of small children may come to realize that she has been reinforcing misbehavior by always focusing immediate attention on the children when they are whining or throwing a temper tantrum. To modify the children's behavior, she could use the method of **extinction,** which would involve a consistent policy of *(always / sometimes / never)* focusing attention on them while they are whining or throwing a tantrum.

19. A parent who decides to stop rewarding misbehavior with attention may at first have no difficulty staying firm with this plan. But if the child's misbehavior persists, the parent might occasionally step in with candy, a toy, or a pleasant activity, with the intent of distracting the child. Instead of extinction, the occasional reinforcement of the misbehavior constitutes of **schedule of** *(partial or intermittent / continuous)* **reinforcement.** This practice could be expected to *(encourage / discourage)* repetition of the unwanted behavior, because research shows that partial reinforcement generally *(increases / decreases)* **resistance to extinction**.

20. In the example just given, the child has received *(positive / negative)* **reinforcement** (presentation of candy or a toy or a favorite activity after the misbehavior), and the parent has received *(positive / negative)* **reinforcement** (relief from the child's irritating crying or whining) after the *(operant / respondent)* behavior of presenting the distracting treat. Since both the parent's and child's behaviors are followed by some type of reinforcement, we would expect these behaviors would be likely to be *(repeated / discontinued)* in the future. The fact that each person's behavior is followed by some type of reinforcement may help to explain why parents fall into short-sighted parenting patterns that encourage undesirable behaviors in their children, and why some children form the habit of throwing temper tantrums. The general principle is that *(positive / negative / both positive and negative)* **reinforcement** encourage(s) the repetition of the particular behavior

that was reinforced. Ginger Osborne reminds us in the video that to reinforce means to *(strengthen / weaken)*. With the emphasis on this part of the terminology, it seems easier to remember that **reinforcers**, whether positive or negative, always serve to *(strengthen / weaken)* the behavior they follow.

21. One particular schedule of partial reinforcement results in especially high rates of responding and great resistance to extinction. If, for example, a reinforcer is presented first after 2 occurrences of the behavior, then after 6, then 4, 8, 5 responses, and so on—on an unpredictable basis but averaging out to one reinforcement per 5 responses, this scheme would qualify as a *(fixed / variable) (ratio / interval)* schedule of reinforcement—the same **schedule of reinforcement** that encourages the high and persistent rates of responding observed in *(gamblers playing slot machines / workers paid on a piecework basis)*.

22. Another partial reinforcement schedule involves reinforcing the first response occurring after a specified period of time has elapsed. Once again, the time period can be predictable and consistent, or unpredictable and inconsistent. If a constant time period must elapse before the operant behavior yields reinforcement, we call this a *(fixed / variable) (ratio / interval)* schedule of reinforcement.

23. **Secondary or _____ reinforcers** are those that have no inherent reinforcing value, but have acquired reinforcing value through a past association with a _____ **reinforcer.** For example, a delicious dessert presented to a child who has just asked "May I please have dessert?" could serve as a *(primary / conditioned)* **reinforcer** for making polite requests. Money presented after a child finishes cleaning his room, if it increases the likelihood of room cleaning in the future, would qualify as a *(primary / conditioned)* **reinforcer.**

24. If used effectively, **punishment** *(increases / decreases)* the occurrence of the operant behavior it follows. In this respect, its effects on operant behavior are *(the same as / opposite to)* the effects of **negative reinforcement**.

25. Parents' occasional use of physical punishment may not do any long-term harm to a child, and may sometimes even be effective if combined with other positive parenting techniques. But experts have pointed out physical punishment can have disadvantages and unwanted side effects. Some of the disadvantages of physical punishment are that it: _____
_____
_____
_____
_____
_____
_____

26. As an alterative to physical punishment, a parent can modify the behavior of a child by using such discipline techniques as: _____
_____
_____
_____
_____
_____
_____

27. Eminent psychologist B.F. Skinner, a strict *(behaviorist / cognitivist / psychoanalyst)*, *(denied / acknowledged)* the existence of mental and biological processes, but strongly *(advocated / opposed)* the view that such processes should be included in explanations of conditioning and other behavioral processes. In contrast, many other psychologists *(have / have not)* found it reasonable to include _____ **processes** such as thoughts, perceptions, knowledge, and expectations, in their explanations of learning.

28. When food rewards begin to be placed in the goal box of a maze, rats that have repeatedly explored that same maze in the past without any food reward suddenly begin to perform *(as well as / more poorly than)* animals that have been given food in the goal box on all their previous trials in the maze. For cognitively-oriented psychologists, these findings suggest that learning was indeed taking place during the initial unrewarded runs through the maze, but that it was _____ **learning**—learning that

was not manifested until reinforcement provided the incentive to display what had been learned.

29. Cognitive psychologists have also shown that rewards can differ in their effect, depending on individuals' perceptions of their own motives for performing a task. Rewards may not always boost performance, but can at times reduce *(extrinsic / intrinsic)* **motivation** for the task, especially if the rewards are improperly applied or excessive. When people come to perceive an external reward as their reason for engaging in an activity, a(n) *(reduction / enhancement)* of intrinsic interest, termed the

    _____ **effect**, can often follow.

30. Although Skinner believed that his principles of behavior applied *(to only a few / to most / equally to all)* species, research on a variety of species has brought the recognition that an animal's natural tendencies— its **biological** _____—can make operant conditioning of some behaviors easier than others. For example, pigeons can more readily learn to *(flap their wings / make pecking motions)* to obtain food, and can more easily learn to *(flap their wings / make pecking motions)* to avoid shock.

31. Many of Skinner's critics viewed the application of operant conditioning principles to the human domain as *(advancing / threatening)* freedom and responsibility, but Skinner continued to see operant conditioning principles as broadly applicable to real-life settings. Programs designed around Skinner's principles—in the workplace, in education, in athletics, and in parenting—have demonstrated that behavior is most likely to improve significantly when performance goals are very *(general / specific)* and *(measurable / vague)*, when the level of expected performance is systematically increased in *(small / large)* steps, and when performance feedback or reinforcement is *(immediate / delayed)*, as demonstrated in Edward Taub's stroke rehabilitation program, shown in the video.

Learning by Observation

32. Beyond classical and operant conditioning, another type of learning has been described and extensively researched by Stanford University psychologist **Albert** _____, whose famous "Bobo doll" experiment was a powerful demonstration of the principles of _____ **learning** or modeling.

33. Neuroscientists have even discovered a potential neural basis for observational learning in finding so-called _____ **neurons** in the *(motor / sensory / visual)* cortex of monkeys and of humans, which are observed to become active when an individual is either performing a particular motion or watching another individual perform that same motion.

34. Although observational learning has been observed in a *(small / large)* number of nonhuman species, it is perhaps most noticeable in humans. The classic Bobo doll experiment revealed that young children were very *(likely / unlikely)* to imitate the style of behavior they had observed in an adult model who had displayed a series of *(aggressive / polite)* actions toward an inflated doll.

35. Bandura's subsequent research demonstrated that we are particularly likely to imitate the behavior of a model if the model is perceived as *(powerful / weak)*, especially when we have a *(warm and close / neutral / cold and detached)* relationship with the model and if we perceive the model as *(similar to / different from)* ourselves. Furthermore, imitation is more likely if the observer sees the model being *(reinforced / punished)* after displaying the behavior.

36. Observational learning can help to explain a wide array of *(antisocial / prosocial / antisocial and prosocial)* behaviors. Models for prosocial behavior are especially effective if their actions and their words are *(consistent / inconsistent)*.

37. **Correlational research** studies have revealed that the amount of television viewing time in teens *(is / is not)* a significant predictor of aggressive behavior. Since correlational studies provide *(sufficient /*

insufficient) evidence for cause and effect relation-ships, formal *(experiments / surveys)*, with participants randomly assigned to groups have been *(important / unnecessary)* as a way to explore the causal links between the viewing of media violence and the expression of aggressive behavior.

38. A large body of research data confirms that exposure to media portrayals of violence *(causes / does not cause)* increased likelihood of aggression in viewers. The viewing of violence tends to *(sensitize / desensitize)* viewers to the damaging effects of violence and to *(encourage / inhibit)* imitation of the aggressive behavior that has been viewed.

39. In the video, David Myers explains that in compari-son to passive viewing of violence, active partici-pation in playing violent video games produces *(stronger / weaker)* effects on aggression.

40. Observational learning offers more than just a way to understand destructive or antisocial behavior. Principles of observational learning have also been put into effect in large-scale programs to encourage helping or _____ **behavior.** For example, serial television dramas have been designed to encourage observational learning of prosocial be-havior in countries such as _____ and _____. Designed around principles derived from Bandura's research on *(classical condi-tioning / observational learning / operant conditioning)*, these programs present viewers with images of a better life, steps they can take to bring about positive changes, and strategies for overcoming impediments they might encounter along the way. For example, in *(Ethiopia / India / Indonesia / Nigeria)*, a drama involving popular characters Taru and her mother appears to have inspired such positive social changes as literacy programs for adults and more widespread opposition to practices that discriminate against girls.

SELF TEST

Read each question and circle the letter of the best answer. When you have completed the Self Test, check your answers against the key at the end of this lesson. If you have answered any items incorrectly, review the appropriate materials to correct misunderstandings and cement your knowledge.

1. Psychologists define learning as
   a. any type of formal education.
   b. any relatively permanent change in behavior that is based on experience.
   c. any improvement in behavior.
   d. any performance change, including that which is due to maturation, motivational change, or fatigue.

2. Classical conditioning was first carefully researched by
   a. B. F. Skinner.
   b. E. L. Thorndike.
   c. E. C. Tolman.
   d. Ivan Pavlov.

3. Ivan Pavlov's ground-breaking research on con-ditioning focused primarily on the modification of
   a. the knee jerk reflex in humans.
   b. the eye blink reflex in humans.
   c. conditioned taste aversions in coyotes.
   d. the salivary reflex in dogs.

4. Associative learning includes
   a. classical conditioning and operant conditioning.
   b. classical conditioning and observational learning.
   c. operant conditioning and observational learning.
   d. classical conditioning, operant conditioning, and observational learning.

5. Classical conditioning has taken place when
   a. a reflexive response automatically follows a specific stimulus.
   b. a certain stimulus acquires the ability to bring out a response that previously did not occur when that same stimulus was presented.
   c. the strength of a voluntary behavior changes because certain consequences have followed that behavior.
   d. individuals begin to imitate behavior they have observed in someone else.

6. Each day, Kristen hears her husband Larry's car coming up the driveway less than a minute before he comes in the door and gives her a hug and a kiss. She always feels happy and excited when greeting and embracing Larry. Recently, however, Kristen has realized that her feelings of excitement and happiness begin when she hears the sound of Larry's car coming up the driveway. These positive feelings in response to the sound of Larry's car can best be explained on he basis of
   a. operant conditioning.
   b. observational learning.
   c. classical conditioning.
   d. latent learning.

7. Linda has experienced so much pleasure and enjoyment during her many visits to her favorite beach that simply hearing the phrase "Crane Beach" gives her a bit of a relaxed, happy feeling and brings a little smile to her face. The name of her favorite beach has become a _____ for pleasure and enjoyment.
   a. conditioned response
   b. unconditioned response
   c. conditioned stimulus
   d. unconditioned stimulus

8. Seven-year-old Nick has learned that when his father speaks to him using his full name, "Nicholas Spencer Wilson," he is about to be harshly criticized and spanked. On the other hand, when his father addresses him simply as "Nick," his father is likely to remain relaxed and friendly. Anytime he hears his father use a sharp voice and address him as "Nicholas Spencer Wilson," he feels anxious and tense, suggesting that the process of _____ has taken place.
   a. discrimination.
   b. generalization.
   c. spontaneous recovery.
   d. operant conditioning.

9. Extinction of a classically conditioned response occurs when
   a. the neutral stimulus becomes a conditioned stimulus.
   b. the UCS is no longer presented along with the CS, and the strength of the CR declines.
   c. the CS is no longer presented at all, and the UCS gradually becomes weaker over time.
   d. the UCS no longer produces the UCR.

10. In the video, David Myers describes an incident in which a car ran through a stoplight in front of him and hit his car. After that accident he felt tense and anxious whenever he was near that intersection. The fact that he also felt tense and anxious when near any intersection that resembled the one where his auto accident occurs represents
    a. spontaneous recovery.
    b. discrimination.
    c. shaping.
    d. generalization.

11. In the video, John Cacioppo and Travis Gibbs discuss racial prejudice as
    a. rooted in associative learning, but also able to be changed through a process of learning.
    b. an innate tendency that cannot be modified through any known form of learning.
    c. a deeply ingrained pattern of attitudes that cannot be changed, regardless of the principles of learning.
    d. based on operant conditioning.

12. Classically conditioned taste aversions can be acquired
    a. even when the onset of illness occurs several hours after tasting a particular food.
    b. only if illness begins within minutes after tasting a particular food.
    c. even if illness occurs several days after tasting a particular food.
    d. only if the individual clearly understands what actually caused the illness.

13. Research has revealed that we more readily acquire associations between a light and an electric shock than between a flower and an electric shock. This observation has led to the suggestion that associations between certain stimuli may be
    a. subject to instinctive drift.
    b. prohibited.
    c. evolutionarily disadvantageous.
    d. biologically predisposed.

14. Which of the following is an example of respondent behavior?
    a. After a seal balances a ball on its nose, the trainer tosses a fish to the seal.
    b. Three-year-old Susie asks politely for a cookie and is given one.
    c. As a stiff breeze hits Rod's face, his eyelids momentarily close.
    d. All of the above exemplify respondent behavior.

15. When a laboratory rat in an operant conditioning chamber received food after an average of ten presses on a lever, but with variations in how many presses are required for each separate reinforcement, this represents a _____ schedule of reinforcement.
    a. fixed interval
    b. variable interval
    c. fixed ratio
    d. variable ratio

16. When a parent gives a teenager a dollar after cleaning his room each day, and the payment is found to be effective in increasing the child's room cleaning behavior, the schedule of reinforcement in effect most closely resembles
    a. continuous reinforcement.
    b. a fixed interval schedule.
    c. a variable interval schedule.
    d. a variable ratio schedule.

17. When a hungry laboratory rat in a Skinner box is given food first on each occasion when it moves toward the lever, then only when it touches the lever lightly, and finally only after it has pressed the lever firmly, the process being used to train the rat to press the lever is
    a. secondary reinforcement.
    b. shaping.
    c. negative reinforcement.
    d. conditioned reinforcement.

18. Which of the following best exemplifies negative reinforcement?
    a. Four-year-old Katherine reaches into the cookie jar, and receives a swift slap on the hand, discouraging her future attempts to swipe cookies.
    b. Ten-year-old Winnie falls off the merry-go-round on the playground and scrapes her knee; now she is afraid of the merry-go-round.
    c. Brad picks up his six-month-old daughter, Valentina, and smiles at her; Valentina smiles back at him.
    d. Ralph has an uncomfortable tickle in his throat until he puts a cough drop in his mouth and gets rapid relief from the discomfort; Ralph now carries cough drops and uses them whenever this discomfort occurs.

19. Miss Lau began giving out small award certificates to her first-graders who stayed in their seats and worked quietly. At the end of the day, the certificates could be traded in for treats or small toys. She observed that after beginning to do this, more of the children stayed in their seats and worked diligently. Using operant conditioning terms, the award certificates served as _____ to shape and maintain desired behavior in Miss Lau 's students.
    a. conditioned reinforcers
    b. primary reinforcers
    c. negative reinforcers
    d. extinction

20. Which of the following is a disadvantage of using physical punishment in disciplining children?
    a. Physical punishment can encourage aggressive behavior because it provides a model for use of aggression to deal with problems.
    b. Physical punishment may suppress the undesirable behavior temporarily, but the same behavior can reappear when the punisher is not present.
    c. Physical punishment can generate fear, a sense of helplessness, and lowered self-esteem.
    d. All of the above.

21. Watson and Pavlov adopted the perspective known as ____, and they ___ the use of mentalistic concepts to explain learning.
    a. psychoanalysis…strongly advocated
    b. behaviorism…reluctantly accepted
    c. behaviorism…firmly opposed
    d. psychoanalysis…had no opinion about

22. Biological predispositions in operant conditioning have been highlighted by recent researchers in observing that
    a. latent learning can be demonstrated after rats have made many runs through a complex maze with no food reward provided in the goal box.
    b. any species of animal can learn to perform just about any behavior that is followed by a food reward.
    c. a pigeon can be more easily trained to perform a pecking behavior to get a food reward than to flap its wings to get a food reward.
    d. all of the above.

23. Recent research has revealed the existence of mirror neurons, which are located in the _____ of the brain, and which become more active when an individual _____.
    a. motor cortex…either observes a particular action being performed or performs that same action
    b. somatosensory cortex… either observes a particular action being performed or performs that same action
    c. visual cortex… sees a reflection in a mirror
    d. auditory cortex…sees a reflection in a mirror

24. A child is particularly likely to imitate behavior he or she observes in a model
    a. if the model is observed being rewarded after displaying the observed behavior.
    b. if the model is observed being punished after displaying the observed behavior.
    c. if the child is told not to imitate the observed behavior.
    d. under none of the above conditions.

25. In the video, Albert Bandura comments that "television violence is an excellent teacher," explaining that it
    a. discourages aggression by clearly and realistically showing the negative side to violence—that decent people can truly be harmed by violent behavior, and that it is no way to solve problems.
    b. encourages aggression by exposing children to various forms of aggression, by desensitizing them so they are no longer as upset by it, and by associating aggression with virtue by showing "good guys" killing off "bad guys."
    c. simply serves as a harmless but absorbing and action-packed form of entertainment without really changing the way people think about the world.
    d. induces enough fear about violence that children who have watched televised violence are actually much less likely than others to display aggressive behavior.

ANSWER KEY FOR THE ACTIVE REVIEW EXERCISES

1. relatively permanent; behavior; experience; conditioning; [1] Textbook, Video 11
2. Pavlov; 1898; dogs; salivary; classical; [1] Textbook, Video 11
3. Watson; behaviorism; unnecessary; [1] Textbook
4. could; are; can; [1] Video 11
5. unconditioned; unconditioned; conditioned stimulus; acquisition; [3] Textbook
6. can; generalization; [3] Textbook, Video 11
7. extinction; response; extinction; conditioned; neutral; [3] Textbook
8. sheep; lithium; unconditioned; conditioned; conditioned response; [4] Textbook, Video 11
9. only one or two; evolution; predisposition; [5] Textbook, Video 11
10. predispositions; snakes and spiders; [6] Textbook, Video 11
11. B. F. Skinner; [1] Textbook, Video 11
12. consequence; strengthens; weaken; [7] Textbook, Video 11
13. respondent; [7] Textbook
14. (a) operant; (b) respondent; (c) respondent; (d) operant; (e) respondent; (f) operant; (g) respondent; (h) operant; [7] Textbook; Video 11 [If you had difficulties here, review the HINT given in the Instructions for this exercise to get an explanation of the operant / respondent distinction.]
15. shaping; approximations; short; faster; longer; Textbook, [8] Video 11
16. all; extinction; [8] Textbook
17. will; partial reinforcement (or intermittent reinforcement); [7] Textbook
18. never; [9] Textbook
19. partial or intermittent; encourage; increases; [8, 9] Textbook
20. positive; negative; operant; repeated; both positive and negative; strengthen; strengthen; [9] Video 11, Textbook
21. variable ratio; gamblers playing slot machines; [8, 9] Textbook
22. fixed interval; [8, 9] Textbook
23. conditioned; primary; primary; conditioned; [10] Textbook
24. decreases; opposite to; [11] Textbook, Video 11
25. *Your answer should include several of the following ideas on punishment:* (1) suppresses but does not eliminate the unwanted behavior; (2) can teach aggressiveness as a way of dealing with problems; (3) can bring about fear and avoidance of the punitive person; (4) can generate negative feelings about the self, resentment, and even a sense of helplessness and depression if the punishment is unpredictable and inescapable; (5) is not an effective teaching tool, because it informs the punished individual about what *not* to do; unlike reinforcement, punishment by itself does not point the way toward acceptable behavior.; Textbook, Video 11
26. *Your answer should include several of the following ideas:* (1) reinforcing other behaviors that are more desirable; providing attention and other rewards when acceptable behavior occurs; (2) changing the negative phrasing of threats of punishment to positive expectations (indicating privileges that will be made available when proper behavior occurs, rather than warning about what privileges will be withdrawn if misbehavior occurs); (3) using the time-out procedure to remove the child from the area where misbehavior can be reinforced; (4) restricting privileges when misbehavior occurs; (5) reasoning with the child, and in the process, communicating norms or social expectations; [11] Textbook, Video 11
27. behaviorist; acknowledged; opposed; have; cognitive; [12] Textbook
28. as well as; latent; [8, 12] Textbook
29. intrinsic; reduction; overjustification; [12] Textbook
30. equally to all; predispositions; make pecking motions; flap their wings; [13] Textbook
31. threatening; specific; measurable; small; immediate; [14] Textbook, Video 11
32. Bandura; observational; [16] Textbook, Video 11
33. mirror; motor; Textbook
34. large; likely; aggressive; [16] Textbook, Video 11
35. powerful; warm and close; similar to; reinforced; [16] Textbook, Video 11
36. antisocial and prosocial; consistent; [17] Textbook, Video 11
37. is; insufficient; experiments; important; [17] Textbook, Video 11
38. causes; desensitize; encourage; [17] Textbook, Video 11
39. stronger; [17] Video 11
40. prosocial; Mexico; India; observational learning; India; [17] Textbook, Video 11

ANSWER KEY FOR THE SELF TEST

Item #	Answer	Learning Outcome #	Source	Item #	Answer	Learning Outcome #	Source
1.	b	1	Textbook, Video 11	14.	c	7	Textbook
2.	d	1	Textbook, Video 11	15.	d	8	Textbook
3.	d	2	Textbook, Video 11	16.	a	8	Textbook
4.	a	2	Textbook, Video 11	17.	b	8, 9, 10	Textbook, Video 11
5.	b	2	Textbook, Video 11	18.	d	9	Textbook, Video 11
6.	c	2, 3, 4	Textbook, Video 11	19.	a	9, 10	Textbook, Video 11
7.	c	3	Textbook	20.	d	11	Textbook, Video 11
8.	a	3	Textbook	21.	c	12	Textbook
9.	b	3	Textbook	22.	c	13	Textbook
10.	d	3, 4	Video 11	23.	a	15	Textbook
11.	a	4	Textbook, Video 11	24.	a	16	Textbook, Video 11
12.	a	4, 5, 6	Textbook, Video 11	25.	b	17	Video 11
13.	d	5, 6	Textbook, Video 11				

Lesson 12 (Memory)

The Mind's Storehouse

Assignments

Reading: Chapter 9, "Memory" in *Psychology* by David Myers (Modules 24, 25, 26, 27, and 28 in the modular version of *Psychology*)

Video: Episode 12, "The Mind's Storehouse"

LEARNING OUTCOMES

Familiarize yourself with the Learning Outcomes for this lesson before you begin the assignments. Return to them to check your learning after completing the Steps to Learning Success. Careful work on these materials should equip you to accomplish the outcomes.

The Phenomenon of Memory (Module 24)

1. Describe examples and cases that illustrate the extremes of memory and forgetting.

2. Explain encoding, storage, and retrieval and discuss the relationships among these processes.

3. Summarize the basic features of the three-stage information processing model developed by Atkinson and Shiffrin.

Encoding: Getting Information In (Module 25)

4. Distinguish between automatic and effortful information processing, and provide examples of each.

5. Explain how rehearsal influences ability to remember, and discuss how rehearsal is involved in overlearning, the next-in-line effect, the spacing effect, and the serial position effect.

6. Distinguish between visual, acoustic, and semantic encoding and compare their influence on ability to remember.

7. Review evidence on the impact of mnemonic devices, imagery, and organization on memory.

Storage: Retaining Information (Module 26)

8. Compare the capacity and duration of storage for iconic and echoic sensory memory, short-term memory, and long-term memory, and describe the relationship between these processes.

9. Summarize evidence relating memory to neural processes, brain areas, and hormones.

10. Describe and compare implicit and explicit memory, and offer examples of each.

Retrieval: Getting Information Out (Module 27)

11. Distinguish between recall, recognition, and relearning tests of memory, and provide examples of each.

12. Identify and discuss retrieval cues, context effects, and state-dependent and mood-congruent memory.

13. List and explain the mechanisms involved in forgetting, providing examples and evidence for each.

Memory Construction (Module 28)

14. Explain memory construction and reconstruction, and describe how misinformation, suggestibility, and source amnesia can contribute to memory distortion.

15. Discuss evidence bearing on the controversial claim that memory for traumatic experiences may be repressed and then later recovered in therapy.

16. Demonstrate your familiarity with how-to-study tips that are based on memory research.

ACTIVE REVIEW

Each item in this section is based on material presented in the video or the textbook assignment for this lesson, or both. Complete this section, referring as needed to your notes or the source materials themselves. Answers are provided at the end of this lesson.

The Phenomenon of Memory

1. In the opening of the video episode, Elizabeth Loftus makes the point that memory *(is / is not)* just a literal recording and playback.

2. People who were old enough at the time of the assassination of John F. Kennedy may remember an array of tiny details about where they were and what they were doing at the time they heard the news. In the textbook, memory for such incidental details surrounding an experience that has high emotional impact is called _____ _____.

3. The framework used to organize ideas for this lesson is based on Atkinson's and Shiffrin's _____-_____ **processing model of memory**. Fill in the first column of the table below, listing the stages of processing suggested by the Atkinson and Shiffrin model. Place these stages in the proper order, from when information stimulates the senses to its more permanent storage. Then complete the remaining two columns, comparing the storage duration and capacity for each of the memory stages listed.

Name of Stage	Duration	Capacity

4. Just as computers first take in data and store it in coded form before the information can be accessed, human memory can be viewed as involving three different phases. The process of getting information into memory is called _____. The process of holding or retaining information over a period of time is known as _____. After information has been encoded and stored, the process of getting it back out of storage is termed _____.

Encoding: Getting Information In

5. Ebbinghaus conducted some of the earliest studies of memory. Among other things, his studies of his own memory for **nonsense syllables** demonstrated that the more he practiced, the *(stronger / weaker)* was his memory for the list of nonsense syllables. In repeating the nonsense syllables over and over to himself, Ebbinghaus was engaging in _____, a type of *(effortful / automatic)* processing.

6. In addition to the amount of effort applied in repeated rehearsal, what are some of the factors that enhance the ability to remember information?

_____

_____

_____

7. Researchers have found that **massing** of study time (studying in long uninterrupted periods, as students do when they "cram" for a test) is *(more / less)* effective than spacing studying over time. Furthermore, studying information twice in the same place *(is / is not)* as effective as studying it in two different locations.

Storage: Retaining Information

8. Memories are thought to be recorded in the brain through changes at **synapses**, which are the points of communication between individual *(neurotransmitters / neurons / nerves)*. Research with the California sea

slug, *Aplysia*, has demonstrated that when learning takes place, certain synapses are repeatedly activated. This repeated activation promotes a process known as _____ _____, which makes those particular synapses easier to activate for a time after this repeated stimulation.

9. The middle part of the *(parietal / temporal / occipital)* **lobe** has been found to be extremely important in memory—especially an area known as the *(hippocampus / corpus callosum / hypothalamus)*.

10. Surgery patient **H.M.** had brain surgery to treat his very severe *(amnesia / epileptic seizures / schizophrenia)*. After the surgery, H.M.'s IQ and language were *(normal / deficient)*, his memories for previous experiences were mostly *(normal / impaired)*, and his ability to make new **explicit memories** was *(normal / impaired)*. This case reveals that the hippocampus *(is / is not)* the place where memories are located, because H.M. was observed to have fairly *(good / poor)* memory for his childhood after damage to the hippocampus.

11. Clive Wearing had a form of brain damage that was *(similar to / different from)* H.M.'s, which in Clive Wearing's case resulted from **encephalitis**. Summarize the major features of Clive Wearing's case (as shown in the video and described by Deborah, Clive's wife). _____

_____

_____

_____

_____

_____

12. Despite the critical importance of the **hippocampus** to *(explicit / implicit)* memory, different brain areas, for example the *(prefrontal cortex / postcentral gyrus / hypothalamus)*, hold on to the information needed for working memory. Other subcortical structures—for example, the amygdala—allow us to interact with the world emotionally. Still other brain areas within the *(cerebrum / cerebellum / corpus callosum)* are important in storing memories for learned responses such as the conditioned eyeblink response, which is a type of *(explicit / implicit)* memory.

13. Hormonal activity is also important to memory. Interesting or emotionally exciting events activate the **amygdala** (located in the _____ **lobe**) and prompt the release of stress hormones such as **adrenalin** and _____, which course through the bloodstream and can instruct the brain to store information more permanently. But too high a level of **glucocorticoid** hormones can interfere with functioning of the hippocampus, impairing memory under *(higher / moderate / lower)* levels of emotional arousal.

Retrieval: Getting Information Out

14. When we can remember a conversation we have had and can describe it a few hours later, this would qualify as a demonstration of *(explicit / implicit)* memory. When our performance reveals that we can still ride a bicycle or ski down a slope, or when we seem to know what to do in a driving emergency, we are exhibiting *(explicit / implicit)* memory, which is also sometimes called **procedural memory**.

15. One way to test the strength of memory is through tasks that require a reconstruction of previously presented information, as in an essay or a fill-in test item. Such tasks test our *(recall / recognition / relearning)*. Another method of testing memory, exemplified by multiple-choice or matching tests, requires the person to select the previously learned information from an array of choices. This would be the *(recall / recognition / relearning)* method of testing memory. A major difference between recall and recognition testing is that recognition testing provides *(more / fewer)* **retrieval cues**.

16. **Forgetting** is sometimes based on **encoding failure**—a failure in getting information *(into / out of)* memory storage. On other occasions, we forget be-

cause we lack essential retrieval cues that are needed to bring information *(into / out of)* memory storage.

17. List several examples of the types of cues that can help us to bring information out of our memories.

_____

_____

_____

_____

_____

_____

18. Another explanation for forgetting is **interference**. Previously established memories may interfere with the ability to remember more recent experiences, a phenomenon known as _____ _____. When more recent memories inhibit the ability to remember previously established memories, it is termed _____ _____. For example, a mother who wants to call her 5-year-old child in from the back yard, but at first mistakenly calls out her 7-year-old child's name, has momentarily experienced _____ interference. Someone unable to remember a previous phone number several years after thoroughly learning a newer phone number, has experienced _____ interference.

Memory Reconstruction

19. In the past several decades, considerable research attention has been focused on issues surrounding the **accuracy of eyewitness testimony** and claims of **recovered memories**. This research has revealed that established memories *(can / cannot)* be contaminated, distorted, transformed, or supplemented by new input. According to comments in the video made by memory researcher **Elizabeth Loftus**, it is *(relatively easy / difficult / impossible)* to contaminate someone's memory—to change details or to plant entirely false scenarios into their minds. In other words, memories, once formed, are quite *(stable / subject to change)* and *(literal / reconstructive)*.

20. In a classic study on memory reconstruction, Loftus and Palmer (1974) showed films of traffic collisions, and afterwards asked the viewers to estimate how fast the cars were going at the time of impact. Even though all participants had viewed the same film footage, participants who were asked how fast the cars were going when they "smashed into each other" tended to give *(higher / lower)* estimates of speed than did those who were asked about the speed when the cars "hit each other."

21. It was Sigmund _____ who advanced the idea that a person could undergo traumatic events such as severe abuse or witnessing a murder, and then actively prevent any memory of the emotionally painful events from coming to consciousness. He called this kind of forgetting _____. In the video, Elizabeth Loftus and James McGaugh assert that available scientific evidence *(does / does not)* support the idea of massive **repression** of extremely unpleasant memories.

22. Several prominent legal cases have been built around the claim that a person can repress the memory of a traumatic event and then much later recover that memory during, for example, psychotherapy. According to memory researcher Elizabeth Loftus, techniques such as **hypnosis**, **"truth serum,"** **guided imagery**, or **dream interpretation** can *(increase / decrease)* suggestibility and make contamination of memories and beliefs *(easier / more difficult)*.

23. Describe the **case of Gary Ramona** and his daughter **Holly Ramona**, and relate this case to skeptics' challenges regarding the **recovered memory** phenomenon and research on the **misinformation effect**. _____

_____

_____

_____

_____

_____

SELF TEST

Read each question and circle the letter of the best answer. When you have completed the Self Test, check your answers against the key at the end of this lesson. If you have answered any items incorrectly, review the appropriate materials to correct misunderstandings and cement your knowledge.

1. Flashbulb memory refers to the tendency to remember clearly a collection of details that might otherwise be forgotten, based on
   a. an emotionally striking experience or event.
   b. numerous repetitions of a particular experience or event.
   c. the misinformation effect.
   d. effortful processing.

2. Which of the following represents the appropriate sequence for the basic phases of the memory process?
   a. Storage, retrieval, encoding
   b. Storage, encoding, retrieval
   c. Retrieval, encoding, storage
   d. Encoding, storage, retrieval

3. One way to keep information available in short-term memory is to continue repeating it mentally, a process known as
   a. reinstatement.
   b. recall.
   c. rehearsal.
   d. relearning.

4. Which of the following represents the order of information flow in Atkinson and Shiffrin's classic three-stage model of memory processing?
   a. Maintenance rehearsal, elaborative rehearsal, retrieval
   b. Episodic memory, semantic memory, procedural memory
   c. Implicit memory, explicit memory, plicit memory
   d. Sensory memory, short-term memory, long-term memory
   e. Recognition, relearning, recall

5. In the video episode, James McGaugh refers to very early memory research published in 1885 by Ebbinghaus, which demonstrated that
   a. memory is a literal recording of events we have experienced.
   b. studying a particular subject always in the same place improves ability to remember what has been studied.
   c. basic memory ability cannot be improved upon, even with extensive practice and use of what might seem to be helpful memory strategies.
   d. the more fully something is learned, the longer it will be remembered.

6. Research on the "spacing effect" has demonstrated that we are likely to retain information more successfully when we study repeatedly and
   a. gradually reduce the amount of time between study sessions.
   b. gradually increase the amount of time between study sessions.
   c. study in a relaxed way, while "spacing out"– paying only minimal attention to what we are studying.
   d. study in the same space at the library over and over, rather than varying the location of study.

7. Leon was at a social gathering where he was introduced to eight unfamiliar people who were standing together in a group. Although he listened carefully and repeated each name after he heard it, a short time later he realized that he could recall only the first two names and the last three names, but could not remember the names of the people in the middle of the group. Leon's experience seems to reflect a typical
   a. flashbulb memory.
   b. serial position effect.
   c. mnemonic strategy.
   d. spacing effect.

8. Which type of encoding listed below involves associating information with its meaning?
   a. Visual encoding
   b. Semantic encoding
   c. Acoustic encoding
   d. Shallow processing

9. Iconic memory
   a. is one type of sensory memory.
   b. occurs after brief presentation of a visual stimulus.
   c. holds information more briefly than echoic memory.
   d. all of the above.
   e. none of the above.

10. According to the experts interviewed in the video episode, which of the following factors can enhance memory under certain conditions?
   a. Repetition or increased duration of exposure to information
   b. Emotional impact or significance
   c. Meaningfulness or understanding of the information
   d. All of the above
   e. None of the above

11. In a research study conducted by Penfield (1969), certain neurosurgery patients reported complex sensory experiences (hearing a mother calling her little boy, for example) when electrical stimulation was applied to specific regions of the cerebral cortex. Scientists reviewing Penfield's results have recently concluded that such sensory experiences probably represent
   a. echoic memories.
   b. the most common outcome for patients treated with this kind of electrical stimulation.
   c. memories of experiences stored in the brain long ago and reactivated by the electrical stimulation.
   d. dream-like states induced in the patient rather than literal memories of real past experiences.

12. After extensive research on the effects of damage to the cerebral cortex in rats that had previously learned the path through a maze, Karl Lashley (1950) concluded that
   a. memory depends entirely on the functioning of a single, specific area of the frontal cortex.
   b. memory does not involve the cerebral cortex.
   c. memories are not located in any one specific region of the cortex.
   d. destruction of even one tiny area of the cortex, regardless of its location, results in a complete loss of memory.

13. Recent research has suggested that _____ is a physical process in the brain that may be critical to the formation of new memories.
   a. long-term potentiation
   b. short-term potentiation
   c. subliminal perception
   d. operant conditioning

14. According to the comments of Michael Rugg in the video, implicit memory generally involves
   a. skills or procedures we know how to do but can't actually capture in a verbal description.
   b. information that is retrieved with effort and with conscious awareness that the information was present in our memory.
   c. retrieval failure.
   d. information that is stored in long-term memory that has never previously been stored in short-term memory.

15. David Myers describes neurologist Oliver Sacks' patient Jimmie, who suffered brain damage that resulted in extreme difficulties in his memory for events he experienced after the brain injury. Patients such as Jimmie have been found to have greater deficits in their _____ memory than in their _____ memory.
   a. explicit … implicit
   b. implicit … explicit
   c. long-term … short-term
   d. procedural … episodic

16. Various experts in the video episode spoke about the critical role of the brain area called the hippocampus, which
   a. serves as the actual storage site for newly formed memories.
   b. facilitates the storage of newly acquired explicit information in other areas of the brain.
   c. allows us to retrieve our implicit memories, including information about how to perform new sequences of skilled movements.
   d. does all of the above.

17. According to descriptions given in the video, after his brain surgery in 1953, patient H.M was never again able to
   a. ride a bicycle.
   b. form new explicit memories.
   c. remember anything about his childhood.
   d. remember the face of a new person he met, even though he displayed normal ability to remember their names and their voices.

18. According to Michael Rugg, very high concentrations of the stress hormones known as glucocorticoids can
    a. interfere with the functioning of the hippocampus, and therefore can interfere with memory under high arousal levels.
    b. improve the ability to establish memories.
    c. heighten arousal levels but do not affect memory.
    d. improve long-term memory without affecting short-term memory.

19. Infantile amnesia
    a. occurs only in children who have been severely abused in infancy.
    b. can be treated successfully if a psychotherapist uses the technique of hypnosis to recover lost childhood memories.
    c. may occur because of the immaturity of the cerebellum during the first few years of life.
    d. may occur because of the immaturity of the hippocampus during the first few years of life.

20. During the last hour of the day at his office, Louis thought of several work-related tasks he would need to complete while at home that same evening. But when he arrived at his house after the 20-minute drive, he found himself having quite a lot of trouble remembering the tasks he had thought of at the office. Because of the shift in the setting from office to home, perhaps the most reasonable explanation for Louis' failure to recall his list of tasks is that
    a. retrieval cues that were available at his office are not available in the context of his home.
    b. proactive interference has occurred.
    c. the method of loci has prevented recall from occurring.
    d. his arrival at home has primed him to forget.

21. When given a series of pictures to choose from, a surprising number of people have difficulty recognizing the correct pattern of elements that make up a common object such as a penny. Errors in correctly recognizing objects we encounter on a daily basis suggests that many instances of failure to remember may be traced to
    a. storage decay.
    b. repression.
    c. encoding failure.
    d. retroactive interference.

22. Elizabeth Loftus' research on eyewitness testimony has demonstrated that
    a. the testimony of an eyewitness is always highly inaccurate.
    b. once a memory has been encoded through the witnessing of an event, the memory tends to be quite durable and resistant to change.
    c. wording of questions can have a significant effect on what an eyewitness reports about an incident.
    d. children can provide much more accurate eyewitness testimony than adults.
    e. the only important factor affecting the accuracy of eyewitness testimony is the amount of time that has passed between the witnessing of the event and the report that is made.

23. When a previously formed memory interferes with the ability to recall a more recently formed memory, the process is known as
    a. proactive interference.
    b. repression.
    c. retroactive interference.
    d. long-term potentiation.

24. According to the author of the textbook, one of the best strategies you can use to improve your memory for information you study in textbooks is to
    a. simply read and then repeatedly reread the assigned material.
    b. test your ability to recall what you have read as you study, to become aware of what you already know and what you do not yet know.
    c. aim to recognize the information instead of trying to recall it.
    d. use speed-reading techniques to get through the material as quickly as possible.
    e. give yourself a pep-talk, because it is very important to feel confident even when your understanding of the material is somewhat weak.

25. Elizabeth Loftus and John Palmer (1974) conducted research in which they first showed people films of automobile accidents. Later, participants' "eyewitness" reports revealed
    a. equally serious distortions of fact in all groups, regardless of the wording of the questions.
    b. highly detailed and remarkably accurate reports in over 98 percent of the cases.
    c. higher estimates of the speed of the vehicles when the questions asked about seeing the cars "smash" into each other than when asked about seeing the cars "hit" each other.
    d. a lower likelihood of saying they saw broken glass if they had been asked about seeing the cars "smash" (instead of "hit") each other.

ANSWER KEY FOR THE ACTIVE REVIEW EXERCISES

1. is not; [2] Video 12
2. flashbulb memory; [1] Textbook
3. three-stage; Sensory store (sensory memory) / Very brief – several hundred milliseconds / Very large; Short-term store (short-term memory) / Up to about 30 seconds or so / Very limited (only a few items– about 5–9 random digits, for example); Long-term store (long-term memory) / Up to many years / Essentially unlimited; [3] Textbook, Video 12
4. encoding; storage; retrieval; [2] Textbook, Video 12
5. stronger; rehearsal; effortful; [4] Textbook
6. *Your answer should mention factors such as* attention, emotional impact, meaning, imagery, organization of the information, and/or mnemonic devices; [5, 6, 7] Textbook, Video 12
7. less; is not; [5] Video 12
8. neurons; long-term potentiation; [8, 9] Textbook
9. temporal; hippocampus; [9] Textbook, Video 12
10. epileptic seizures; normal, normal, impaired; is not, good [8, 9, 10] Textbook, Video 12
11. similar to; As a result of encephalitis, British musician Clive Wearing had damage to the hippocampus. The result was a very serious impairment of memory, leading to a constant state of confusion because newly registered information all fades very rapidly. (For example, after ten minutes spent sitting on a park bench with his wife, he doesn't remember how he got there or how long he has been there.) Still, he remains fully able to recognize his wife, to use language normally, and to conduct musical works that he learned before his brain damage. [9] Video 12
12. explicit; prefrontal cortex; cerebellum; implicit memory [9, 10] Textbook, Video 12
13. temporal; cortisol; higher; [9] Textbook, Video 12
14. explicit; implicit; [10] Textbook, Video 12
15. recall; recognition; more; [11, 12] Textbook
16. into; out of; [12, 13] Textbook
17. *Your list should include items such as:* context cues that match the conditions under which we encoded the memory (for example, the weather or the colors or items of furniture in the room); a physiological state that matches the state under which we encoded the memory (for example, being influenced by caffeine if caffeine was in the body during encoding); and a mood while trying to retrieve information that matches the mood we were in during encoding (as shown in studies of mood-congruent memory). [12] Textbook, Video 12
18. proactive interference, retroactive interference, proactive, retroactive; [13] Textbook
19. can; relatively easy; subject to change; reconstructive; [14] Textbook, Video 12
20. higher; [14] Textbook
21. Freud; repression; does not; [15] Textbook, Video 12
22. increase; easier; [15] Textbook, Video 12
23. Holly Ramona, daughter of winery executive Gary Ramona, entered therapy while in college. As her therapy proceeded, Holly became convinced that her father had sexually abused her during her childhood, but that she had repressed the memories of the abuse until recently. After Gary Ramona had been accused of child sexual abuse, sustaining considerable damage to his family, his reputation, and his career, he responded by suing Holly's therapist, accusing her of planting false memories in his daughter's mind. Gary Ramona won this lawsuit and was awarded half a million dollars in damages.

    Psychologists acknowledge that abuse happens. But today, instead of simply accepting Freud's largely unsubstantiated idea that memories of extremely painful episodes are routinely repressed, memory researchers have reason to consider an alternative explanation for the recovered memory phenomenon, acknowledging research showing that suggestibility can be involved in reshaping peoples' memories, and that misinformation provided to a person can lead to the development of false memories. [15] Video 12

ANSWER KEY FOR THE SELF TEST

Item #	Answer	Learning Outcome #	Source	Item #	Answer	Learning Outcome #	Source
1.	a	1	Textbook	14.	a	10	Video 12
2.	d	2	Textbook, Video 12	15.	a	9, 10	Textbook
3.	c	4	Textbook	16.	b	9, 10	Textbook, Video 12
4.	d	3, 8	Textbook, Video 12	17.	b	9, 10	Video 12
5.	d	4, 5	Textbook, Video 12	18.	a	9	Textbook, Video 12
6.	b	5, 16	Textbook, Video 12	19.	d	9, 10	Textbook
7.	b	5	Textbook	20.	a	12, 13	Textbook, Video 12
8.	b	6	Textbook	21.	c	13	Textbook
9.	d	8	Textbook	22.	c	14	Textbook, Video 12
10.	d	4, 6, 7	Textbook, Video 12	23.	a	13	Textbook
11.	d	9	Textbook	24.	b	16	Textbook
12.	c	9	Textbook	25.	c	14, 15	Textbook
13.	a	9	Textbook				

Lesson 13 (Thinking and Language)

Thinking and Language

> **Assignments**
>
> **Reading:** Chapter 10, "Thinking and Language," in *Psychology* by David Myers (Modules 29 and 30 in the modular version of *Psychology*)
>
> **Video:** Episode 13, "Thinking and Language"

LEARNING OUTCOMES

Familiarize yourself with the Learning Outcomes for this lesson before you begin the assignments. Return to them to check your learning after completing the Steps to Learning Success. Careful work on these materials should equip you to accomplish the outcomes.

Thinking (Module 29)

1. Define **cognition**.

2. Describe how **prototypes**, hierarchies, and categories contribute to the formation of **concepts**.

3. Explain the various ways in which problem solving is accomplished, including **algorithms**, **heuristics**, and **insight**.

4. Discuss **confirmation bias** and **fixation**, the two obstacles to problem solving; contrast the two methods of fixation discussed in the text—**mental set** and **functional fixedness**.

5. Compare and contrast the various ways we can error when we use heuristics, including the Kahneman and Tversky examples from the text: **representativeness heuristic**, **availability heuristic**, and **anchoring**, discussed in the video lesson.

6. Define **overconfidence** in the context of decision-making, and discuss both its pitfalls and positive consequences.

7. Explain **framing** and how it can be used to influence others to accept or reject a particular point of view.

8. Compare **belief bias** to **belief perseverance** and explain how the latter can be remedied.

Language (Module 30)

9. Define **language** and identify its various components, including **phonemes**, **morphemes**, **grammar**, **semantics**, and **syntax**.

10. Summarize the typical progression of language development from infancy to elementary school age, including such concepts as **babbling** and **telegraphic speech**.

11. Differentiate between the Skinner and Chomsky theories of language acquisition in children and discuss the importance of statistical learning and critical periods in childhood language development.

Thinking and Language (Module 30)

12. Summarize the hypothesis of **linguistic determinism** and discuss the benefits of exceptional language skills, including the ability to communicate in more than one language. List examples from the text and video in which language is connected to culture, and how language may influence thinking.

13. Provide examples that demonstrate the value of thinking in images.

14. Describe the case of Genie seen in the video; discuss conclusions that can be drawn from the case and why it was such a unique opportunity for researchers studying thinking and language.

Animal Thinking and Language (Module 30)

15. Identify and explain the five cognitive skills shared by humans and great apes.

16. Discuss claims that suggest some animals have the capacity for language; outline arguments that refute such claims.

ACTIVE REVIEW

Each item in this section is based on material presented in the video or the textbook assignment for this lesson, or both. Complete this section, referring as needed to your notes or the source materials themselves. Answers are provided at the end of this lesson.

Thinking

1. **Cognition** refers to the mental activities associated with _____, knowing, remembering, and _____. Cognitive processes involve the formation of _____, which are mental groupings of similar objects, events, or people.

2. We divide concepts into categories. That our concept of animals may be divided into wild or domesticated and that domesticated animals may then be divided into pets and farm animals demonstrates that we subdivide concepts into a(n) _____ (mental subdivisions). Once a concept is defined, we create a mental image that we consider the best example of this category, called a(n) _____. Once an item is placed into a category, our memory of the concept shifts *(toward / away from)* that mental image.

3. There are multiple methods of solving problems. One is to follow a(n) _____, which is a methodical, logical procedure that guarantees an eventual solution. Another method we might employ is _____, in which certain solutions are eliminated and an area in which a solution is considered most likely to be found is the object of focus. Trial and error is then used to solve the problem. Still another way of problem solving is using sudden flashes of inspiration called _____.

4. We sometimes lack objectivity when solving problems. Preconceived ideas about a situation may cause us to pay attention only to information that confirms existing ideas while discounting or ignoring information to the contrary. This phenomenon is known as _____ _____. Another impediment to problem solving is _____, which is the inability to see a problem from a fresh perspective. Two ways in which this occurs are **mental set** and **functional fixedness**. If, while cooking on the grill, we search everywhere for a spatula while ignoring the nearby tongs, we are a victim of *(a mental set / functional fixedness)*. Similarly, if we approach a problem while trying to use a solution that worked previously, we are fixated by *(a mental set / functional fixedness)*.

5. Researchers Daniel Kahneman and Amos Tversky explained that solving problems with **heuristics** can sometimes get us into trouble. If asked, for example, to name a species of birds, we may leave out those birds that vary from our **prototype**, such as penguins and geese. In this example, we're adhering to the *(representativeness / availability)* heuristic. Another example of heuristic error is demonstrated by someone who sees a horrific plane crash on the news and then cancels an upcoming flight, opting to drive instead. This decision, which completely ignores the more dire statistics about driving in an automobile, would be an example of the *(representativeness / availability)* heuristic.

6. The tendency to trust our intuitive heuristics and confirm our beliefs are further evidence of our _____, or tendency to be more sure than correct about the accuracy of our judgments. People who favor this tendency find it *(easier /*

more difficult) to make tough decisions and seem *(more / less)* credible.

7. The way an issue is presented may have an effect on decision-making about that issue. This is called _____. For example, we would be more likely to judge a product as *(unfavorable / favorable)* if it is presented as having a "95% success rate" than if it is presented as having a "5% failure rate," even though the two statistics are identical.

8. The tendency for preexisting beliefs to distort logic or make invalid conclusions seem valid is called _____ _____. This is contrasted with the tendency to cling to a belief despite evidence disproving it, which is called _____ _____. In order to remedy this phenomenon, research has found it helps to imagine that the *(opposite finding was true / same evidence was framed differently)*.

Language

9. The most tangible indication of our thinking power is **language**. Elements critical to language include **syntax**, **semantics**, **grammar**, **phonemes**, and **morphemes**. The smallest distinctive sound unit is called a _____. The smallest unit in language that carries meaning is called a _____. The word *kite*, for example, has three distinctive _____, but if the "*i*" sound stands alone as a pronoun, linguists refer to it as a _____. Languages must have a system of rules that enables us to communicate with and understand others called _____. Rules that govern combining words into grammatically sensible sentences are called _____, while the set of rules by which we derive meaning from morphemes, words, and sentences in a given language is called _____.

10. The development of language in children goes from simplicity to complexity. Around four months of age, babies enter the _____ _____, during which they typically utter very simple consonant-vowel pairs. Around the time of their first birthday, babies have associated words with meanings and enter the _____-_____ _____, perhaps pointing and identifying, "Daddy!" At around 18 months, they move beyond one-word sentences and enter the _____-_____ _____. Typically noun-verb combinations, this kind of speech resembles that used in a telegram and is thus referred to as _____ _____. By early elementary school, children can typically form and understand complex sentences.

11. Keeping to theories he developed on the subject of conditioning, behaviorist B.F. Skinner believed that language developed as an example of association, imitation, and _____ conditioning. Linguist Noam Chomsky feels Skinner's views were too simplistic. He believes our brains are hard-wired for language acquisition and contain a sort of language acquisition device, or *("syntax sponge" / "switch box")*, that aids in understanding and producing language.

12. Cognitive scientists notice that babies as young as seven months old are able to analyze the sounds and syllables that are more likely to go together as well as tell the difference between word breaks and sound sequences. Researchers refer to this analysis as the _____ _____ of human speech, which appears to be the brain's way of mastering grammar. Though we can learn a second language at an older age, some believe babies and young children enter a _____ period in which absorbing language is natural. The window to this period appears to close gradually after age seven. This was demonstrated in the video with the case of Genie, who was largely deprived of language until age 14. After eagerly absorbing the words and meanings for a variety of objects, Genie was able to communicate with speech *(and included / but did not include)* the connector words that make grammatically correct sentences.

Thinking and Language

13. Benjamin Lee Whorf's theory of linguistic determinism hypothesized that *(thinking / language)* determines how we *(think / speak)*. For example, when Arabic

speakers, who read from right to left, see the sentence "The girl pushes the boy," they mentally picture the girl on the *(left / right)* side of the boy, as opposed to English speakers who read from left to right. Researchers have also found that increased vocabulary and learning a second language *(increased / had no effect on)* childrens' aptitude scores.

14. Most people think not just in words, but also in pictures. Brain imaging studies suggest that when we mentally visualize an activity, the brain activation *(is identical to / differs slightly from)* when we actually perform the activity.

15. According to Susan Curtiss in the video, researchers learned several things from the special case of Genie. First, language is *(not the same as / synonymous with)* communication. Also, the fact that Genie did not know language *(impaired / did not impair)* her from completing complex hierarchical and spatial tasks.

Animal Thinking and Language

16. While some may dispute the claim that animals can think, evidence finds that great apes do share five cognitive abilities with humans. First, the fact that these animals are able to sort items such as cats, dogs, chairs, and flowers into categories shows they are able to form _____. Second, when Psychologist Wolfgang Kohler watched caged chimpanzees try to retrieve fruit using a series of sticks, they seemed to experience the "aha!" moment when solving the puzzle, which implied they can experience _____. Third, the fact that chimpanzees choose such appropriate items as reeds and stones to perform tasks shows their ability to use _____. Fourth, that different species of apes seem to pass along different tool uses, grooming styles, and other actions, shows evidence they pass along _____ innovations to their peers and young. Finally, many believe that the great apes' ability to use deception, empathy, and imitation and to inspect themselves, implies they have a theory of _____.

17. When asked to retrieve an item, many animals show they understand words and phrases and can infer meaning from human language. But many argue that the only thing these animals learn is to respond to cues, and imitae their trainers' signs in order to receive reward. The phrasing of "you tickle" and "tickle you" has completely different meanings, yet might be signed by a chimp interchangeably. This shows animals lack human *(syntax / subtlety)*.

Self Test

Read each question and circle the letter of the best answer. When you have completed the Self Test, check your answers against the key at the end of this lesson. If you have answered any items incorrectly, review the appropriate materials to correct misunderstandings and cement your knowledge.

1. Which of the following activities would <u>least</u> likely be associated with cognition?
   a. Thinking
   b. Walking
   c. Remembering
   d. Speaking

2. Which of the following statements is <u>not</u> true of prototypes?
   a. A prototype is a mental "best example" of a category.
   b. Once we have placed an item into a category our memory of that item will drift away from the prototype of the item.
   c. Matching items into prototypes makes it easy and quick to include items into categories.
   d. Matching items into prototypes can lead to judgment errors or overlooking other possible options.

3. Melissa is asked to determine which U.S. state has the highest average temperature. Before beginning her search, she checks a map and eliminates all states that do not border Mexico or the Gulf, then searches for temperatures in the remaining states. Which method has Melissa employed in solving the problem?
   a. Insight
   b. Fixation
   c. Algorithm
   d. Heuristics

4. Which of the following is an advantage of solving a problem using the algorithm method versus using heuristics?
   a. Using an algorithm is faster than heuristics
   b. Using an algorithm guarantees a solution
   c. Using an algorithm is less work than heuristics
   d. None of the above

5. Which of the following best defines confirmation bias?
   a. A tendency to overestimate the accuracy of one's beliefs or judgments
   b. A tendency for one's preexisting beliefs to distort logical reasoning
   c. A tendency to search for information that confirms one's preconceptions
   d. A tendency to cling to one's initial beliefs even after they have been discredited

6. Which of the following best describes fixation?
   a. The inability to see a problem from a new perspective
   b. The tendency to search for information that confirms one's preconceptions
   c. The tendency to be more confident than correct
   d. None of the above

7. Which type of fixation is the tendency to approach a problem in a particular way, often a way that has been successful in the past?
   a. Functional fixedness
   b. Availability heuristic
   c. Framing
   d. Mental set

8. Which of the following are the two ways of misusing heuristics that are presented in the text?
   a. Mental set and functional fixedness
   b. Belief bias and belief perseverance
   c. Overconfidence and confidence bias
   d. Representativeness and availability

9. Mrs. Hanson makes a plane reservation to fly from Miami to Nashville to visit her son. When she sees a news story about a plane crash, she cancels her flight and opts to drive instead. Her son reassures her about the statistical safety of air travel, but Mrs. Hanson ignores the data. It would appear her decision was based on the
   a. availability heuristic.
   b. mental set.
   c. representativeness heuristic.
   d. confirmation bias.

10. In the video, Daniel Kahneman talks about a study in which people were first asked to write down the last 4 digits of their social security number, then asked if they thought the number of physicians in Manhattan was higher or lower than that number. When asked to estimate the number of physicians in Manhattan, people's guesses tended to remain correlated to their social security number, despite its irrelevance to the question! This demonstrated the phenomenon of
    a. mental set.
    b. availability heuristic.
    c. representativeness heuristic.
    d. anchoring.

11. According to the text, which of the following is <u>not</u> true of overconfidence?
    a. Overconfidence is the tendency to overestimate the accuracy of one's beliefs and judgments.
    b. People who are overconfident find it easier to make tough decisions.
    c. People who are overconfident are perceived by others to be less credible.
    d. People who err on the side of confidence tend to be happier.

12. In the video, Daniel Kahneman talks about how doctors phrase the survivability of a certain surgery. Patients responded more positively to being told they had a "90% survival rate," than if they were given a "10% mortality rate." This demonstrates the power of
    a. framing.
    b. mental set.
    c. belief bias.
    d. heuristics.

13. The tendency for one's preexisting beliefs to distort logical reasoning, sometimes by making invalid conclusions seem valid, or valid conclusions seem invalid is
    a. belief perseverance.
    b. mental set.
    c. belief bias.
    d. overconfidence.

14. Which of the following is the best definition of belief perseverance?
    a. The tendency for preexisting beliefs to distort logical reasoning, sometimes by making invalid conclusions seem valid, or valid conclusions seem invalid
    b. Clinging to one's initial conceptions after the basis on which they were formed has been discredited
    c. Seeking only evidence that supports previously-held beliefs
    d. None of the above

15. Which of the below is the best definition of language?
    a. Spoken or written words, and the ways they are combined to communicate meaning
    b. A set of rules by which meaning is derived from morphemes, words, and sentences
    c. A cultural means of communication based on early cave drawings
    d. Spoken, written, or signed words, and the ways they are combined to communicate meaning

16. In a language, which of the below represents the smallest distinctive sound unit?
    a. Phoneme
    b. Morpheme
    c. Nouns
    d. Articles and pronouns

17. A morpheme is defined in a language as
    a. the smallest unit that carries meaning.
    b. the smallest distinctive sound unit.
    c. a system of rules that enables us to communicate with and understand others.
    d. none of the above.

18. The rules of syntax refer to the rules we use to
    a. derive meaning from morphemes, words, and sentences.
    b. order words in a sentence.
    c. derive meaning from phonemes.
    d. both a and b are correct.

19. Which stage of language development begins around the age of 18 months?
    a. Babbling stage
    b. Cooing stage
    c. One-word stage
    d. Two-word stage

20. At approximately what age does the three-word stage of language development begin?
    a. One year
    b. 18 months
    c. 36 months
    d. There is no three-word stage

21. In the text and video, linguist Noam Chomsky asserted that the human capacity for developing language is natural and hardwired. He likens our language acquisition abilities to a sort of
    a. bottle that is filled up with the right kind of experiences to develop language.
    b. computer terminal where words are typed in the keyboard and processed by the brain.
    c. "switch box" with switches that must be set for the language we learn.
    d. color copier that scans information and stores it in memory for processing.

22. What hypothesis supposes that language determines how we think?
    a. Statistical learning
    b. Critical period
    c. Linguistic relativism
    d. Linguistic determinism

23. As described by Susan Curtiss in the video, which of the following describes the peak of Genie's language ability?
    a. Genie never gained the ability to speak
    b. Genie was able to communicate with one and two-word sentences
    c. Genie was able to form complex sentences, but left out the small connector words typical to proper grammar
    d. Genie was able to use flawless American sign language

24. Which of the following lists all five of the cognitive traits great apes share with humans?
    a. Use tools, display insight, pass along cultural innovations, and have a theory of mind
    b. Ability to form concepts, use tools, display insight, pass along cultural innovations, and have a theory of mind
    c. Ability to form concepts, use tools, communicate language, pass along cultural innovations, and have a theory of mind
    d. Ability to form concepts, use tools, display insight, express empathy, and have a theory of mind

25. Which of the following is not true regarding apes and sign language?
    a. People who know sign language are able to "eavesdrop" on chimps signing to each other and have near-perfect agreement on what the chimps are saying
    b. A baby chimp brought into the area of the signing chimps has learned to sign simply by observing the other chimps
    c. Unlike human babies, baby chimps raised without language seem able to gain language competence as adults
    d. Apes are able to combine words creatively

ANSWER KEY FOR THE ACTIVE REVIEW EXERCISES

1. thinking, communicating; concepts; [1, 2] Textbook
2. hierarchy; prototype; toward; [2] Textbook
3. algorithm; heuristics; insight; [3] Textbook
4. confirmation bias; fixation; functional fixedness; a mental set; [4] Textbook, Video 13
5. representativeness; availability; [5] Textbook, Video 13
6. overconfidence; easier, more; [6] Textbook, Video 13
7. framing; favorable; [7] Textbook, Video 13
8. belief bias; belief perseverance; opposite finding was true; [8] Textbook, Video 13
9. phoneme; morpheme; phonemes, morpheme; grammar; syntax, semantics; [9] Textbook
10. babbling stage; one-word stage; two-word stage; telegraphic speech; [10] Textbook, Video 13
11. operant; "switch box"; [11] Textbook, Video 13
12. statistical learning; critical; but did not include; [11, 14] Textbook, Video 13
13. language, think; right; increased; [12] Textbook
14. is identical to; [13] Textbook
15. not the same as; did not impair; [14] Video 13
16. concepts; insight; tools; cultural; mind; [15] Textbook
17. syntax; [16] Textbook

ANSWER KEY FOR THE SELF TEST

Item #	Answer	Learning Outcome #	Source	Item #	Answer	Learning Outcome #	Source
1.	b	1	Textbook	14.	b	8	Textbook
2.	b	2	Textbook	15.	d	9	Textbook
3.	d	3	Textbook, Video 13	16.	a	9	Textbook
4.	b	3	Textbook	17.	a	9	Textbook
5.	c	4	Textbook, Video 13	18.	b	9	Textbook
6.	a	4	Textbook	19.	d	10	Textbook
7.	d	4	Textbook, Video 13	20.	d	10	Textbook
8.	d	5	Textbook	21.	c	11	Textbook, Video 13
9.	a	5	Textbook, Video 13	22.	d	12	Textbook
10.	d	5	Video 13	23.	c	14	Video 13
11.	c	6	Textbook	24.	b	15	Textbook
12.	a	7	Textbook, Video 13	25.	c	16	Textbook
13.	c	8	Textbook				

Lesson 14 (Intelligence)

The Search for Intelligence

> **Assignments**
>
> **Reading:** Chapter 11, "Intelligence," in *Psychology* by David Myers (Modules 31, 32, and 33 in the modular version of *Psychology*)
>
> **Video:** Episode 14, "The Search for Intelligence"

LEARNING OUTCOMES

Familiarize yourself with the Learning Outcomes for this lesson before you begin the assignments. Return to them to check your learning after completing the Steps to Learning Success. Careful work on these materials should equip you to accomplish the outcomes.

What is Intelligence? (Module 31)

1. Define **intelligence** and explain its contextual and non-concrete nature.

2. Discuss ways that the concept of intelligence might vary from one culture to another, and suggest attributes that might be deemed "more intelligent" by some cultures than others.

3. Describe **intelligence tests** and discuss Alfred Binet's reasoning for creating the first such test.

Is Intelligence One General Ability or Several Specific Abilities? (Module 31)

4. Explain how factor analysis lead Spearman to conclude that there is only one form of **general intelligence**, or **g**.

5. Discuss **savant syndrome** and how it supports Howard Gardner's theory of multiple intelligences.

6. Compare and contrast Gardner's theory of **multiple intelligences** with Sternberg's **triarchic theory**, and discuss examples of each.

7. Understand the skills involved in emotional intelligence and discuss how they could have value in everyday situations.

Intelligence and Creativity (Module 31)

8. Define **creativity** and describe its relationship to intelligence.

9. Discuss the five components of creativity and how these components can be used to foster creativity at school and in the workplace.

Is Intelligence Neurologically Measurable? (Module 31)

10. Cite several examples in which neuroscientists found the brain anatomy of exceptionally intelligent people to differ from that of people of more average intelligence.

11. Discuss the ways in which faster brains may be more intelligent brains and the implications of these findings to the various theories of intelligence.

Assessing Intelligence (Module 32)

12. Understand the concept of **mental age** and explain the purpose of Alfred Binet's first intelligence test.

13. Define the intelligence quotient and recall Lewis Terman's reasoning for creating the **Stanford-Binet**.

14. Explain the difference between **aptitude** tests and **achievement** tests.

15. Define the concepts of **standardization, reliability,** and **validity** and discuss their importance in intelligence testing.

16. Describe the normal curve created by standardized test results and explain how the curve illustrates scores that are above and below average.

17. Identify and distinguish between **content validity** and **predictive validity**.

18. Discuss the predictive validity of general aptitude tests and why their predictive value diminishes as the test takers get older.

The Dynamics of Intelligence (Module 32)

19. Contrast the stability of intelligence test scores at ages four and seven with those of high school and college students.

20. Discuss the advantages and pitfalls of intelligence testing and the tracking that results with the creation of gifted and talented programs that are popular in many schools across the country.

Genetic and Environmental Influences on Intelligence (Module 33)

21. Discuss heritability in relation to intelligence, using examples of the strong genetic influence on various traits of intelligence.

22. Using examples, detail the impact of substandard environments on intelligence in early childhood, as well as the changes that occur after educational interventions.

23. List and discuss the variety of environmental factors that contribute to the average differences in ethnic and group test scores.

24. Compare the genders in terms of the various areas in which their intelligence test scores differ, including areas of math, spelling, spatial abilities, and emotional intelligence.

25. Identify ways in which aptitude tests might be biased and discriminatory.

26. Define **stereotype threat** and give examples of situations in which it might change the behavior of an individual.

ACTIVE REVIEW

Each item in this section is based on material presented in the video or the textbook assignment for this lesson, or both. Complete this section, referring as needed to your notes or the source materials themselves. Answers are provided at the end of this lesson.

Introduction

1. The author of the textbook defines **intelligence** as the ability to *(adapt to new situations / learn from experience / adapt to new situations and learn from experience)*.

2. According to Robert Sternberg in the video, the standardized tests of today primarily measure *(practical intelligence / memory and analytical abilities / multiple intelligences)*.

What Is Intelligence?

3. Using a statistical method called **factor analysis,** *(Alfred Binet / Charles Spearman / Howard Gardner)* determined that high proficiency in some mental abilities predicted high proficiency in others, which led to the idea that there is only one intelligence, referred to as **general intelligence**, or **g**.

4. Given what we know about "**g**," performance on a test of **general intelligence** *(should / should not)* predict success in other mental abilities.

5. According to *(Howard Gardner's / Robert Sternberg's / Charles Spearman's)* theory of **multiple intelligences**, we do not have one intelligence, but many—each relatively *(independent of / correlated with)* the others.

6. As Joyce Bishop says in the video, the theory of multiple intelligences can be applied to how students learn. While all students can benefit from a variety of study methods, those who excel in verbal linguistics should be especially sure that they *(never miss a lecture / pace while studying)*.

7. Robert Sternberg *(agrees / disagrees)* with Howard Gardner's idea that there are several different forms of intelligence and divides intelligence into *(2 / 3 / 8)* categories. As reinforced in the video, the analytical skills displayed by "Alice" *(were / were not)* reflected in her performance on intelligence tests.

8. As seen in the text and video, though the **practical intelligence** of Sternberg's theory (the **triarchic theory**) does not show up on typical **aptitude tests**, practical intelligence seemed to predict *(managerial and employmeng success / creative talents / math ability)*.

9. In the video, Peter Salovey ponders why very intelligent people sometimes do "not-so-smart" things or have difficulty in their personal lives. He speculates this could be traced to a lack of *(creative intelligence / academic intelligence / emotional intelligence)*.

10. Among the components of **emotional intelligence** are the ability to perceive emotions, understand emotions, and *(regulate / critique / predict)* emotions.

Intelligence and Creativity

11. **Creativity** is defined as the ability to produce ideas that *(lead to job success / are novel and valuable / follow well-defined rules)*. In general, intelligence test performance *(correlates / does not correlate)* with performance on creativity tests.

12. Among the five components of creativity discussed in the text are expertise, imaginative thinking skills, a venturesome personality, *(intrinsic / extrinsic)* motivation, and a creative environment. Research shows that people tend to be *(more / less)* creative when they think their work will be evaluated.

Is Intelligence Neurologically Measurable?

13. In post-mortem brain studies of intelligent people, it has been found that people with more education have *(more / fewer)* synapses in the brain. The cause of this is *(genetics / experience / inconclusive)*.

14. Neuroscientists testing brain function have found a correlation between intelligence test scores and _____ speed and processing or neurological speed. That is, they found that more intelligent subjects react more *(quickly / slowly)* to simple tasks than their lower scoring counterparts.

Assessing Intelligence

15. Researchers are quick to remind people that intelligence is not a "thing" but is instead defined by a(n) *(intelligence / achievement / personality)* **test**, the scores of which can be compared with others to find an average. In France, **Alfred Binet** set out to find an unbiased method of determining a child's *(IQ / mental age / practical intelligence)* by creating the first aptitude test. Binet hoped his test would *(identify children who would perform poorly in school / weed out children with inferior genes)*.

16. The **Stanford-Binet** created by *(Howard Gardner / Charles Spearman / Lewis Terman)* became the widely-used American version of Binet's intelligence test. As testing became more widespread, other factors were added such as the calculating of a(n) *(base intelligence / intelligence quotient)*, which was a person's **mental age** divided by their chronological age, then multiplied by 100. Most current intelligence tests *(use / no longer use)* this calculation to arrive at a person's final score.

17. Stanford Professor **Lewis Terman** helped the U.S. Government develop new tests that were administered *en masse* to U.S. immigrants and army recruits during World War I. To some, the results of these tests indicated *(that Army volunteers were less intelligent than those drafted / the inferiority of non-Anglo-Saxon cultures)*. In this manner, Terman's use of intelligence tests probably would have been *(praised / condemned)* by Alfred Binet.

18. Standardized tests of today are generally divided into two categories. *(Achievement / Aptitude)* tests are intended to reflect what the individual has learned,

while *(achievement / aptitude)* tests set out to predict a person's ability to learn a new skill.

19. The **WAIS**, which stands for the _____ _____ _____ _____ is the most *(widely used / controversial)* intelligence test of today and provides *(an overall intelligence score / a score measuring several important abilities / both an overall score and a score measuring several important abilities)*. Using this format, a subject whose verbal comprehension score was dramatically lower than scores in their other abilities might indicate *(a test bias in that area / a reading or language disability)*.

20. In order for an intelligence test to be widely accepted, it must meet three criteria. _____ refers to the process of making scores meaningful by comparing them to a pre-tested standardized group. _____ refers to the extent to which a test predicts or measures what it is supposed to. A test is said to be _____ if it yields dependably consistent scores.

21. The **normal curve** refers to the pattern created by a bell-shaped distribution of scores around the average score, regardless of what is being measured. On intelligence tests, the assigned average score is *(50 / 100 / 150)*. Therefore, a test score that falls in the widest (or tallest) portion of the curve would be *(below average / about average / above average)*.

22. The "Flynn effect" refers to the fact that over the years, performance on intelligence tests has been *(improving / declining)*. In order to keep the average score near 100, intelligence test scales must periodically be _____.

23. To check a test's **reliability**, researchers might *(give the same test twice / compare test scores with IQ scores)*. The more the two scores correlate, the higher the reliability.

24. As noted in the text, using an inaccurate tape measure would mean your measurements would have a high *(reliability / validity)* but a low *(reliability / validity)*.

Validity is broken down into two categories. An eye test that evaluates vision would be said to have *(content validity / predictive validity)*. An aptitude test, on the other hand, must <u>specifically</u> have *(content validity / predictive validity)* in order to forecast future achievement. Tests such as the SAT and GRE have *(greater / less)* **predictive validity** than do aptitude tests given during the early school years. A test loses its predictive validity when a *(wide / narrow)* the range of people are used to validate it.

The Dynamics of Intelligence

25. According to the text, the fact that a baby is an "early talker" is a *(good / poor)* predictor of future intelligence. After age seven, intelligence test scores tend to *(rise steadily / remain consistent)*.

26. Researchers verify validity of intelligence tests when they compare groups at the two extremes of the normal curve. Individuals who score very low on intelligence tests and have difficulty adapting to independent living are considered to have *(mental retardation / Down syndrome)*. An extra chromosome 21 is the cause of *(Down syndrome / savant syndrome)*.

27. In Lewis Terman's famous 1921 study of children with IQs over 135, the children were *(more likely / no more likely)* to attain higher levels of education than their peers with more average IQs.

Genetic and Environmental Influences on Intelligence

28. As stated in the text, intelligence test scores of identical twins raised <u>together</u> *(were virtually identical / had only average similarities)*. Behavior geneticists also notice that as adopted children reach adulthood it is the *(genetic / environmental)* influences that become more obvious.

29. Using Mark Twain's hypothetical idea that we raise boys in barrels until age 12, we would expect any differences in their intelligence to be of purely *(genetic / environmental)* influence. By the same token, if

identical twins were raised in very different environments, we would expect their age 12 score variations to be purely of *(genetic / environmental)* influence.

30. According to the text, malnutrition, sensory deprivation, and social isolation are examples in which environment can *(override / enrich)* genetic influences on intelligence. Given the research on "enriched" environments, we might predict that a mother who exposes her baby to Beethoven *(would / would not)* affect the child's intelligence or musical abilities.

31. In the video, both Angela Ginorio and Claude Steele credit the rising math scores of women in the past 15 years to *(genetics / environmental and social interventions)*.

32. Racial and ethnic groups differ in their averages on intelligence tests. For example, the scores for whites on intelligence tests are centered around the average of *(85 / 100 / 50)* while the average for American Blacks is roughly centered around *(85 / 100 / 50)*. In infant intelligence measures, however, black babies scored *(higher than / lower than / equally as well as)* white babies. It is important to remember that individual genetic differences <u>within</u> a race are *(much greater than / not as great as)* differences <u>between</u> races.

33. List several factors that could contribute to the average test score differences between blacks and whites, Asians and whites, etc. _____

_____

_____

_____

_____

_____

34. Among the many gender differences in the various components of mental ability, it has been found that *(boys / girls)* are better spellers, *(boys / girls)* excel at verbal ability, *(boys / girls)* excel at detecting emotions,

and high school *(boys / girls)* are better at the math portion of the SAT. Some researchers have suggested that prenatal hormones may contribute to the better *(male / female)* performance in spatial abilities.

35. The group differences in intelligence test outcomes often lead to charges of bias in the intelligence tests. Racial group differences *(are / are not)* found in non-verbal test items. If test results do, in fact, reflect unequal experience and opportunities of different groups, then we have *(reason / no reason)* to conclude a test is biased. If a test predicts achievement for women but not for men, then the test would be considered *(biased / invalid / both biased and invalid)*.

36. In the video, Claude Steele's test of **stereotype threat** revealed that the stereotype of women performing poorly on a difficult math test had *(significant / no)* negative impact on women's test performance. Similarly, it was found that blacks scored *(higher / lower)* when tested by blacks than when tested by whites.

37. According to Claude Steele, individuals who are encouraged to believe in their potential and to be confident that they <u>can</u> succeed are found to perform *(better / worse)* on intelligence tests despite the threat of a stereotype. Without such interventions, researchers believe that the test performance of these individuals would continue to erode, and that they would run a risk of "disidentifying" with *(school achievement / their own race or ethnic group)*.

38. Myers reminds us that intelligence test scores reveal *(only one / many / all)* element(s) of an individual's personal capabilities. Intelligence test scores can be *(related / unrelated / all important)* to certain aspects of life success.

SELF TEST

Read each question and circle the letter of the best answer. When you have completed the Self Test, check your answers against the key at the end of this lesson. If you have answered any items incorrectly, review the appropriate materials to correct misunderstandings and cement your knowledge.

1. Which pair of researchers in the history of intelligence testing most closely *agree* on the idea that inteligence is not just a single entity measurable with one kind of test?
   a. Charles Spearman and Howard Gardner
   b. Howard Gardner and Robert Sternberg
   c. Alfred Binet and Lewis Terman
   d. L.L. Thurstone and Charles Spearman

2. Which of the following abilities is <u>not</u> typically tested on a standardized college entrance exam?
   a. Creativity
   b. Memory skills
   c. Math skills
   d. Verbal linguistic skills

3. In the video, Sternberg's student with practical intelligence, "Celia," did very well in the job market. Why was this so?
   a. Her creative skills helped her find novel ways to get her foot in the door.
   b. Her common sense and practical skills helped her identify potential employers and what they were looking for.
   c. Her charming personal skills enabled her to take down the emotional barriers of her interviewers.
   d. She always looked good in an interview when she went in after Paul.

4. Which of the following best explains why Alfred Binet created the first intelligence test?
   a. To identify children who would need extra help in school
   b. To identify children from lower socio-economic groups in order to isolate them from the gifted and talented students
   c. To compare the abilities of French children with those of German and American students
   d. To identify children in the education system who might hold back the grade averages of more intelligent students

5. Of the following, which would be the best example of someone with savant syndrome?
   a. James is 33 years old and has been diagnosed with Down syndrome. Though he scores very low on intelligence tests, he works three days at the local grocery store where he bags groceries and stocks shelves.
   b. Ruthie is 7 years old. She is already reading at a high school level and her violin teacher says she's a prodigy. She scores very well on intelligence tests and is an advanced student.
   c. Mavis is 28 years old. Her parents don't feel she'll ever be able to live on her own without assistance. Though Mavis scores very low on intelligence tests, she has an uncanny ability to remember minute details and can recite back a very long list of numbers after viewing the list only briefly.
   d. Simon is a 45-year-old construction worker. After a head injury at work, Simon is unable to form any new long-term memories. He scores a little below average on intelligence tests.

6. Which of the following is <u>not</u> a component of creativity discussed in the text?
   a. A well-developed base of knowledge
   b. Imaginative thinking skills
   c. A venturesome personality
   d. Extrinsic motivation

7. According to the text, people with exceptional intelligence have been found to have several differences in brain anatomy from those of more average intelligence. Which of the following was true according to the Canadian study that examined Einstein's brain?
   a. Einstein's brain was 15 percent larger in the areas associated with mathematical processing and spatial information.
   b. Einstein's brain was heavier than the average brain.
   c. Einstein's brain had a 15% thicker cerebral cortex
   d. Einstein's brain had more "white matter" over grey matter

8. Which of the following best explains why Lewis Terman created the Stanford-Binet intelligence test?
   a. Binet's norms for age did not apply well to American students in California
   b. Because *mental age* did not translate well to America, he invented the concept of IQ and included it in his own test
   c. Binet's entire test was done in French and had to be translated
   d. Most of the questions in Binet's test referred to European number systems and landmarks

9. Which of the following would be a valid argument <u>against</u> tracking students' intelligence test scores and placing them into certain programs in the education system?
   a. Such programs might question the validity of intelligence tests
   b. Higher-scoring individuals may feel bored or unchallenged if placed in classes with lower-scoring students
   c. Such programs may give special attention to students who need a little extra help in school
   d. Such systems may promote segregation since minorities are more likely to be placed in lower scoring groups

10. Which of the following would <u>not</u> be an example of an environmental influence on intelligence?
    a. Malnourishment in children
    b. Infants who are not picked up or touched by caregivers
    c. Infants with an extra chromosome 21
    d. Children whose school is adjacent to a noisy, busy airport

11. According to the text, which of the following is true of programs such as Head Start?
    a. High-quality preschool programs give a small boost to emotional intelligence
    b. The aptitude benefits of Head Start decline as time passes
    c. Participation in such programs decreases a child's likelihood of repeating a grade
    d. All of the above

12. One of the job candidates in the video, noticing the body language of her interviewer, compliments him on his tie in order to lighten his mood. This action demonstrates skills associated with
    a. emotional intelligence.
    b. analytical intelligence.
    c. verbal linguistic intelligence.
    d. bodily-kinesthetic intelligence.

13. Aptitude tests are intended to do which of the following?
    a. Determine IQ
    b. Predict future ability to learn a skill
    c. Assess learning
    d. None of the above

14. A review board that created an intelligence test in 1995 checks the data from the previous year and notes that students from all over the country are averaging a score of 103 on the test. In 1995, the average score was 100. Based on this data, which of the following conclusions might the company reach?
    a. It is time to restandardize their test.
    b. Their test lacks content validity.
    c. Their test is no longer reliable.
    d. Their test has become too difficult.

15. The change in the average score above could best be attributed to
    a. an increase in the number of people taking their test.
    b. students taking advantage of extra credit.
    c. recent improvements in test standardization.
    d. the Flynn effect.

16. A common physical cause of mental retardation is
    a. a depressed environment for learning.
    b. teachers who don't help their students fulfill their potential.
    c. savant syndrome.
    d. an extra 21st chromosome.

17. Which of the following ideas about average group intelligence test scores is <u>not</u> correct?
    a. Asian students perform more poorly than North American students on math achievement and math aptitude.
    b. Individual differences within a race are greater than overall differences between races.
    c. The average score for American Blacks is lower than the average for American Whites on intelligence tests.
    d. Millions of blacks have higher IQs than the average white person.

18. A test question that measures spatial ability would most likely require
    a. listing all the possible uses for a brick.
    b. mentally rotating an object.
    c. reading a paragraph and then summarizing its content.
    d. matching emotions to facial expressions.

For each of the abilities listed below, indicate which sex displays the greater aptitude.

    a. male
    b. female

19. Spelling

20. Verbal ability

21. Nonverbal memory

22. Sensation

23. Spatial aptitudes

24. Emotion-detecting ability

25. Which of the following best describes stereotype threat?
    a. The self-fulfilling effect of a negative stereotype
    b. The steadily rising test scores of women and minorities
    c. Men who feel guilty because they are superior at math underperforming in other areas
    d. Stereotyped ethnic groups being less likely to show up for scheduled intelligence tests

ANSWER KEY FOR THE ACTIVE REVIEW

1. adapt to new situations and learn from experience; [1] Textbook, Video 14
2. memory and analytical abilities; [3] Video 14
3. Charles Spearman; [4] Textbook, Video 14
4. should; [4] Textbook, Video 14
5. Howard Gardner's; independent; [5, 6] Textbook, Video 14
6. never miss a lecture; [5, 6] Video 14
7. agrees; 3; were; [6] Textbook, Video 14
8. managerial and employment success; [6] Textbook, Video 14
9. emotional intelligence; [7] Video 14
10. regulate; [7] Textbook, Video 14
11. are novel and valuable; correlates; [8] Textbook
12. intrinsic; less; [9] Text
13. more; inconclusive; [10] Textbook
14. perceptual; quickly; [11] Textbook
15. intelligence; mental age; identify children who would perform poorly in school; [12, 13]Textbook
16. Lewis Terman; intelligence quotient; no longer use; [12, 13] Textbook
17. the inferiority of non-Anglo-Saxon cultures; condemned; [12, 13] Textbook
18. achievement; aptitude; [14] Textbook
19. Wechsler Adult Intelligence Scale; widely used; both an overall score and a score measuring several important abilities; a reading or language disability; [16] Textbook
20. Standardization; Validity; reliable; [15] Textbook
21. 100; about average; [16] Textbook
22. improving; restandardized; [19] Textbook
23. give the same test twice; [15] Textbook
24. reliability; validity; content validity; predictive validity; less; narrow; [15] Textbook
25. poor; remain consistent; [18, 19] Textbook
26. mental retardation; Down syndrome; [19] Textbook
27. more likely; [19, 20] Textbook
28. were virtually identical; genetic; [21] Textbook
29. genetic; environmental; [21, 22] Textbook
30. override; will not; [22] Textbook
31. environmental and social interventions; [22] Video 14
32. 100; 85; equally as well as; much greater than; [23] Textbook
33. *Answers should include some of these elements:* Some group differences are genetically based, but among the variety of factors, most are probably environmental. Black, white, and Asian students may have vast differences in terms of educational opportunity, quality, and experience. Some communities may hold education in a higher regard than others. Aspects of stereotype threat could also come into play when it comes to testing. Asian students attend school 30 percent more days than other ethnicities. People of mixed ethnicities may vary which race they declare themselves. [22, 23] Textbook, Video 14
34. girls; girls; girls; boys; male; [23] Textbook
35. are; no reason; both biased and invalid; [25] Textbook
36. significant; higher; [26] Textbook, Video 14
37. better; school achievement; [23, 26] Textbook, Video 14
38. only one; unrelated; [6, 7] Textbook

ANSWER KEY FOR THE SELF TEST

Item #	Answer	Learning Outcome #	Source	Item #	Answer	Learning Outcome #	Source
1.	b	6	Textbook, Video 14	14.	a	15	Textbook
2.	a	8	Textbook, Video 14	15.	d	19	Textbook
3.	b	6	Video 14	16.	d	21	Textbook
4.	a	3	Textbook, Video 14	17.	a	23	Textbook
5.	c	5	Textbook, Video 14	18.	b	24	Textbook
6.	d	9	Textbook	19.	b	24	Textbook
7.	a	10	Textbook	20.	b	24	Textbook, Video 14
8.	a	13	Textbook	21.	b	24	Textbook
9.	d	20	Textbook	22.	b	24	Textbook
10.	c	22	Textbook	23.	a	24	Textbook, Video 14
11.	d	22	Textbook	24.	b	24	Textbook
12.	a	7	Video 14	25.	a	26	Textbook, Video 14
13.	b	14	Textbook				

Lesson 15 (Motivation)

In the Driver's Seat

Assignments

Reading: Chapter 12, "Motivation and Work" in *Psychology* by David Myers (Modules 34, 35, 36, and 37 in the modular version of *Psychology*)

Video: Episode 15, "In the Driver's Seat"

LEARNING OUTCOMES

Familiarize yourself with the Learning Outcomes for this lesson before you begin the assignments. Return to them to check your learning after completing the Steps to Learning Success. Careful work on these materials should equip you to accomplish the outcomes.

Perspectives on Motivation (Module 34)

1. Define **motivation** from a psychological perspective and list some of the basic needs discussed in the textbook and video.

2. Apply Colin Camerer's platonic charioteer metaphor to examples used in the video (i.e. oxygen deprivation, eating disorders, belonging)—and explain aspects of those examples that might reflect action of the brain's prefrontal cortex or limbic system.

3. Define **instinct** and discuss its relation to the instinct theory and the evolutionary perspective.

4. Explain the concept of **homeostasis** in relation to the **drive-reduction theory** and how drives and **incentives** can motivate behavior.

5. Discuss how arousal relates to motivation, using examples.

6. Explain Maslow's **hierarchy of needs** and discuss why some needs take priority over others.

Hunger (Module 35)

7. Discuss the physiology of hunger, including how the brain monitors **glucose** and regulates the body's need to take in nutrients.

8. Discuss the influence of culture on taste preference, as well as evolution's influence on our need for high calorie foods.

9. Explain the difference between **anorexia nervosa** and **bulimia nervosa** and list some of the factors that influence each of the eating disorders.

Sexual Motivation (Module 36)

10. Describe elements of the **sexual response cycle,** how the sex hormones **estrogen** and **testosterone** can influence sexual behavior and discuss ways in which the genders differ in sexual motivation and partnership.

11. List factors that contribute to teen pregnancy and the various influences on sexually transmitted diseases.

12. Discuss the social and physiological findings of research in the area of **sexual orientation**.

The Need to Belong (Module 36)

13. Discuss the survival value of the need to belong, as well as the social value assigned to having attachments and to not having attachments.

Motivation at Work (Module 37)

14. Define **flow** and discuss the ways its presence or absence affects students, workers, employers, and overall happiness.

15. Define **industrial-organizational psychology** and discuss research done in some of its sub-fields such as **personnel psychology**.

16. Differentiate between **task leadership** and **social leadership** and discuss ways in which managers can get the most out of the people they employ.

ACTIVE REVIEW

Each item in this section is based on material presented in the video or the textbook assignment for this lesson, or both. Complete this section, referring as needed to your notes or the source materials themselves. Answers are provided at the end of this lesson.

Perspectives on Motivation

1. **Motivation** is defined as a need that _____ and _____ behavior. According to Peter Ditto and Derek Denton in the video, the basic biological motivators include: _____, _____, _____, salt and mineral appetites, hunger for oxygen, and avoidance of change in body temperature. These kinds of basic needs are generated from the _____ _____ in the brain, as opposed to the prefrontal cortex.

2. The influence of Charles Darwin popularized the labeling of human behavior as (*instincts / incentives*). The trend faded as scientists found that labeling behavior did not explain it. A complex behavior must be rigidly patterned throughout a species and be unlearned in order to be considered an (*instinct / incentive*).

3. According to the **drive reduction theory**, our physiological aim is _____, which means to maintain a balanced, or constant, internal state. The best example of this would be a thermostat, which might activate the heat or air conditioning in order to maintain room temperature. Our behavior is also pulled by _____, which are positive or negative stimuli that lure or repel us.

4. Abraham Maslow described our motivations as being a _____ ___ _____.

Though not a fixed pyramid of priorities, when more basic physiological needs near the bottom of the pyramid, such as _____ and _____, are satisfied, then needs of safety and belonging might be pursued. At the top of the pyramid we generally see needs of _____-_____, or the need to live up to one's full potential.

Hunger

5. Areas of the brain, mainly the (*hypothalamus / corpus callosum / cortex*) automatically control hunger. The body maintains **homeostasis** partly by monitoring _____, which is the form of sugar that circulates throughout the body providing it with energy. Some theorize that the body has a "weight thermostat" meant to keep us at a specific weight, or _____ _____, with hunger and energy expenditure modulated to maintain that weight. Researchers also monitor a person's _____ _____ _____, or resting rate of energy expenditure.

6. As confirmed in the video by Peter Ditto's cookie experiment, the presence or aroma of tasty food can act as an (*instinct / incentive*) and lead us to take risks for the reward of food. When presented with an abundance of tasty foods, we tend to (*overeat / maintain the body's set point*). As Ginger Osborne states, our evolutionary ancestors might have preferred (*high / low*) fat and calorie foods if they feared they would not eat again for a time.

7. Though preferences for salts and sweets appear to be universal, food preference varies according to

culture. We are *(more / less)* likely to try foods that are unfamiliar.

8. Applying Colin Camerer's platonic charioteer metaphor, a person would be using the brain's *(prefrontal cortex / limbic system)* in order to resist the more "instinctual" appetite for food. The eating disorder characterized by dieting or starving to lower weight, yet still feeling overweight is *(anorexia nervosa / bulimia nervosa)*. The eating disorder characterized by overeating and then vomiting, fasting, and/or exercising excessively is *(anorexia nervosa / bulimia nervosa)*. The disorder in which weight tends to fluctuate close to the norm is _____ _____. Images in the media of the ideal weight *(do / do not)* have an influence on eating disorders. Researchers *(do / do not)* see a genetic influence on eating disorders.

Sexual Motivation

9. Famous sex researchers Masters and Johnson broke down the **sexual response cycle** into four stages: _____, _____, _____, and _____. At the resolution phase, both sexes enter the _____ _____, in which they are unable to complete another orgasm. Sex becomes a motivator during *(childhood / adolescence / adulthood)*. *(Testosterone / Estrogen)* activates the male sex characteristics, while *(testosterone / estrogen)* promotes the sexual receptivity in females. Normal fluctuations of the male sex hormone in men *(do / do not)* affect the desire for sex.

10. According to Michael Bailey, in general *(men / women)* seek a partner who is younger than them, while *(men / women)*, usually seek an older mate. Both sexes want their partner to be faithful, but sexual fidelity is more important than emotional fidelity to *(men / women)*. Despite this fact, *(men / women)* have a higher interest in casual, uncommitted sex.

11. American teens have *(higher / lower)* rates of intercourse when compared to European teens, and have *(higher / lower)* rates of pregnancy and abortion. Many factors contribute to this statistic, including the American teen's use of *(alcohol / birth control)*, which inhibits judgment.

12. Factors contributing to teen abstinence include high _____, involvement in religion, *(mother / father)* presence, and participation in service learning programs.

13. Enduring sexual attraction to either one's own or the opposite sex defines one's _____ _____. According to the textbook and the video, *(men / women)* have a more bisexual arousal pattern, demonstrating their sexuality is more plastic.

14. According to Michael Bailey and David Myers in the video, sexual orientation *(is / is not)* a choice. Researcher Simon LeVay discovered a group of cells in the _____ (part of the brain) that was larger in straight men than in gay men. Other research suggests that homosexual men are *(more / less)* likely to have neuroanatomy similar to a woman's. Researchers find many correlations connected to sexual orientation, including the fact that men with older brothers are slightly more likely to be *(heterosexual / homosexual)*. Evidence also suggests that prenatal hormones play a role in determining the sexual orientation of a fetus. It appears to be the case that our *(genes / environment / genes and environment)* determine sexual orientation.

The Need to Belong

15. As Derek Denton says in the video, the deep need to be accepted by others appears to be *(unique / not unique)* to humans. For our ancestors, being alone or ostracized *(aided / was detrimental to)* survival. The **social pain** felt by Alfred Nunes in the video—due to his isolation in prison from his loved ones—demonstrates society's hope that incarceration can *(motivate*

corrective action / protect the public from criminals like him). Evidence also shows that those who are socially accepted are *(more / less)* prone to depression, and *(more / less)* likely to have better health.

Motivation at Work

16. The application of psychological concepts and methods to human behavior in the workplace is _____-_____ **psychology**. One of its subfields is **personnel psychology**, which applies psychological methods to selecting and evaluating _____. The other subfield is _____ **psychology**, which examines organizational influences on workers and facilitates organizational change.

17. Mihaly Csikszentmihalyi's research centers on the concept of _____–a focused state of consciousness where a person's skills are fully engaged, with diminished awareness of self and time. According to the text and video, employers may want to *(encourage / discourage)* **flow** experiences in their employees, as those who experienced flow had *(higher / lower)* self-esteem and made *(more / less)* mistakes in their work. Those who experienced flow appeared to be _____ motivated and thus *(more / less)* likely to be focused on their pay.

18. When examining employee selection, **personnel psychologists** have found that informal interviews are *(more / less)* helpful than information such as aptitude tests and work samples. Interviewers who "trust their gut" are *(more / less)* apt to predict a worker's successful match to the job situation. In contrast to informal interviews, psychologists have developed a _____ _____, which asks the same questions of every applicant and rates them on established scales. Personnel psychologists also study performance appraisals and find that **360-degree feedback**, in which you rate the performance of *(yourself / your supervisor / yourself and your supervisor and all your coworkers)* fosters *(more / less)* open communication in the job setting.

19. Psychologists define _____ _____ as the desire for significant accomplishment and attaining a high mastery and standard. According to Diego Pizzagalli in the video lesson, this kind of goal-directed motivation is a product of the *(limbic system / prefrontal cortex)*.

20. Researchers have found that the "100 Best Companies to Work For" *(have / do not have)* higher than average returns for their investors.

21. Leadership styles vary. Managers who utilize *(task / social)* **leadership** excel at setting standards, organizing work, and keeping workers focused on goals. Bosses who use *(task / social)* **leadership** are better at team-building and mediating conflicts, and have a more democratic style. As David Myers states in the video, employers who *(use task leadership / share authority)* with their employees give them a sense of ownership in the company, which helps motivate job performance.

SELF TEST

Read each question and circle the letter of the best answer. When you have completed the Self Test, check your answers against the key at the end of this lesson. If you have answered any items incorrectly, review the appropriate materials to correct misunderstandings and cement your knowledge.

1. A complex behavior that is rigidly-patterned throughout a species and is unlearned is a(n)
   a. incentive.
   b. instinct.
   c. motivator.
   d. emotion.

2. According to the metaphor of the platonic charioteer in the video lesson, which part of the brain represents *reason*?
   a. The limbic system
   b. The prefrontal cortex
   c. The hippocampus
   d. The corpus callosum

3. Peter Ditto describes an experiment in the video in which participants are asked to play a card game for a reward of cookies. Participants who were able to *see* or *smell* the cookies were more likely to risk losing the game. The presence of the cookies in this experiment acted as
   a. an incentive.
   b. an instrument of homeostasis.
   c. an instinct.
   d. a drive-reduction.

4. An older hunger theory proposes that there is a "weight thermostat" and that the body will strive to maintain weight at a(n)
   a. basal metabolic rate.
   b. set point.
   c. optimum level according to height.
   d. level that anticipates a glucose deprivation.

5. According to the text and video lesson, which of the following is not a true statement regarding hunger?
   a. People given an excess of salt develop a taste for excessively salty foods.
   b. In order for a full stomach to turn off eating, it needs to take in one-third extra calories.
   c. When given an abundance of tasty foods, we are more than likely to overeat.
   d. All of the above are true.

6. Which of the following specifically describes anorexia nervosa?
   a. Weight fluctuates within the normal ranges.
   b. Weight drops significantly below normal.
   c. Sufferers may use laxatives and exercise excessively.
   d. None of the above

7. Of the following statements, which is not believed to be true about eating disorders?
   a. They center around body image and self worth
   b. Genes may contribute to the likelihood of eating disorders
   c. Mothers who are preoccupied with their own appearance may influence their daughter's susceptibility to eating disorders
   d. They indicate a history of childhood sexual abuse

8. The American sexual researcher who pioneered studies on sexual behavior in the 1940's was
   a. Alfred Kinsey.
   b. William Masters (of Master's and Johnson).
   c. Michael Bailey.
   d. Dr. Joyce Brothers.

9. Which of the following describes the sexual response cycle, in its proper order?
   a. Resolution phase, excitement phase, orgasm, plateau phase
   b. Excitement phase, orgasm, plateau phase, resolution phase
   c. Excitement phase, plateau phase, orgasm, resolution phase
   d. Excitement phase, orgasm, refractory period, plateau phase

10. Which part of the sexual response cycle is characterized by the genitals first becoming engorged with blood?
    a. Excitement phase
    b. Plateau phase
    c. Refractory period
    d. Orgasm

11. Which of the following is not true of estrogen?
    a. In most mammals, injecting estrogen promotes sexual receptivity
    b. It is found only in females
    c. In most mammals, estrogen levels peak at ovulation
    d. All of the above are true

12. Which statement about the use of birth control by American teens is not true?
    a. Teens who feel guilty about sexual activity are less likely to carry condoms.
    b. Sexually active teens are more likely to use alcohol.
    c. Most teens overestimate the sexual activity of their peers.
    d. Open discussion of contraceptives among teens does not increase their likelihood of using them.

13. Which of the following has been proven to be a factor in teen girls abstaining from sex?
    a. The presence of a father in the home
    b. Activity in sports programs
    c. The late onset of puberty
    d. The genetic persistence of virginity

14. According to both the text and the video, more and more evidence suggests that sexual orientation is
    a. not a matter of choice.
    b. determined randomly.
    c. determined very specifically by genes.
    d. determined by the relationship with the father.

15. According to the video lesson, which statement is more true regarding casual sex, or sex in an uncommitted relationship?
    a. Straight men are more approving of casual sex
    b. Gay men are more approving of casual sex
    c. Straight women are more approving of casual sex
    d. Both gay and straight men are more approving of casual sex than women

16. Which of the following would be an evolutionary reason we are instilled with a need to belong?
    a. Connecting with others aided in hunting and gathering food
    b. Social bonds helped protect offspring from predators
    c. Cooperation with others helped create an environment that supported reproduction and survival
    d. All of the above

17. In the video, Alfred Nunes hopes the birth of his son will
    a. be the motivator that makes him correct his ways and never return to prison.
    b. motivate the prison authorities to be more lenient with him.
    c. motivate his son to abide by the laws.
    d. motivate his wife to come visit the prison more often.

18. Which of the following is not true of people who are married?
    a. They are less likely to die an early death
    b. They are less likely to be depressed
    c. They are a higher risk for suicide
    d. All of the above are true

19. According to findings in the computer experiment described by Csikszentmihalyi in the video,
    a. people who are paid more are more likely to experience flow while on the job.
    b. students who experienced flow made less mistakes in the computer task.
    c. students who experienced flow took more time to complete the computer task.
    d. students who experienced flow did not enjoy the computer task.

20. Which of the below best describes the application of psychological concepts and methods to optimizing human behavior in the workplace?
    a. Personnel psychology
    b. Organizational psychology
    c. Sports psychology
    d. Industrial-organizational psychology

21. Which of the following is a sub-field of industrial-organizational psychology?
    a. Psychiatry
    b. Forensic psychology
    c. Organizational psychology
    d. None of the above

22. A desire for significant accomplishment; for mastery of things, people, or ideas; and for attaining a high standard is the definition of
    a. flow experience.
    b. social leadership.
    c. employee engagement.
    d. achievement motivation.

23. According to the study of businesses in India, Taiwan, and Iran that is described in the text, the most effective managers demonstrated which kind of leadership?
    a. Task leadership
    b. Social leadership
    c. Both task and social leadership
    d. Charisma

24. According to the text, an effective manager would be best served by not doing which of the following?
    a. Send employees to seminars to work on their weak areas
    b. Focus training on people's strengths
    c. Catch an employee doing something right and reward them for it
    d. Set specific, challenging goals

25. Which of the following tactics might increase employee satisfaction in the workplace?
    a. Form an agreement so the worker can profit from the company's success
    b. Give clear and, when possible, positive feedback on performance
    c. Allow employees flexible hours
    d. Any of the above could increase job satisfaction

ANSWER KEY FOR THE ACTIVE REVIEW EXERCISES

1. energizes, directs; thirst, hunger, sex; limbic system; [1, 2] Textbook, Video 15
2. instincts, instinct; [3] Textbook
3. homeostasis, incentives; [4] Textbook
4. hierarchy of motives; hunger, thirst, self-actualization; [6] Textbook
5. hypothalamus, glucose, set point, basal metabolic rate; [7] Textbook
6. incentive, overeat, high; [4, 7, 8] Textbook, Video 15
7. less; [8] Textbook, Video 15
8. prefrontal cortex, anorexia nervosa; bulimia nervosa; bulimia nervosa; do; do; [9] Textbook, Video 15
9. excitement phase, plateau phase, orgasm, resolution phase; refractory period; adolescence; Testosterone; estrogen; do not; [10] Textbook
10. men, women; men; men; [10] Video 15
11. lower, higher; alcohol; [11] Textbook
12. intelligence, father; [11] Textbook
13. sexual orientation; women; [12] Textbook, Video 15
14. is not; hypothalamus; more; homosexual; genes and environment; [12] Textbook, Video 15
15. not unique; was detrimental to; motivate corrective action; less, more; [13] Textbook, Video 15
16. industrial-organizational; employees; organizational; [15] Textbook, Video 15
17. flow; encourage, higher, less; intrinsically, less; [14] Video 15
18. less; less; structured interview, yourself and your supervisor and all your coworkers, more; [15] Textbook
19. achievement motivation; prefrontal cortex; [15] Textbook, Video 15
20. have; [15] Textbook
21. task; social; share authority; [16] Textbook, Video 15

ANSWER KEY FOR THE SELF TEST

Item #	Answer	Learning Outcome #	Source
1.	b	2	Textbook
2.	b	2	Video 15
3.	a	4	Textbook, Video 15
4.	b	7	Textbook
5.	d	7, 8	Textbook, Video 15
6.	b	9	Textbook, Video 15
7.	d	9	Textbook
8.	a	10	Textbook
9.	c	10	Textbook
10.	a	10	Textbook
11.	b	10	Textbook
12.	d	11	Textbook
13.	a	11	Textbook
14.	a	12	Textbook, Video 15
15.	d	12	Video 15
16.	d	13	Textbook, Video 15
17.	a	13	Video 15
18.	c	13	Textbook
19.	b	14	Video 15
20.	d	15	Textbook
21.	c	15	Textbook
22.	d	15	Textbook
23.	c	16	Textbook
24.	a	15	Textbook
25.	d	15	Textbook

Lesson 16 (Emotion)

Emotions

Assignments

Reading: Chapter 13, "Emotion," in *Psychology* by David Myers (Modules 38, 39, and 40 in the modular version of *Psychology*)

Video: Episode 16, "Emotions"

LEARNING OUTCOMES

Familiarize yourself with the Learning Outcomes for this lesson before you begin the assignments. Return to them to check your learning after completing the Steps to Learning Success. Careful work on these materials should equip you to accomplish the outcomes.

Theories of Emotion (Module 38)

1. Name the three basic components of **emotion** and relate each to an emotional incident you have witnessed or experienced.

2. Explain the role that emotion plays in social relationships.

3. Briefly state Charles Darwin's primary thesis in *The Expression of Emotion in Man and Animals,* and how it supported his theory of evolution.

4. Identify the four criteria Paul Ekman uses to distinguish emotions from other states.

5. Differentiate between the **James-Lange** and **Cannon-Bard theories** of emotion, and compare the arguments they used to support their original theories to recent research findings.

6. Briefly describe Schachter and Singer's two-factor theory of emotion.

Embodied Emotion (Module 38)

7. Compare the roles of the autonomic nervous system's sympathetic and parasympathetic divisions in regulating physiological arousal.

8. Indicate the role that arousal plays in performance.

9. Recognize the physiological similarities and differences among specific emotions.

10. Describe the spillover effect and its impact on our experience of emotion.

11. Contrast the responses that Zajonc and Lazurus would give to the question "Must cognition precede emotion?"

Expressed Emotion (Module 39)

12. Describe the function of **nonverbal** expressions and gestures in communication, and recognize factors that influence our ability to decipher non-verbal cues.

13. Summarize the comparative skills of men and women in expressing, detecting, and regulating emotion.

14. Compare the ways in which people from different cultures display and interpret expressions of emotion, and at what level any variations that may exist translate into differences in the emotional system.

15. Explain briefly how expressions of emotion and the physiology of emotion help ensure our continued existence.

16. Relate the contagious nature of emotions to such concepts as **facial feedback**.

Experienced Emotion (Module 40)

17. Name the emotions that are generally considered basic, recognizing that opinions among researchers vary as to which and how many emotions should be included on that list.

18. Indicate the two basic dimensions along which emotions can be differentiated, and what these measures tell researchers.

19. Explain the significance of the "peculiar longevity of things not so bad" discussed by Daniel Gilbert.

20. Connect the adaptive emotion fear to its biological roots, physiological expression, and development as a learned behavior.

21. Briefly summarize research related to anger, the **catharsis** hypothesis, and forgiveness.

22. List factors that appear to have a major bearing on our **subjective well-being**, and those that do not.

23. Explain the relativity of happiness based on the **adaptation-level phenomenon** and the **relative deprivation principle**.

ACTIVE REVIEW

Each item in this section is based on material presented in the video or the textbook assignment for this lesson, or both. Complete this section, referring as needed to your notes or the source materials themselves. Answers are provided at the end of this lesson.

Theories of Emotion

1. Emotions are an adaptive response. If you're driving late at night and an animal darts across the road a few feet in front of your car, you will undoubtedly experience the three components of emotion:

   _____ _____ (heart pounding), _____ _____ (foot jams on brake, hands grip steering wheel to execute sharp turn), and _____ _____ (sense of fear).

2. Dacher Keltner introduces the idea that emotions are also _____ sensory systems that help us form attachments and create cooperative communities.

3. British naturalist Charles Darwin extended this view to other species in *The Expression of Emotion in Man and Animals* written in 1872. Darwin's argument that humans and other animal species have similar emotions fit his thesis regarding _____. One emotion that clearly exists across species is _____. There may be less similarity among species when the emotion is more _____.

4. Emotions researcher Paul Ekman establishes four criteria to distinguish emotion from other states. An emotion, he says, is _____; we don't say "Now I'm going to be happy, or how about a little bit of fear?" Fear is influenced by both our **phylogeny** (the evolutionary development of our species) and our **ontogeny** (what happened to us in the course of growing up). Emotions are _____ without our being able to witness the process or influence it much. Emotions are not private. There's a _____, generally a facial expression, that informs others what's going on. Emotions (do / do not) tell us their cause.

5. One of the oldest controversies regarding emotion centers on the timing of our feelings in relation to the physiological responses that accompany emotion. William James and Carl Lange believed that we feel emotion *(before / after / at the same time as)* our bodies respond. Walter Cannon and Philip Bard disagreed. They argued that we feel emotion *(before / after / at the same time as)* our bodies respond.

6. A second, more recent controversy has to do with the connection between thinking and emotion. Stanley Schachter and Jerome Singer maintained that two factors were essential in experiencing emotion:
   (1) _____ _____ and
   (2) a cognitive _____ of the emotion.

Embodied Emotion

7. Emotions *(do /do not)* have distinctive physiologies. In general, it is the _____ _____ _____ that controls arousal. Its sympathetic division directs the adrenal glands to release stress hormones, which increases _____ _____, _____ _____, and blood sugar levels.

8. When the crisis passes, the parasympathetic division becomes active and _____ the body. Stress hormones already in the blood stream cause the body to slowly *(increase / diminish)* its aroused state. Prolonged physical arousal places a strain on the body.

9. In terms of the brain and emotion, activity in the _____ occurs when someone experiences fear. Negative emotions like disgust tend to promote more brain activity in the *(left / right)* prefrontal cortex. Alert, energetic, positive people show more activity in the *(left / right)* frontal lobe. The job of the _____ is to rein in emotions.

10. Sometimes our interpretation of one event can _____ _____ to the next. As your textbook points out, arousal _____ emotion; cognition _____ it.

11. Must cognition precede emotion? Robert Zajonc contends that emotional reactions can be *(quicker / slower)* than our interpretation of a situation; therefore we feel some emotions *(before / after)* we think. Research on neurological processes in emotion and thinking *(supports / rejects)* his theory. But, says Richard Lazarus, even instant emotional reactions require some sort of cognitive _____.

Expressed Emotion

12. People communicate in two ways: verbally and _____. Research shows that *(men / women)* are *(much / somewhat)* better at decoding emotion, which helps explain their greater emotional literacy.

13. Men are better at *(regulating / expressing)* emotion. They are allowed a *(wide / narrow)* range of emotional options. Janet Shibley Hyde notes that the emotion _____ is considered appropriate for men, but inappropriate for women.

14. Most people find it difficult to detect fake facial expressions. But these skills can be taught, as Paul Ekman and Maureen O'Sullivan demonstrated. Training enabled the researchers to discern lying with over _____ percent accuracy.

15. Subtle facial indicators of emotion may offer a reliable behavioral alternative to current-day _____ _____ tests.

16. The meaning of gestures *(is the same across cultures / varies with the culture)*. What about facial expressions? Paul Ekman and a team of researchers took photographs of people expressing emotion to people in radically different cultures and asked them to identify the emotion. Which emotion does Ekman say is universal? _____ Two other emotions that tend to be recognized across national boundaries are _____ and _____.

17. Despite this universality, Angela Ginorio comments, there are *(major / subtle)* cultural differences in the kinds of situations that elicit the _____ (number) basic emotions.

18. Robert Levenson's research has focused on two different types of cultures: cultures that believe emotions need to be hidden and moderated and cultures that believe emotions should be shared and expressed. People from _____ tend to fall in the first category; people from _____ _____ _____ in the second.

19. At what level do these cultural beliefs translate into differences in the emotion system? Fill out the chart:

Culture influences...	Culture has little effect on...

20. Charles Darwin, nineteenth century emotion researcher, theorized that the ability to convey emotions helped our prehistoric ancestors _____ in the period before they began to communicate in spoken language. That, he reasoned, is why all humans express basic emotions with similar

    _____ _____.

21. It has also been adaptive for us to _____ faces in particular contexts. List two ways in which film and television directors use this phenomenon to induce fear. _____

    _____

    _____

22. How does an expression itself help to ensure our continued existence? What happens when you experience surprise? _____

    _____

    Disgust?_____

    _____

23. Expressions not only reflect emotion. They can also intensify the feelings that accompany them. If you smile or frown, you begin to experience the

    _____ _____. If you make a fearful face and create the physiology of fear in your body, you begin to feel _____. This is called the _____ _____ theory.

24. Experiments have shown that imitating others' expressions tends to *(make us more / keep us from being)* empathetic. This helps to explain why emotions are

    _____.

25. Emotions arise from the interplay of _____,

    _____, and _____ behaviors.

Experienced Emotion

26. There is *(general agreement / some disagreement)* as to which emotions are categorized as basic and which are not. Jot down some of the criteria researchers use to include an emotion in the basic category. _____

    _____

    _____

    _____

27. As we see in the example of the wildebeests approaching the waterhole, most emotions can be measured along two different scales: _____ (high vs. low) and _____ (good vs. bad). In addition, Paul Ekman talks about other dimensions he has researched: the _____ and _____ of our response.

28. If we are aware of the dimensions of our emotional profile, is it possible to regulate our emotions? It's *(hard / easy)* to achieve, said Paul Ekman. It helps if there is *(more / less)* of a gap between impulse and action.

29. Daniel Gilbert notes that we tend to overestimate the intensity and duration of our negative emotions. The "peculiar longevity of things not so bad" refers to the fact that we tend to _____ big events more than little events.

30. List two descriptive terms David Myers uses to depict the role fear plays in our lives: _____

    _____

31. In a series of experiments in the mid-1980s, Susan Mineka observed that most monkeys raised in the lab *(did / did not)* fear snakes, whereas monkeys raised in the wild *(did / did not)*. When the lab-raised monkeys observed their parents' behavior, they developed a

similar pattern of _____. Three months later the behavior *(persisted / disappeared)*.

32. Monkeys who were shown edited videos of monkeys reacting fearfully to flowers *(did / did not)* mimic this behavior. This suggests that this may be an evolutionary fear that helped our ancestors _____.

33. The _____ carries messages from such brain areas as the anterior cingulated cortex to all parts of the brain, allowing us to respond to fearful situations.

34. People who are extremely afraid of certain situations or objects may suffer from chronic _____. At the other end of the spectrum, people who show great heroism or commit criminal acts may appear almost _____. Our _____ background and our _____ contribute to both extremes.

35. To summarize, humans seem to be biologically _____ to acquire some fears. Other fears are learned through _____ and _____.

36. Anger *(is / is not)* included on the basic list of emotions. List at least two physiological markers for anger. _____

37. A suggestion that it is better to voice than to suppress anger would most likely come from someone who is part of *(an individualist / a collectivist)* culture. The assumption is that emotional expression provides an emotional release, or _____. Researchers have found, however, that expressing anger may _____ the conflict and _____ the anger.

38. Robert Levenson says it's critical we fine tune our emotions. Anger that is appropriate for predators may not be appropriate for dealing with _____ _____. Paul Ekman

recommends employing _____ anger—anger that is directed at the action not the actor and promotes reconciliation.

39. What two suggestions do experts offer regarding how to handle anger?
    a. _____
    _____
    b. _____
    _____

40. Charlotte Witvliet distinguishes between what forgiveness is and what it is not. List at least three items that are included on her "forgiveness is not" list.
    _____
    _____
    _____

41. Her research shows that people tend to report lower levels of fear and sadness and greater levels of control and joy when they _____ rather than ruminate about an event. Physiologically, holding a grudge is _____. Granting forgiveness shifts one's emotions in a more _____ direction.

42. Researchers tend to refer to happiness as _____ _____ because it is less ambiguous. The _____ _____ phenomenon illustrates the fact that when people feel happy they are more willing to help others.

43. Separating myth from well-researched studies of temporary moods and long-term life satisfaction shows that people tend to be happier *(earlier / later)* in the day. Stressful events trigger bad moods that tend to last a *(day / week / month)*. People tend to rebound from bad days to a *(less-than-usual / better-than-usual)* good mood. We tend to *(underestimate / overestimate)* the duration of dramatic positive events. Increased affluence has a *(major / minor)* influence on happiness.

44. Which of the following has a greater bearing on our happiness? *(Financial well-being / relationship well-being*

/ job success) Studies that probe differences in happiness between men and women, and between the young and the old reveal distinctions that are *(consistent and significant / erratic and small)*.

45. Surveys that measure subjective well-being (combined happiness and satisfaction) in 82 societies show that the United States and Australia are close to each other in _____ place. Daniel Kahneman suggests that a better approach than asking people to judge their satisfaction with their lives would be to see

_____

_____ .

46. The **adaptation-level phenomenon** describes our tendency to form judgments relative to a neutral level defined by our prior experience. Explain this

principle in your own words and apply it to how you rate your level of happiness. _____

_____

_____

_____

_____

_____

_____

47. In the same manner, explain the concept of **relative deprivation**. _____

_____

_____

_____

_____

_____

SELF TEST

Read each question and circle the letter of the best answer. When you have completed the Self Test, check your answers against the key at the end of this lesson. If you have answered any items incorrectly, review the appropriate materials to correct misunderstandings and cement your knowledge.

1. Emotions are
   a. adaptive responses that enhance our survival.
   b. channels for cognitive information.
   c. attributes unique to the human species.
   d. unconscious reactions.

2. The idea that emotions are social sensory systems that help us form attachments and create cooperative communities
   a. was developed by William James in the 19th century.
   b. is no longer considered valid after decades of study.
   c. is the basis for the research of Paul Ekman.
   d. is a new view of emotion that is currently being researched.

3. Which of the following statements does *not* accurately reflect the similarities between human emotions and the emotions of other animal species?
   a. Humans express emotions in many ways that are similar to animals.
   b. Fear is a species-distinct emotion that requires brain circuitry unique to the animal, whether it's a housecat, human, or cockroach.
   c. Some emotions like shame, guilt, and embarrassment are thought to be distinctly social and distinctly human.
   d. In writing *The Expression of Emotion in Man and Animals,* Charles Darwin attempted to show cross-species connections that supported his view of evolution.

4. Paul Ekman characterizes an emotion as
   a. pre-planned.
   b. influenced by evolutionary development (phylogeny).
   c. private, with little evidence that informs others how we feel.
   d. resisting developmental factors or experience.

5. Which team of researchers proposed that there are two factors involved in emotion–physical arousal and a cognitive label?
   a. William James and Carl Lange
   b. Walter Cannon and Philip Bard
   c. Stanley Schachter and Jerome Singer
   d. Robert Jajonc and Joseph LeDoux

6. Why is the return from a fear response to a calmer, more normal state gradual rather than instantaneous?
   a. Although further release of stress hormones is halted, hormones already in the bloodstream linger awhile.
   b. The parasympathetic division of the ANS is slower to receive signals than the sympathetic division.
   c. It actually takes longer for the heart rate and blood pressure to increase in a crisis situation than it does for them to decrease once the crisis is over.
   d. Our bodies tend to prefer highly aroused states and are reluctant to return to normal.

7. Brain scans and EEG recordings reveal that people who are happy and energetic show greater activity in the
   a. amygdala.
   b. left frontal lobe.
   c. right prefrontal cortex.
   d. right frontal lobe.

8. Which of the following emotional pairs would <u>not</u> appear similar in terms of general autonomic arousal?
   a. Fear and anger
   b. Disgust and joy
   c. Joy and anger
   d. Fear and joy

9. It is not uncommon for riots to occur after a championship game, whatever the sport, whatever the country. This is an example of
   a. the spillover effect.
   b. unsportsmanship-like conduct.
   c. the peculiar longevity of things not so bad.
   d. relative deprivation principle.

10. Which portion of the brain is bypassed when emotions take the shortcut rather than the longer pathway to the emotional experience?
    a. Amygdala
    b. Cortex
    c. Thalamus
    d. Autonomic nervous system

11. Skill in detecting and accurately translating nonverbal clues depends to a large degree on
    a. age, gender, intelligence.
    b. verbal skills.
    c. acuity of sight and perception.
    d. experience, culture, gender.

Match the sex that rates higher in each of areas that follow.

   a. Men
   b. Women

12. Narrower range of emotions

13. Expressing anger

14. More happy recollections

15. The discovery that facial expressions speak a fairly universal language would not have surprised pioneer emotion researcher Charles Darwin. He would have agreed with all but one of the following items. Identify the statement with which Darwin would <u>not</u> have agreed.
    a. Emotions were crucial survival mechanisms for our prehistoric ancestors.
    b. The expression of an emotion intensifies that emotion.
    c. This shared heritage is why all humans communicate basic emotions with similar facial expressions.
    d. Young animals and young babies must be taught to express emotion.

16. The fact that expressions not only communicate emotions but also amplify and regulate them is termed the
    a. emotional control thesis.
    b. facial feedback theory.
    c. catharsis effect.
    d. adaptation-level principle.

17. There is some agreement among researchers regarding how many basic emotions there are, and which emotions should be included on the list. All but one of the following emotions are included on many of the basic lists. Identify the emotion that is <u>not</u> usually included.
    a. Surprise
    b. Jealousy
    c. Contempt
    d. Joy

18. The "peculiar longevity of things not so bad" refers to the fact that
    a. we tend to rationalize small annoyances and ignore larger issues.
    b. we usually ignore insignificant events and dismiss them from our memory.
    c. we underestimate how long a minor negative event might bother us and overestimate how long we would suffer in the wake of a major negative event.
    d. most people lack the skill to rationalize events, large or small.

19. The emotion fear
    a. is an alarm system that prepares our bodies to flee danger.
    b. tends to be non-adaptive.
    c. rarely, if ever, spreads from one person to another.
    d. prevents us from focusing on a problem and developing survival strategies.

20. The basic question Susan Mineka sought to answer in her experiments with monkeys raised in the lab and those raised in the wild was
    a. why lab-reared mice are afraid of snakes whereas monkeys raised in the wild are not.
    b. why lab-reared monkeys who have never seen a snake are as afraid of snakes as their wild-reared parents.
    c. why monkeys raised in a lab setting are not afraid of snakes, while monkeys raised in the wild are.
    d. why monkeys are afraid of snakes.

21. Anger is a basic emotion with defined physiological markers. In the list below, identify the marker that should <u>not</u> be included.
    a. Muscles tightening
    b. Heart pumping
    c. Face loses all color, becomes pale
    d. Higher skin temperature

22. The statement "acting angry can make us feel angrier" is associated with
    a. catharsis theory.
    b. behavior feedback research.
    c. individualized culture credo.
    d. constructive anger.

23. According to research, which of the following factors has the greatest impact on personal happiness?
    a. Job success and financial well-being
    b. Physical attractiveness
    c. Relationship well-being
    d. Gender, age, and educational attainment

24. Rather than ask people how happy they are, Daniel Kahneman suggests looking at
    a. their altruistic acts; how they give of themselves.
    b. what they do with their time.
    c. how many friends and loved ones they have.
    d. the country in which they live.

25. If Jossie feels that her family is much poorer than anyone else in her neighborhood, she might be said to be experiencing what researchers call
    a. the relative deprivation principle.
    b. the green-eyed monster.
    c. the adaptation-level phenomenon.
    d. the theory of relativity.

ANSWER KEY FOR THE ACTIVE REVIEW EXERCISES

1. physiological arousal; expressive behaviors; conscious experience; [1] Textbook
2. social; [2] Video 16
3. evolution; fear; complex; [3] Video 16
4. unbidden; triggered; signal; do not; [4] Video 16
5. after, at the same time; [5] Textbook
6. physical arousal; interpretation; [6] Textbook
7. do; autonomic nervous system; heart rate; blood pressure; [7, 8] Textbook, Video 16
8. calms; diminish; [7, 8] Textbook, Video 16
9. amygdala; right; left; cortex; [9] Textbook, Video 16
10. spill over; fuels; channels; [10] Textbook
11. quicker; before; supports; appraisal; [11] Textbook
12. nonverbally; women; somewhat; [12] Textbook, Video 16.
13. regulating; narrow; anger; [13] Video 16
14. 80 percent; [12] Textbook
15. lie detector; [12] Textbook
16. varies with the culture; anger; happiness and fear; [14] Textbook, Video 16
17. subtle; six; [14] Textbook, Video 16
18. Asian countries like Japan; North America, Western Europe, Australia and New Zealand; [14] Textbook, Video 16
19. [14] Video 16

Culture influences...	Culture has little effect on...
The way we talk about emotions	The way our faces express emotion
The way we label emotions	How our bodies respond to emotion
Beliefs about what makes for a good emotional life	

20. survive; facial expressions; [15] Textbook, Video 16
21. interpret; music growing in intensity, ominous-looking setting, heart-pounding sound effects; [15] Textbook
22. eyes widen to take in more information; nose wrinkles to reduce offensive odor; [15] Textbook
23. corresponding emotion; afraid; facial feedback; [16] Textbook, Video 16.
24. makes us more; contagious; [16] Textbook
25. cognition, physiology, and expressive; [1] Textbook
26. some disagreement; distinct facial signature, cross-cultural similarity, early analog in animals; [17] Textbook, Video 16
27. arousal; valence; speed and duration; [18] Video 16
28. hard; more; [18] Video 16
29. rationalize; [19] Video 16
30. traumatic (poisonous); contagious; an adaptive emotion; alarm system, learned behavior; conditioned behavior; [20] Textbook
31. did not; did; fear; persisted; [20] Textbook, Video 4 (DVD Find Out More, *Is Fear of Snakes Inborn?*)
32. did not; survive; Textbook, [20] Video 4, Video 11
33. amygdala; [20] Textbook, Video 16
34. anxiety; fearless; genetic; experiences; [20] Textbook
35. predisposed, experience, observation; [20] Textbook
36. is; your heart pumping, muscles tightening, face becoming suffused with color and heat; [21] Video 16
37. an individualist; catharsis; escalate; magnify; [21] Textbook
38. loved ones or a boss; constructive; [21] Textbook, Video 16
39. (a) wait before you react angrily (the physiological arousal will taper off); (b) find ways to calm yourself and deal with anger in a way that does not make it habitual or long lasting; [21] Textbook
40. condoning, tolerating, minimizing, excusing, doesn't mean you like the person, does mean reconciling with the offender; [21] Video 16
41. forgivee; stressful; positive; [21] Textbook, Video 16
42. subjective well-being; feel good, do good; [22] Textbook, Video 16
43. earlier; day; better-than-usual; overestimate; minor; [22] Textbook, Video 16
44. relationship well-being; erratic and small; [22] Textbook, Video 16
45. 15th; what their lives are actually like and how they spend their time; [22] Video 16
46. Sample: If you make $7.50 an hour working at the library and earn twice that much a year later doing research for a tech firm, you are no long going to be satisfied with the lower rate. You've adjusted your neutral level and set a new standard. [23] Textbook
47. Sample: A standout quarterback for your college team would not be satisfied with a million dollar signing bonus if someone who graduated two years later received twice as much. [23] Textbook

ANSWER KEY FOR THE SELF TEST

Item #	Answer	Learning Outcome #	Source	Item #	Answer	Learning Outcome #	Source
1.	a	1	Textbook, Video 16	14.	b	13	Textbook, Video 16
2.	d	2	Video 16	15.	d	15	Textbook, Video 16
3.	b	3	Video 16	16.	b	16	Textbook, Video 16
4.	b	4	Video 16	17.	b	17	Textbook, Video 16
5.	b	6	Textbook	18.	c	19	Video 16
6.	a	7	Textbook	19.	a	20	Textbook
7.	b	9	Textbook	20.	c	20	Textbook, Video 4 (Find Out More: *Is Fear of Snakes Inborn?*)
8.	b	9	Textbook	21.	c	21	Textbook, Video 16
9.	a	10	Textbook	22.	b	21	Textbook, Video 16
10.	b	11	Textbook	23.	c	22	Textbook, Video 16
11.	c	12	Textbook, Video 16	24.	b	22	Video
12.	a	13	Textbook, Video 16	25.	a	23	Textbook
13.	a	13	Textbook, Video 16				

Lesson 17 (Stress and Health)

Stressed to the Limit

> **Assignments**
>
> **Reading:** Chapter 14, "Stress and Health," in *Psychology* by David Myers (Modules 41, 42, and 43 in the modular version of *Psychology*)
>
> **Video:** Episode 17, "Stressed to the Limit"

LEARNING OUTCOMES

Familiarize yourself with the Learning Outcomes for this lesson before you begin the assignments. Return to them to check your learning after completing the Steps to Learning Success. Careful work on these materials should equip you to accomplish the outcomes.

Stress and Illness (Module 41)

1. Compare the fields of **behavioral medicine** and **health psychology** and discuss behavior-related causes of illness.

2. Define **stress** and explain, using examples, why a situation can be stressful to one person but not another.

3. Compare and contrast the varied ways people and animals respond to stress, including the fight-or-flight response and behavioral disengagement. Also, explain the **general adaptation syndrome**, and identify the stages of this adaptive response.

4. Detail the effects of stress hormones such as cortisol on various organs and systems of the body.

5. Discuss the health impact of catastrophic events, significant life changes, and everyday stress.

6. Differentiate between **Type A** and **Type B** personalities, and discuss the ways in which stress can contribute to **coronary artery disease**.

7. Explain **psychophysiological illnesses** and the ways that stress can impact aspects of the immune system, including **lymphocytes** and cytokines.

8. Discuss the findings of research on the connection between stress and various diseases including AIDS and cancer.

Coping with Stress (Module 42)

9. Contrast the various ways of **coping**, including **problem-focused coping** and **emotion-focused strategy**.

10. Discuss factors that aid in coping with stress, including control, social support, and **expression** and **suppression** of emotion.

11. Describe the aspects and examples of **resilience** shown in the video and discuss how research on the phenomenon could help psychoneuroimmunology and health psychology in general.

12. Discuss the various ways stress can be managed, including aerobic exercise, **biofeedback**, and meditation.

Modifying Illness-Related Behaviors (Module 43)

13. List reasons people start **smoking** and why it is difficult to stop; discuss strategies for quitting and preventing people from acquiring up the habit.

14. Discuss the social and physiological aspects of fat and obesity, including the role of genes and environment on weight.

15. Discuss the psychology of weight control and the various strategies people can use to lose weight.

ACTIVE REVIEW

Each item in this section is based on material presented in the video or the textbook assignment for this lesson, or both. Complete this section, referring as needed to your notes or the source materials themselves. Answers are provided at the end of this lesson.

Stress and Illness

1. _____ _____ is a subfield of psychology that contributes to _____ _____, which is an interdisciplinary field that integrates behavioral and medical knowledge and applies that knowledge to health and disease. Both fields are concerned with **stress**, which is a *(stimulus / process / response)* by which we perceive and respond to certain events, called stressors, that we appraise as threatening or challenging. In the video, Sheldon Cohen suggests that stress is the extent to which *(demands / ability)* exceed the *(demands / ability)* to cope.

2. Most research involving the stress response system focuses on the *(fight-or-flight / behavioral disengagement / tend and befriend)* reaction. While this reaction causes heart rate to *(increase / decrease)* and readies the body for action, a more slow-acting system in the body eventually releases a stress hormone called _____. Prolonged exposure to this hormone can damage cells in organs as well as cells in specific brain areas such as the _____ and the prefrontal cortex.

3. In the video, Margaret Kemeny more fully explains another stress response system called **behavioral disengagement**. During reaction, an animal may *(avoid / sustain)* direct eye contact, try to make itself *(larger / smaller)* than the dominant animal, and withdraw from the situation, thus conserving its energy.

4. Researcher Hans Selye has outlined what he calls the **general adaptation syndrome**. GAS has three stages, the first being _____, in which the sympathetic nervous system is activated. The second stage, _____, involves the outpouring of hormones, and the third stage, _____,

occurs if the stressor persists. During this last stage, the body systems are vulnerable to illness.

5. The leading cause of death in this country is _____ _____ _____, which is the clogging of the vessels that nourish the heart muscle. A health study by Meyer Friedman and Ray Rosenman divided 3,000 men into two personality categories, Type A and Type B. The Type ___ personalities had more circulating stress hormones, which contributed to a buildup of plaque in the arteries and *(increased / decreased)* the risk of stroke and heart attack. While this type was more easily angered, impatient, and reactive, the Type ___ people were more easygoing and relaxed when challenged by stressors and thus less vulnerable to such diseases.

6. Illnesses such as headaches and hypertension are classified as _____ **illnesses**, which literally means "mind-body" illnesses. As seen in the video lesson, John Cacioppo's team examined the immune system of those who cared for Alzheimer's patients–specifically examining their levels of _____, which are the white blood cells in the immune system that fight bacterial and viral invaders. Research by Sheldon Cohen and others examined the effect of stress on levels of *(cytokines / lymphocytes / microphages)*, which are the actual cause of the symptoms of a cold once exposed to an infection. Producing an excess of these pro-inflammatory agents can cause your cold symptoms to *(lessen / worsen)*. In both experiments, having *(less / more)* stress made test subjects more vulnerable to infection.

7. Researchers also study other diseases to check their vulnerability to stress. Because *(AIDS / cancer / lupus)* is an immune deficiency disease, it is reasonable to assume that stress could hasten the progression of the disease. Evidence has proven this to be *(true / false)*. The link between stress and *(AIDS / cancer / colds)* is conflicting. While rodents given *carcinogens* then exposed to stressful events were more likely to

develop tumors, a similar link in humans is unproven.

Coping with Stress

8. Alleviating stress by emotional, cognitive, or behavioral methods is the definition of _____. There are two ways of dealing with stressors. The first is _____- **focused coping**, in which case the person tries to alleviate the stressor directly. The other is a more _____- **focused strategy** in which the person attempts to avoid or ignore the stressor and attends to their emotional needs related to the stressful reaction.

9. According to Sheldon Cohen in the video lesson, **predictability** in the environment makes a difference in the stress reaction. If we know when the train outside our window will go by, we show *(more / less)* negative reaction to the noise of that train. Researchers also know that having a sense of control over our environment *(increases / decreases)* stressful reactions. Feeling liked, being married, and having close friends and family is a type of control called *(family matters / social support / social coping)*. Those who have strong social ties have been found to have *(higher / lower)* levels of stress hormones circulating in the bloodstream. Margaret Kemeny states in the video that suppression of anger can *(activate / diffuse)* the fight-or-flight reaction.

10. Though efforts to cope with stress can help deflect its effects on the mind and body, sometimes we have no choice but to manage stress and counteract its effects. Exercise, especially _____ _____, which is sustained activity that increases heart and lung fitness, has been shown to help people better manage stressful events. It also *(reduces / cures / increases)* depression and anxiety. Another method of electronically recording, amplifying, and feeding back information regarding changes in the physiological state (such as blood pressure and muscle tension) is called _____. Researchers found the benefits of this method to be overblown. Other methods of managing stress include relaxation and _____, which

is a practice most commonly associated with Buddhist monks and Franciscan nuns.

11. The breast cancer survivors in the video helped explore the psychological concept of _____, which means to bounce back from overwhelming adversity. Central to this concept is that those who survived their cancer were able to find *(meaning / joy)* in their experience.

Modifying Illness-Related Behaviors

12. Health psychologists also endeavor to modify behaviors that lead to poor health. Researchers estimate that the elimination of _____ _____ (common health-related behavior) would increase life expectancy more than any other preventive measure. Many people claim that nicotine is more addictive than _____ (illegal drug). We also know that nicotine *(inhibits / stimulates)* dopamine production in the brain.

13. Obesity is also on the list of targets for health psychology with *(75 / 65 / 45)* percent of Americans classified as overweight. Though fitness matters *(more / less)* to overall health than being slightly overweight, obesity contributes to many diseases and *(increases / decreases)* life expectancy, especially in *(men / women)*.

14. Obesity has both physiological and social effects, with a social bias against overweight *(men / women)* being especially evident in experiments measuring discrimination. People become overweight when they *(consume / expend)* more calories than they *(consume / expend)*. One of the reasons it is so difficult to lose weight is that it requires *(more / less)* calories to maintain body weight than it did to attain it. When someone who is overweight decreases calorie intake, the body reacts as if it's being starved and its metabolic rate *(increases / decreases)*. Though fat cells *(diminish / shrink)*, they never disappear.

15. Studies involving identical twins raised apart show that they are more likely to have *(similar / different)* body weight, which proves a strong *(genetic / environmental)* influence on obesity. However, culture and environment clearly make a difference, as seen

by the fact that women are six times more likely to be obese when they are in a *(higher / lower)* socio-economic class. Compared to the population in the early 1900s, western cultures are eating foods with *(more / less)* calories, while at the same time expending *(more / less)* calories.

16. People who diet often lose weight then *(gain it back / suffer eating disorders)*. Strategies for losing weight include the goal of *(boosting / slowing down)* metabolism, minimizing exposure to tempting foods, and avoiding the temptation of _____ eating.

SELF TEST

Read each question and circle the letter of the best answer. When you have completed the Self Test, check your answers against the key at the end of this lesson. If you have answered any items incorrectly, review the appropriate materials to correct misunderstandings and cement your knowledge.

1. Which of the following would be the best definition for behavioral medicine?
   a. An interdisciplinary field that integrates behavioral and medical knowledge and applies that knowledge to health and disease
   b. A subfield of psychology that provides psychology's contribution to behavioral medicine
   c. The application of psychological concepts and methods to optimizing human behavior in the workplace
   d. The study of the interaction of behavioral, neural, and endocrine factors with the functioning of the immune system

2. Which of the following is <u>not</u> true of stress?
   a. A short-lived stressor can help the immune system to fend off infection.
   b. A short-lived stressor or challenge can motivate positive action.
   c. Living through excessively stressful events can deepen spirituality and add meaning to life.
   d. Continual, long-term stress can strengthen the sympathetic nervous system to create an immune-vigilant state.

3. Sharon parks her car on the street two blocks away from a café where she will meet a friend. As she gets out of the car, she is confronted by a mugger with a knife who demands her purse. In an instant, Sharon's heart races, her breath quickens and her temperature shoots up. When the mugger looks over his shoulder, Sharon bolts down the street to the café

without thinking. This example illustrates which adaptive response?
   a. Fight-or-flight
   b. Behavioral disengagement
   c. Tend and befriend
   d. None of the above

4. Two animals confront each other in the wild. According to Margaret Kemeny in the video, the animal that reacts with behavioral disengagement might do which of the following?
   a. Pull the "look over there!" trick and then run away
   b. Show teeth and ready for attack
   c. Make itself larger by raising arms or arching its back
   d. Make itself small to show the aggressor it is not a threat

5. Which of the below defines the general adaptation syndrome?
   a. Hans Selye's concept of the body's adaptive response to stress in three stages
   b. Walter Cannon's observation of the increase in heart and respiration, etc, that characterizes the fight-or-flight response
   c. The alleviating of stress using emotional, cognitive, or behavioral methods
   d. Alfred Binet's observation that intelligence test scores continue to increase

6. Which stage of the general adaptation syndrome would probably not occur if the stressor was brief or lacked intensity?
   a. Exhaustion
   b. Alarm
   c. Resistance
   d. Infection

7. In the opening of the video, what are the researchers measuring by "stressing out" their test subject?
   a. GAS
   b. Lymphocytes
   c. Cortisol
   d. Cytokines

8. Which of the following do researchers study when examining the human response to stress?
   a. Catastrophes
   b. Significant life changes
   c. Daily hassles
   d. All of the above

9. Which of the below is the best definition of coronary heart disease?
   a. The disruption of the heart's beating and rhythm, which can lead to cardiac arrest
   b. The clogging of the vessels that nourish the heart muscle
   c. The sudden and complete cessation of the heart valve's opening and closing
   d. The quickening of the heart's rhythm, which can quickly lead to exhaustion of the cardiac muscle

10. As researchers discovered the correlation between stress and coronary heart disease, they determined that certain personality types differed in their reactions to stressors. Which type was more susceptible to heart attacks and stroke?
    a. Type A
    b. Type B
    c. Type C
    d. Types A and B were equally susceptible to heart attacks, but had different response patterns

11. Jack is a trader at the New York Stock Exchange. When the market falls quickly, Jack has to continuously relay messages from his boss to the market floor and back, buying and selling so fast that he can barely keep up. At the end of these days, he has intense, painful headaches. Such headaches might be classified as
    a. psychophysiological.
    b. psychosomatic.
    c. a telltale sign of general adaptation syndrome.
    d. an early indication of coronary heart disease.

12. The white blood cells that form in the bone marrow and release antibodies that fight bacterial infections are called
    a. macrophages.
    b. T lymphocytes.
    c. B lymphocytes.
    d. cytokines.

13. According to Sheldon Cohen in the video, the symptoms of a cold are
    a. an indicator of the severity of the infection.
    b. not caused by an infectious agent, but by the immune system's *response* to the infection.
    c. not caused by an infectious agent, but by macrophages, which attempt to "smoke out" the invading agent.
    d. the direct cause of an invader and its attack on the central nervous system.

14. In the video, John Cacioppo describes an experiment done on caregivers of Alzheimer's patients. When screening the caregivers' blood for lymphocytes, what did they find?
    a. Their lymphocytes had overpowered and eliminated cytokine levels
    b. The caregivers had contracted Alzheimer's disease themselves
    c. Their levels of lymphocytes were significantly higher than normal
    d. Their levels of lymphocytes were significantly lower than normal

15. According to evidence presented in both the text and video, which statement is the most accurate regarding the relationship between stress and the immune system?
    a. Stress activates foreign invaders that would otherwise lie dormant
    b. Stress does not cause illness, but restrains the immune system's ability to fight foreign invaders
    c. Foreign agents invade the body and make it more susceptible to stressors
    d. Stressors wear on the body, causing invading agents such as cancer to generate spontaneously

16. Which of the following is not true regarding the connection between stress and cancer?
    a. Stress and negative emotions have been linked to cancer's progression
    b. Tumors developed sooner and grew larger in rats that were stressed and exposed to carcinogens
    c. Stress/cancer studies are difficult to do in real world population studies
    d. Studies are consistent and conclusive that stress increases incidents of cancer in humans

17. James finds his coworker, Laura, to be sour, rude, and unreliable. After talking to her directly only made the situation worse, he now tries to avoid her and seeks advice from others about how to deal with this stress at the office. This <u>new</u> coping strategy would best be described as
    a. problem-focused coping.
    b. emotion-focused coping.
    c. clinical-focused coping.
    d. behavioral disengagement.

18. While Doug is on an important call, construction workers begin using jackhammers on the street in front of his house. Doug's blood pressure goes up and his muscles tense as his irritation increases. Finally, he changes phones and shuts several doors between himself and the outside noise, which helps the situation. What concept does this demonstrate?
    a. Emotion-focused coping
    b. Predictability of the environment
    c. Social support
    d. Control

19. According to information presented in the video, researchers are increasingly interested in those who survive a life-threatening disease and remarkably bounce back to where they were before. This concept of "what doesn't kill me makes me stronger" is known as
    a. thriving phenomenon.
    b. "rubber ball" theory.
    c. resilience.
    d. boomerang effect.

20. In the video, Margaret Kemeny states that people who were able to face a life threatening illness and assign some meaning to it
    a. were less likely to begin smoking.
    b. were more likely to have a *faith factor* in their lives.
    c. seemed to have worse health outcomes than those who didn't look for meaning.
    d. seem to do better physiologically than those who didn't.

21. Which of the factors below might contribute to the fact that those who regularly attend religious services are more likely to live longer?
    a. Church attendees are more likely to have social support
    b. Religions often encourage healthy behaviors
    c. Women are more likely to be active in church and women live longer anyway
    d. All of the above

22. Which of the following is <u>not</u> true of smoking?
    a. Smoking correlates with higher rates of depression and divorce
    b. Most smokers begin the habit during adolescence
    c. Most teen smokers take up the habit due to the power of cigarette advertising
    d. Teens are less likely to smoke if their parents and friends are nonsmokers

23. What happened in the month-long experiment where obese patients had their calories reduced from 3500 to 450?
    a. They steadily lost 6 percent of their weight during the experiment
    b. They lost 6 percent of their weight, then weight loss leveled off
    c. Changes in weight were negligible until the last week when their metabolism boosted
    d. The men lost weight steadily while the women had difficulty

24. Which of the following is <u>not</u> true regarding fat cells?
    a. A typical adult has 30 to 40 billion
    b. The number of fat cells an individual has never increases, only their size increases
    c. The number of fat cells an individual has as an adult never decreases
    d. In obese people, fat cells can swell to two or three times their normal size

25. Which of the following would <u>not</u> be a way to change the environment and affect obesity in our society?
    a. Encourage obese people to accept their weight
    b. The so-called "twinkie tax"
    c. Create a zone around schools that is fast food-free
    d. Ban junk food advertising to kids

ANSWER KEY FOR THE ACTIVE REVIEW EXERCISES

1. Health psychology, behavioral medicine, process, demands, ability; [1, 2] Textbook, Video 17
2. fight-or-flight, increase, cortisol, hippocampus; [3, 4] Textbook, Video 17
3. avoid, smaller; [3] Video 17
4. alarm, resistance, exhaustion; [3] Text
5. coronary heart disease; A; increased, B [6] Textbook, Video 17
6. psychophysiological; lymphocytes; cytokines; worsen; more; [7] Textbook, Video 17
7. AIDS; true; cancer; [8] Textbook, Video 17
8. coping; problem; emotion; [9] Text
9. less; decreases; social support; lower; activate; [10] Textbook, Video 17
10. aerobic exercise; reduces; biofeedback; meditation; [12] Text
11. resilience; meaning; [11] Video 17
12. cigarette smoking; heroin; stimulates; [13] Textbook, Video 17
13. 65; more; decreases; men; [14] Text
14. women; consume, expend; less; decreases; shrink; [14] Text
15. similar, genetic; lower, more, less; [14] Text
16. gain it back; boost, binge; [15] Text

ANSWER KEY FOR THE SELF TEST

Item #	Answer	Learning Outcome #	Source	Item #	Answer	Learning Outcome #	Source
1.	c	1	Textbook	14.	a	7	Video 17
2.	b	2	Textbook	15.	b	7	Video 17
3.	c	2	Video 17	16.	b	8	Textbook
4.	d	3	Textbook, Video 17	17.	d	9	Textbook
5.	c	3	Video 17	18.	a	10	Video 17
6.	d	3	Video 17	19.	d	10	Video 17
7.	d	3	Textbook	20.	c	10	Textbook, Video 17
8.	a	4	Textbook, Video 17	21.	d	13	Textbook, Video 17
9.	a	6	Textbook, Video 17	22.	a	14	Textbook
10.	c	6	Textbook	23.	b	14	Textbook
11.	b	7	Textbook	24.	b	14	Textbook
12.	b	7	Textbook	25.	b	15	Textbook
13.	d	7	Textbook				

Lesson 18 (Personality)

The Enduring Self

Assignments

Reading: Chapter 15, "Personality" in *Psychology* by David Myers (Modules 44, 45, and 46 in the modular version of *Psychology*)

Video: Episode 18, "The Enduring Self"

LEARNING OUTCOMES

Familiarize yourself with the Learning Outcomes for this lesson before you begin the assignments. Return to them to check your learning after completing the Steps to Learning Success. Careful work on these materials should equip you to accomplish the outcomes.

Introduction (Module 44)

1. Discuss **personality**'s essential characteristics and relate them to the examples that introduce the *Inside Out* episode "The Enduring Self."

The Psychoanalytic Perspective (Module 44)

2. Briefly associate Sigmund Freud's background with his development of the theory of **psychoanalysis,** the first comprehensive theory of personality.

3. Recognize Freud's ideas regarding the **unconscious** and the techniques he used to bring these submerged thoughts and feelings to the level of conscious analysis.

4. Differentiate among the interactive roles Freud attributed to the **id**, the **ego**, and the **superego**—the three systems Freud considered basic to personality's structure.

5. Compare Freud's belief that children's personalities develop through psychosocial stages to Hazel Markus' comments regarding the family and the shaping of self.

6. Indicate the role Freud assigned to **defense mechanisms** and provide examples.

7. Draw distinctions between the ideas of **neo-Freudian** and **psychodynamic** theorists and the original work of Sigmund Freud.

8. Summarize Freud's contribution to the study of personality, and how his theories are regarded in light of current-day psychological science.

The Humanistic Perspective (Module 45)

9. Distinguish the **humanistic perspective** on personality from the psychoanalytic approach of Sigmund Freud and the behaviorist approach of B. F. Skinner.

10. Briefly describe Abraham Maslow's concept of **self actualization** and Carl Rogers' **person-centered perspective**.

11. Recognize the contributions of humanistic philosophers to modern culture, and criticisms of some of this perspective's basic tenets.

The Trait Perspective (Module 46)

12. Be aware of the basic difference between the **trait perspective** and the historical psychoanalytic approach to personality.

13. Identify at least two approaches trait researchers use to establish basic personality traits.

14. Describe the extent to which biological factors influence personality traits.

15. Identify the traits researchers have dubbed "the big five" and several endpoints for each dimension.

16. Specify the features required for a high-quality **personality inventory**, and explain why even those attributes cannot guarantee validity.

17. Develop arguments for and against competing points of view in the **person-situation controversy**; include the research related to the consistency of **expressive** and **less-expressive personality styles**.

The Social-Cognitive Perspective (Module 46)

18. Differentiate the **social-cognitive** view on personality from the other perspectives we have explored.

19. Relate the concepts of **reciprocal determinism** and **human agency** to the social-cognitive perspective.

20. Compare **internal locus of control** with **external local of control**, and **optimism** with **pessimism**,

recognizing the effect these states of mind have on the individual and his/her performance.

21. Indicate the major concern that is expressed regarding the social-cognitive perspective.

Exploring the Self (Module 46)

22. Recognize the significance of the **self** in relation to personality, and summarize current research in the field.

23. Relate **high** and **low self-esteem** to an individual's health, performance, and reactions to negative feedback.

24. Discuss **self-serving bias** tendencies and the difference between **secure** and **defensive self-esteem**.

25. Explain how stigmatized groups maintain their level of self-esteem.

ACTIVE REVIEW

Each item in this section is based on material presented in the video or the textbook assignment for this lesson, or both. Complete this section, referring as needed to your notes or the source materials themselves. Answers are provided at the end of this lesson.

Introduction

1. Psychologists define **personality** as a person's characteristic pattern of _____, _____, and _____. The "classroom avengers" that Dr. Jim McGee profiles are generally *(above / below)* average intelligence, *(Caucasion / African American or Latino)* and *(upbeat / depressed)*.

2. Psychotherapist Neil Clark Warren was so concerned about the number of marriages that end in divorce that he conducted what he calls "divorce _____." In about *(40 / 60 / 75)* percent of the cases, he reports, the marriages he studied were in trouble the day they started. That began his search for qualities like _____ _____ that tend to sustain the marriage bond.

3. A practical reason for interest in personality, says Daniel Weiss, is the fact that different _____ are related to _____. As an example, he cites test pilot Chuck Yeager who, when the X2 he

was flying was plunging toward earth, was not _____. He was methodically reviewing his *(checklist / escape procedures)*, hoping something would work before he hit the ground.

The Psychoanalytic Perspective

4. The psychologist most often recognized historically is _____ _____, an Austrian physician whose theories were an outgrowth of his work with people suffering from nervous disorders. His attempts to understand his patients' conditions, which seemed to have no _____ basis, led to the development of his theory of _____, the first comprehensive theory of personality.

5. If these disorders had no clear physical cause, Freud reasoned, they must have a _____ basis, deeply buried in the patient's *(conscious / unconscious)* mind. Freud used _____ _____ and _____ _____ to trace at these thoughts back to their source in the unconscious for analysis.

6. Freud compared the mind to a/an _____. Our *(conscious / unconscious)* awareness is visible above

the surface, but underneath is a much larger *(conscious / unconscious)* area full of troublesome passions and thoughts we constantly try to *(enhance / repress)*. This effort is never completely _____.

7. Personality, according to Freud, results from the conflict between three interacting systems: the _____, which unconsciously seeks immediate gratification of its sexual and aggressive drives; the _____, our conscious, moral sense of right and wrong; and the _____, which attempts to ameliorate the conflict between the impulses of the first and the restraints imposed by the second as well as the outside world.

8. It was Freud's contention that children develop through **psychosexual stages**. Failure to progress through a stage successfully may cause a person to become stuck or _____ in that stage, and result in _____ behavior.

9. Hazel Markus agrees with Freud's belief that if you want to understand a person, you must look into their _____ context. However, the Freudian model sees the self as much more _____. He thought that once your personality is shaped, you are then *(free to make changes / stuck with it)*. We see the self as much more *(fixed / malleable)*.

10. In order to keep ourselves from becoming anxious as a result of the ongoing conflict between the id and the superego, Freud said, the ego employs protective defense mechanisms such as _____ (banishing anxiety-arousing thoughts from consciousness), _____ (attributing behaviors I don't like in myself to other people), and _____ (justifying our actions with explanations that stray from the truth).

11. Although neo-Freudians and contemporary psychodynamic psychologists agree with some of Freud's ideas regarding the unconscious and the shaping of _____ and attachments in childhood, most feel that _____ and _____ are not the driving forces that Freud thought. Your text also notes that projection-type tests often used to uncover hidden feelings and motivations *(are / are not)* well known for _____ (accuracy of their predictions) or _____ (consistency of their results). In light of recent research, how do psychologists today view Sigmund Freud? As you re-read and re-listen to some of the overarching assessments provided in the text chapter and video, fill in the chart below.

Critics of Freud's Theory of Psychoanalysis contend...	Supporters of Freud's Theory of Psychoanalysis claim...

The Humanistic Perspective

12. In the 1960s some personality psychologists became disenchanted with Freud's *(positive / negative)* views of personality and B. F. Skinner's brand of _____. These _____ psychologists focused on *(sick / healthy)* people and their drive for self-determination and self-realization.

13. Abraham Maslow proposed that people are motivated by a hierarchy of needs ranging from basic _____ needs to the highest step in the hierarchy—the need for _____. Achieving one set of needs allows us to focus on the next category in the sequence. Maslow developed his ideas by studying *(healthy / unhealthy)* individuals rather than people who are *(productive / troubled)*.

14. Carl Rogers *(agreed / disagreed)* with Maslow that people are basically *(good / bad)* and seek **self-actualization.** People can achieve growth and fulfillment if they are nurtured by people who are _____ (open and self-disclosing), _____ (offering what Rogers called unconditional positive regard), and _____ (listening and sharing our feelings)

15. Both Maslow and Rogers believed that a person's _____ is the essential feature of their personality. Today's _____ _____, as David Myers points out, are carrying on this legacy by studying the roots of positive well–being, and thinking about how we can nurture human virtues. How is the humanistic perspective currently perceived by psychological scientists? As you study and think about this section, fill in the chart below.

Influence of Humanistic Psychology	Criticisms of Humanistic Psychology

The Trait Perspective

16. Today's personality researchers are more interested in investigating the basic _____ of personality than in constructing grand _____. One of the ways people have studied personality is to try to see if they can identify behavior patterns in people that are _____ over _____.

17. There are a number of approaches researchers have used to isolate basic personality **traits**. One method is to place individuals at points on several _____ dimensions simultaneously. Another is to apply a _____ analysis to identify key dimensions of personality, such as _____-introversion, or emotional stability-_____.

18. Many traits have _____ underpinnings. As Terry Sejnowski explains in the video, there's a clear _____ component that has to do with set points for our different neuromodulatory systems. That *(is / is not)* to say that these systems are set for good, especially when context and culture come into play. Jerome Kagan illustrates this fact in his research with children who begin life with a very low threshold of excitability in the amygdala, and are considered _____. But, as he emphasizes, this shyness can be _____.

19. One of the most popular lists of personality traits is known as the Big Five. Peter Salovey uses the acronym OCEAN, and David Myers the word CANOE as prompts to help us remember what they are. See if you can identify the traits:

    _____ _____

    _____ _____

    _____

20. In recent years **personality inventories** have become an increasingly *(rare / common)* way to measure a wide range of feelings and behaviors. Items on the **MMPI**, a widely used assessment tool, are empirically derived; the tests are _____ scored. Objectivity *(does / does not)* guarantee validity. Why? People may not answer truthfully. Joyce Bishop notes that it's important to take a careful look at the results of any inventory or assessment to see

    _____.

21. Critics of the trait perspective note that although a person's basic traits may *(change / persist)* over time, their specific _____ tend to *(vary / remain constant)* from situation to situation, depending on the environment. Thus, critics contend, traits *(are / are not)* good predictors of behavior. Trait researchers insist that on _____, behavior tends to be

fairly _____. This disagreement is known as the **person-situation controversy**.

22. Researchers who have studied expressive and _____ expressive personality styles have demonstrated how *(consistent / inconsistent)* traits can be in various situations. It seems that we have *(amazing / little)* voluntary control over our expressiveness.

23. Think about Daniel Weiss' question regarding whether or not these dimensions or traits add up to a personality. In addition to the social self that people see, is there an internal self that is private? Even you may not always see or understand it. Is what happens outside our awareness important to personality? *(Yes or No?)*

The Social-Cognitive Perspective

24. The **social-cognitive perspective** on personality proposed by Albert Bandura applies the principles of _____ and _____ to the study of personality. Personalities are shaped by feelings and thoughts, the environment, and our _____.

25. Social-cognitive researchers are interested in how people are affected by their _____. By observing people in _____ situations, they can predict how they will _____ in similar situations.

26. Think about Dr. Bandura's own life path, which he related in the video. Is there anything in his story that would suggest he would become a noted psychologist and researcher? What does he indicate would have been a more likely scenario?_____

_____

_____

27. Dr. Bandura's own experience is one of the reasons he has such faith in human **agency**. He calls the process of interacting with our environment

_____ _____.

Different people, for example, choose different _____. Our personalities shape how we _____ and react to events. In addition, our personalities help create _____

to which we react. As David Myers observes in your text, "… we are both products and the architects of our environment."

28. The term _____ **locus of control** refers to people who believe that, to a large extent, they control their own destinies. When people feel buffeted by outside forces beyond their ability to manage, the locus of control is referred to as _____. When faced with a series of such events, both people and _____ tend to resign themselves to the situation and adapt a passive state of _____

_____.

29. "The most central and pervasive mechanism of agency," Dr. Bandura notes, "is people's belief in their efficacy." Without that they have no _____ to act or persevere in the face of difficulties. In terms of performance, moderate optimism has _____ effects; _____ tends to take the opposite path.

30. Critics of the social-cognitive perspective charge that researchers are so focused on the *(situation / person)* that they lose sight of the *(situation / person)*. Among the areas this perspective ignores are _____ _____, _____, and biologically-influenced _____.

Exploring the Self

31. Hazel Marcus refers to the self as our operating center, the _____ of thoughts, feelings, and actions. It is a product of the various interactions and experiences we have, as well as a(n) _____ that helps us make sense of everything that surrounds and affects us.

32. One research study, cited in your textbook, refers to the spotlight effect. This is the tendency to *(overestimate / underestimate)* the extent to which others notice our appearance, performance, and mistakes. In one study only _____ percent of a class noticed when their classmates walked in self-consciously wearing Barry Manilow T-shirts.

33. Recent research by Dr. Marcus and her colleagues focuses on the idea of *(a unitary self / multiple selves)*. This concept is particularly *(appealing / bothersome)* to the Latino community, says Angela Ginorio, because it is future-oriented and developed in the context of _____ _____. She also notes that this idea is much *(more / less)* predictive of behavior for Latinos than self-esteem.

34. Jot down some of the dividends that are associated with a healthy self image, or high self-esteem.

    _____

    _____.

    Low self-esteem tends to be linked to:

    _____

    _____.

35. Contemporary researchers *(agree / doubt)* that high self-esteem is an armor that shields children from life's problems. Self-esteem reflects _____ and it does not help a child to artificially inflate it. Over time, Travis Gibbs notes, we may learn to pay less attention to *(internal / external)* feedback and become more comfortable with *(internal / external)* judgments. The textbook terms that _____ self esteem.

36. James Blascovich contrasts the reactions of people with high or low, stable or unstable self esteem. Research demonstrated that people with unstable high self esteem were much *(more / less)* threatened by negative performance feedback than people with stable _____ self esteem.

37. Dr. Gibbs points out that children with high self esteem will become more proficient in a particular area with *(positive / negative)* feedback. Why? Because *(positive / negative)* feedback shuts down the information search. For children with low self esteem, negative feedback *(improves / adversely affects)* their performance.

38. Self-serving bias, the tendency to perceive ourselves _____, means that we are *(more / less)* likely to accept credit for successes than we are for failures. We also like to see ourselves as _____ than _____ drivers or, or applying David Myers' example to you, _____.

39. Stigmatized groups—ethnic minorities, the disabled, women—may have a *(much higher / somewhat lower)* self esteem than most people think. As Claude Steele notes, people in these groups base their self esteem on achievements that are not devalued and _____ or downplay those that are.

SELF TEST

Read each question and circle the letter of the best answer. When you have completed the Self Test, check your answers against the key at the end of this lesson. If you have answered any items incorrectly, review the appropriate materials to correct misunderstandings and cement your knowledge.

1. Which of the following represents the definition contemporary psychologists use to describe personality?
   a. An individual's thoughts and actions that are controlled by the unconscious
   b. The conflict between our biological impulses and the social restraints we place on them
   c. The temperament we are born with
   d. An individual's characteristic pattern of thinking, feeling, and acting

2. Freud crafted his theory of psychoanalysis when
   a. patients asked him for help in understanding their unsettling dreams.
   b. he could find no physiological reason for his patients' nervous disorders.
   c. the field seemed ready for a comprehensive theory of personality.
   d. he was dissatisfied with the minimal attention given to mental illness.

3. Freud would categorize the strong desire to go out and party with friends as a natural function of the
   a. id.
   b. superego.
   c. ego.
   d. preconscious.

4. In comparison to Freud, how do contemporary psychologists view the unconscious mind?
   a. The troublesome feelings that dominate the unconscious exert a powerful influence on our lives.
   b. We process enormous amounts of information outside of our awareness.
   c. People try to block or repress unacceptable thoughts and passions that dominate the unconscious mind.
   d. "Slips of the tongue" and the content of dreams provide the trained psychotherapist with a glimpse into the unconscious mind of a patient.

5. Like Freud, contemporary psychologists acknowledge the importance of the family context in understanding the personality of an individual, but unlike the Freudian model, they see personality as much
   a. more fixed.
   b. less complex.
   c. more malleable.
   d. more aggressive and sexual.

6. In order to keep ourselves from becoming anxious as a result of the ongoing conflict between the id and superego, Freud theorized that the ego employs
   a. protective defense mechanisms.
   b. alter egos to confuse the id and superego.
   c. mind games that direct attention away from the conflict.
   d. a neutral approach that allows us to rationally deal with the inner conflict.

7. Your boyfriend, in the throes of a major meltdown, accuses you of being angry all the time. What defense mechanism is he using?
   a. Rationalization
   b. Displacement
   c. Repression
   d. Projection

8. The humanistic perspective on personality
   a. has a more negative view of human nature and personality than Freud's psychoanalytic theories.
   b. is scientifically objective in contrast to B. F. Skinner's behaviorism.
   c. regards self-concept—how we respond to the question "Who am I?"—as an essential component of personality.
   d. enjoys widespread support among psychological scientists today.

9. In light of recent research, which of the following statements should <u>not</u> be included in a summary of how psychologists today view Sigmund Freud?
   a. Many of Freud's basic ideas cannot be verified by scientific methods; they offer only after-the-fact explanations.
   b. Development is lifelong, not fixed in childhood as Freud maintained.
   c. Current research does not support Freud's view that the unconscious mind is seething with sexual and aggressive motives.
   d. There is no credible research that supports Freud's ideas about repressed memories and other defense mechanisms designed to defend the unconscious or protect self esteem.

10. Attribute the following statement to the humanistic psychologist(s) below: "People are basically good, and have an enormous capacity to grow and achieve their potential."
    a. Abraham Maslow
    b. Carl Jung
    c. Carl Rogers
    d. both Carl Rogers and Abraham Maslow

11. The set points for our neuromodulatory systems are
    a. genetically derived.
    b. static over time.
    c. the same for all people.
    d. not statistically relevant to personality.

Match the trait dimension with the description below.

   a. Extraversion
   b. Neuroticism
   c. Conscientiousness
   d. Agreeableness

12. Joseph is suspicious of anyone who walks down his street.

13. Even in an emergency situation, Zoe seems calm and collected.

14. Cody is the life of the party.

15. Gina keeps losing her driver's license.

16. All but one of the following apply to personality inventories. Which item does <u>not</u> belong?
    a. Personality inventories are questionnaires that ask people to respond to items that measure a broad range of feelings and behaviors.
    b. Respected inventories like MMPI are empirically derived and objectively scored.
    c. MMPI measures abnormal personality tendencies rather than normal personality traits.
    d. The objectivity employed in creating the MMPI guarantees the validity of the test.

17. In studying expressive and less-expressive styles, researchers have found
    a. just how inconsistent traits can be in various situations.
    b. that we have little voluntary control over our expressiveness.
    c. that expressive and less-expressive traits tend to be consistent in a variety of contexts.
    d. both b and c.

18. Personality, according to social-cognitive researchers, is influenced by all but one of the following. Identify the <u>incorrect</u> item.
    a. Feelings and thoughts
    b. Unconscious motivations
    c. The environment
    d. Our behavior

19. Social-cognitive researchers observe people in _____ situations.
    a. real
    b. contrived
    c. controlled
    d. emotional

20. You might logically predict that Albert Bandura, having grown up in a small village in Alberta, Canada, would _____. He actually became _____.
    a. follow the pattern of his community; a labor negotiator.
    b. work in the fields, play pool, and drink; a professor and researcher.
    c. become an environmentalist; an industrialist psychologist.
    d. emigrate as had his parents; disenchanted with his adopted country and return to Alberta.

21. Albert Bandura cites the H. G. Wells quotation "Reasonable people adapt to the world; unreasonable ones try to change it." This is an example of
    a. external locus of control.
    b. reciprocal determinism.
    c. human agency.
    d. unconscious motivation.

22. The research related to multiple selves by Hazel Markus and her colleagues
    a. is an example of dissociative identity disorder.
    b. has been discounted by the Latino community.
    c. causes confusion in a world that is already diverse.
    d. illustrates that there are many equally viable ways of being.

23. Which of the following statements regarding self-esteem is <u>most</u> accurate?
    a. High self-esteem is an armor that shields children from life's problems.
    b. Self-esteem emerges from reality; it does not help a child to artificially inflate his or her accomplishments.
    c. Secure self esteem is dependent on external evaluations.
    d. Defensive self esteem is less egotistical, less focused on maintaining status whatever the cost.

24. Groups that face discrimination—stigmatized groups—a have a higher level of self-esteem than people think. They tend to base their self esteem on achievements that are _____ and _____ those that are.
    a. not devalued; downplay
    b. common to all groups; concentrate on
    c. devalued; ignore
    d. of little importance to them; focus on

25. Travis Gibbs points out that children with high self esteem will become more proficient in a particular area with ____ feedback because ____ feedback shuts down the impetus to dig deeper.
    a. positive; negative
    b. no; too much
    c. negative; positive
    d. detailed; unsubstantiated

ANSWER KEY FOR THE ACTIVE REVIEW EXERCISES

1. thinking; feeling, acting; above; Caucasion; depressed; [1] Textbook, Video 18
2. autopsy; 75%; emotional stability; [1] Video 18
3. traits; performance; anxious; checklist; [1] Video 18
4. Sigmund Freud; physical; psychoanalysis; [2] Textbook, Video 18
5. psychological; unconscious; free association; dream interpretation; [3] Textbook, Video 18

6. iceberg; conscious; unconscious; repress; successful; [3] Texbook; Video 18
7. id; superego; ego; [4] Textbook, Video 18
8. fixated; maladaptive; [5] Textbook
9. family; fixed; stuck with it; malleable; [5] Video 18
10. repression; projection; rationalization; [6] Textbook, Video 18
11. personality; sex; aggression; are not; validity; reliability; [7] Texbook

Critics of Freud's theory of psychoanalysis contend...	Supporters of Freud's theory of psychoanalysis claim...
Many of Freud's basic ideas cannot be verified by scientific methods; they offer only after-the-fact explanations.	Freud used psychoanalysis as a way to provide meaning to human existence, not as predictive science.
Current research does not support Freud's view that the unconscious mind is "seething with sexual and aggressive motives." It sees a cooler unconscious that is processing a lot of information automatically.	Freud drew attention to the unconscious, the struggle to cope with anxiety, and the conflict between biological impulses and social restraints...all valued contributions.
There is no credible research that supports Freud's ideas about repressed memories and other defense mechanisms linked to defense of the unconscious.	Research does support defense mechanisms that seem to be designed to protect self esteem.
Development is lifelong, not fixed in childhood; we gain gender identity earlier than Freud thought, even without a same sex parent present.	"If you're doing psychoanalytic work, somewhere at the heart of it" is the work of Sigmund Freud.

12. negative; behaviorism; humanistic; healthy; [9] Textbook, Video 18
13. physiological; self-actualization; healthy; troubled; [10] Textbook

14. agreed; good; genuine; accepting; empathetic; [10] Textbook
15. self-concept; positive psychologists; [10] Textbook, Video 18

Influence of Humanistic Psychology	Criticisms of Humanistic Psychology
Impact evident in counseling and education, in nurturing children and motivating employees	Concepts vague and subjective
Has become the basis for much of today's popular psychology.	Individualist, self-centered values can lead to selfishness and erosion of moral restraints.
Self-acceptance, supporters argue, is first step to loving others.	Naïve and optimistic; fails to appreciate human capacity for evil.

16. dimensions; theories; stable; time; [12] Textbook, Video 18
17. trait; factor; extroversion; instability; [13] Textbook
18. biological; genetic; is not; shy; conquered; [14] Textbook, Video 18
19. openness; conscientiousness; extraversion; agreeableness; neuroticism; [15] Textbook, Video 18
20. common; objectively; does not; what this tells me about myself; [16] Textbook, Video 18
21. persist; behaviors; vary; are not; average; consistent; [17] Textbook, Video 18
22. less; consistent; little; [17] Textbook
23. yes; [17] Video 18

24. learning; cognition; behavior; [18] Textbook, Video 18
25. environment *or* surroundings; real; behave; [18] Textbook, Video 18
26. working in the fields; playing pool; drinking excessively; [19] Video 18
27. reciprocal determinism, environments, interpret, situations; [19] Textbook
28. internal; external; animals; learned helplessness; [20] Textbook, Video 18
29. incentive; positive; pessimism; [20] Textbook, Video 18
30. situation; person; unconscious motives; emotions; traits; [21] Textbook

31. organizer; mediator; [22] Textbook, Video 18
32. overestimate; 23; [22] Textbook
33. multiple selves; appealing; social relations; more; [22] Textbook, Video 18
34. Answers include fewer sleepless nights, less pressure to conform; persistence at difficult tasks, less shy and lonely; answers include unhappiness, despair, social rejection; [23] Textbook

35. doubt; reality; external; internal; secure; [24] Textbook, Video 18
36. more; high; [23] Video 18
37. negative; positive; adversely affects; [23] Video 18
38. favorably; more; better; average; students; [24] Textbook, Video 18
39. much higher; ignore; [2] Textbook, Video 18

ANSWER KEY FOR THE SELF TEST

Item #	Answer	Learning Outcome #	Source	Item #	Answer	Learning Outcome #	Source
1.	d	1	Textbook, Video 18	14.	d	15	Textbook, Video 18
2.	b	2	Textbook	15.	a	15	Textbook, Video 18
3.	a	4	Textbook	16.	d	16	Textbook, Video 18
4.	b	3	Textbook, Video 18	17.	d	17	Textbook
5.	c	5	Textbook, Video 18	18.	b	18	Textbook, Video 18
6.	a	6	Textbook, Video 18	19.	a	18	Textbook
7.	d	6	Textbook, Video 18	20.	b	19	Video 18
8.	c	9	Textbook	21.	c	20	Video 18
9.	d	8	Textbook, Video 18	22.	d	22	Video 18
10.	d	10	Textbook	23.	b	24	Textbook, Video 18
11.	a	14	Textbook, Video 18	24.	a	25	Textbook, Video 18
12.	c	15	Textbook, Video 18	25.	c	23	Video
13.	b	15	Textbook, Video 18				

Lesson 19 (Anxiety and Personality Disorders)

Out of Balance

> **Assignments**
>
> **Reading:** "Perspectives on Psychological Disorders," "Anxiety Disorders," and "Personality Disorders" in Chapter 16 of David Myers' *Psychology* (Modules 47, 48, and 49 in *Psychology in Modules*)
>
> **Video:** Episode 19, "Out of Balance"

LEARNING OUTCOMES

Familiarize yourself with the Learning Outcomes for this lesson before you begin the assignments. Return to them to check your learning after completing the Steps to Learning Success. Careful work on these materials should equip you to accomplish the outcomes.

Perspectives on Psychological Disorders (Module 47)

1. Specify the criteria used to distinguish a **psychological disorder** (like depression) from the normal fluctuations that are a part of everyday living.

2. Describe how opinions related to the cause of psychological disorders have changed through the years; cite the causal factors recognized today by psychological science.

3. Recognize the role of **DSM-IV** in classifying psychological disorders.

4. Be aware of the potential benefits and possible disadvantages of using diagnostic labels, citing specific research studies.

Anxiety Disorders (Module 48)

5. Briefly summarize the characteristics of **anxiety disorders** and how these disorders differ from normal feelings of stress and apprehension.

6. Give examples of the symptoms of **generalized anxiety disorder** and **panic disorder**.

7. Distinguish the experience of **phobias** from the normal sensation of fear.

8. Describe the symptoms of and physiological basis for **obsessive compulsive disorder**.

9. Recognize the symptoms of **post-traumatic stress disorder**, and the factors that account for why some people will develop **PTSD** and others will not.

10. Summarize the contributions of conditioned and observational learning to the development of anxiety disorders.

11. Discuss the role that natural selection, genetics, and brain function play in the development of anxiety disorders.

Personality Disorders (Module 49)

12. Identify the disruptive patterns that characterize the major types of **personality disorders**.

13. Recognize the differences among personality disorders linked to **anxiety**, to **eccentric behaviors**, and to **dramatic or impulsive behaviors**.

14. Develop a verbal profile of someone with **antisocial personality disorder**, and state the biological and environmental factors that contribute to it.

ACTIVE REVIEW

Each item in this section is based on material presented in the video or the textbook assignment for this lesson, or both. Complete this section, referring as needed to your notes or the source materials themselves. Answers are provided at the end of this lesson.

Perspectives on Psychological Disorders

1. The line between normal and abnormal, Samuel Baronds observes, is blurry. **Psychological disorders** are just _____ of thoughts, feelings, and actions we all experience.

2. What are the criteria that tip the scale one way or the other? One factor, notes Elaine Walker, is the statistical _____ of the behavior or set of behaviors. If it gets in the way of a person's _____ and _____ functioning, Michael Otto adds, if it is an unusual behavior that's _____, it is more likely to be categorized as a psychological disorder.

3. The criteria, or _____, used to classify a behavior as deviant vary from culture to culture and

with _____. For example, _____ was classified as an illness for over 20 years, from 1952 to 1973. A superb athlete may be exhibiting behavior that deviates from the norm; the difference is it does not cause the athlete _____.

4. Prior to the time we had labels for mental illness, all abnormal behavior was perceived from the perspective of _____. "The devil made him do it!" But with the passage of time, and further observation and study, people began to look at these deviances as illnesses of the mind—psychopathologies that need to be _____ on the basis of _____ and cured through _____, sometimes including treatment in a psychiatric hospital.

5. Today, psychologists believe that serious mental disorders involve both biological and psychosocial components. Fill in the chart that follows, listing contributors to psychological disorders in each of the categories.

Biological influences	Psychological influences	Social-cultural influences

6. The American Psychiatric Association's *Diagnostic and Statistical Manual of Mental Disorders*, called **DSM-IV-TR**, describes *(200 / 300 / 400)* disorders and their *(cause / prevalence)*. It uses _____ definitions that help mental health workers diagnose people with greater _____ than once was true.

7. Why bother to group and make categories? It aids in _____ and _____. But there's also a downside, Michael Otto notes—the sense that some of the lines that have been drawn are *(real / artificial)*, creating _____ out of

continuums. What is starting to emerge from the field of affective neuroscience is a more precise means of categorizing psychiatric disorders by looking at dysfunctions in the _____.

8. Some people are concerned about the negative fallout from such labeling. For example, as James Jones relates, African Americans are often diagnosed with _____, but seldom diagnosed with _____ or _____ disorders. Is that because the incidences are dissimilar, he asks,

or because they're looking at different things and not taking into account relevant cultural disparities?

9. Your textbook notes several classic experiments, one in which eight quite *(normal / disturbed)* people went to the admissions office of a mental hospital complaining of hearing voices. All were diagnosed as mentally *(gifted / ill)*. When they were released 19 days or so later, the clinicians were able to "discover" the _____ for each of their disorders. Not only can labels _____ perceptions; they can change reality.

10. A major struggle in psychiatry, Andrew Leuchter states, is overcoming the _____ associated with mental illness. People don't want to come in for _____ because they think their co-workers, friends, and family will think *(more / less)* of them if they admit they need _____. Kay Redfield Jamison talks about the personal ramifications of having a serious psychological disorder. How would you handle some of the issues she raises?

Anxiety Disorders

11. Anxiety, says James McGee is a *(normal / abnormal)* part of the human condition. We have _____ as a species to be *(brave / scaredy cats)*; it protects us from danger and helps us survive. **Anxiety disorders**, in contrast, are distressing, _____ anxiety or _____ behaviors that *(increase / reduce)* anxiety.

12. **Generalized anxiety disorder** is chronic _____ about a number of life events, beyond that which is normal. The worry seems to take on a life of its own and no longer has an _____ function. People feel *(occasionally / continually)* tense and apprehensive. They may show physical signs such as _____ _____.

13. Susan Mineka compares a **panic attack** to the experience of hiking on a mountain trail and having a bear start chasing you, only there is _____ _____. The experience *(strikes suddenly / evolves slowly)*, is devastating, and *(lingers / disappears)*. This rapid mobilization of the fight or _____ fear response is accom-

panied by a number of physical reactions. List at least two. _____ _____

14. **Phobias** focus anxiety on specific _____, _____, or _____. It is a(n) *(rational / irrational)* fear that *(does / does)* not disrupt behavior. A strong fear can often become a phobia if it brings about a(n) *(natural / unnatural)* desire to avoid the object or situation. Three of the most common phobias are _____ _____ _____.

15. **Obsessive-compulsive disorders** (**OCD**) are conditions characterized by unwanted _____ thoughts and _____. These compulsive rituals are designed to *(eradicate / neutralize / magnify)* the obsessive thoughts and images. For 2 to 3 percent of the population, the rituals become so time-consuming that effective functioning becomes *(somewhat impaired / impossible)*.

16. Jeffrey Schwartz points out that OCD is a neuropsychiatric condition. People really do experience the intrusive thoughts and urges as *(ordinary / nonsensical)*. Brain images of people with OCD show that parts of the brain that monitor our actions and check for errors are *(sluggish / overactive)*. Dr. Schwartz uses the term "brain lock" to describe the situation. The brain is stuck in gear and an error detection message keeps _____ over and over again.

17. Nightmares, intrusive thoughts and images, and the re-experiencing of a traumatic event that a person witnessed but could not _____ are symptoms that characterize _____ _____ _____. A second type of response Daniel Weiss describes has to do with _____, a swinging back and forth between whether or not the traumatic event actually happened.

18. About ____ percent of women and _____ percent of men develop PTSD following a traumatic event. In research conducted by Metin Basoglu and Susan Mineka, the single best predictor of who did not

develop PSTD was level of _____
_____. Another factor that
Daniel Weiss mentions is _____ to other
traumatic events, modified by whether or not there
was some kind of symptomatic response.

19. Researchers have linked anxiety with the classical
_____ of fear. Conditioned fears
may exist long after we have forgotten what caused
them. Some fears may be linked by stimulus
_____; a fear of heights may
link to a fear of flying even though the person has
never flown. Reinforcement helps *(maintain / get rid
of)* the fear. Fear is also learned by _____
others who are afraid, as we saw in Susan Mineka's
experiments with wild- and lab-reared monkeys and
snake fear.

20. From a biological perspective, fear is a _____
mechanism. Natural selection and
_____ have played a major role in
tendency to fear certain things and not others.
Phobias tend to focus on _____ faced by
our ancestors; compulsive behaviors on acts that
(contribute to / inhibit) our survival.

21. Some people may be _____ predisposed
to particular fears or a high level of anxiety. Vulnerability rises when the relative is an _____
_____.

22. Anxiety disorders tend to be _____. They
don't go away unless they are treated. People with
various anxiety disorders show increased activity in
the _____ and associated regions. Many
have more than one anxiety disorder, either concur-
rently or at some point in their lives, as well as
_____ _____. Why do these dis-
orders tend to co-occur? A common factor tends to
be the personality trait _____.

Personality Disorders

23. Personality disorders represent dysfunctional
patterns of thinking, feeling, and acting that impair

one's *(social / cognitive)* functioning. They are princi-
pally disorders of the self that are _____
_____ in origin. These repeated, *(short- /
long-)* term behavior patterns cause distress to the
_____ as well as to others.

24. Personality disorders tend to cluster around several
different facets of behavior. People who are *(confron-
tational / avoidant)* fear rejection and have trouble
dealing with other people. They are part of a group of
personality disorders that expresses _____.
A second group exhibits _____ behavior
such as emotional disengagement. Do you remember
James Masterson's story about the business executive
who didn't get the CEO position?

25. A third cluster demonstrates dramatic or _____
_____ behaviors. For example, those with
_____ personality disorder exag-
gerate their own importance, as sometimes occurs in
the field of _____. But, as Dr. Masterson
cautions, narcissism by itself *(is / is not)* pathologic.
There is no life without _____narcissism,
having a sense of oneself as competent and capable.

26. Most troubling is the _____ personality
disorder, a person whose lack of _____
can be glaringly apparent even before the age of ___.
Antisocial personalities _____ *and* _____
little, as evidenced by their acts of brutality, and their
lack of concern or remorse. Most criminals *(do / do
not)* fit this profile.

27. PET scans of some murderers with antisocial personality disorder show *(decreased / increased)* activity in the
frontal cortex, a brain area that helps control
impulsive, _____ behavior. There is no
_____ for violent criminal behavior, but studies
have shown that _____ _____
can interact with _____ influences
to produce such antisocial behavior.

SELF TEST

Read each question and circle the letter of the best answer. When you have completed the Self Test, check your answers against the key at the end of this lesson. If you have answered any items incorrectly, review the appropriate materials to correct misunderstandings and cement your knowledge.

1. Psychological disorders
   a. affect 450 million people worldwide.
   b. have statistics similar to heart disease and cancer in terms of years lost to disabilities and death.
   c. occur primarily in the United States and countries of Western Europe; many countries of the world report no incidences.
   d. both a and b

2. Prior to the time we had labels for mental illness, all abnormal behavior was perceived from the perspective of
   a. evolution.
   b. religion.
   c. psychopathology.
   d. biopsychosocial phenomenon.

Today's psychologists believe that serious mental disorders involve biological, psychological, and social-cultural components. Link each item below with one of the influences.

   a. biological influences
   b. psychological influences
   c. social-cultural influences

3. "We have evolved as a species," comments Jim McGee, "to be scaredy cats."

4. Jamie is convinced that he cannot succeed in school no matter what he does or how hard he tries.

5. Jose's doesn't understand his Ecuadorian grandmother's belief that black magic, which she calls *susto,* is destroying her family.

6. Kendra keeps reliving the experience of being attacked by a pack of dogs.

7. Tanya, a young teenager, is worried about her vulnerability for schizophrenia. Her mother was diagnosed with the illness at 19.

8. DSM-IV uses _____ to help mental health workers diagnose people with greater reliability than once was true.
   a. causal factors
   b. behavioral definitions
   c. psychologists' reports
   d. actual case studies

9. Why is the labeling of psychological disorders so troubling to mental heath professionals?
   a. Labels create preconceptions that guide what we see and how we interpret behaviors.
   b. Labels can stigmatize a person and affect how others react to them.
   c. The "insanity" label used in some legal defenses raises both moral and ethical questions.
   d. All of the above.

10. Which of the following pairs of disorders are included in the category of anxiety disorders?
    a. Phobias and depressions
    b. Panic and bipolar disorders
    c. Obsessive compulsive disorder and agoraphobia
    d. Generalized anxiety and personality disorders

11. All but one of the following is a symptom of generalized anxiety disorder. Identify the item that should <u>not</u> be included.
    a. Uncontrollable, inappropriate laughter
    b. Frequently feeling tense and apprehensive
    c. Chronic worry that no longer has an adaptive function
    d. Difficulty in concentrating

12. In comparison to the source of panic attacks, the source of post-traumatic stress disorders is undoubtedly
    a. real.
    b. imaginary.
    c. less debilitating.
    d. faked.

13. Phobias focus anxiety on specific
    a. objects.
    b. activities.
    c. situations.
    d. All of the above

14. Brain images of people with OCD show that parts of the basal ganglia and frontal cortex are
    a. sluggish.
    b. overactive.
    c. missing.
    d. enlarged and misshapened.

15. The fact that a fear of heights may link to a fear of flying although a person has never been aboard an airplane is an example of
    a. stimulus generalization.
    b. the copycat syndrome.
    c. reinforcement.
    d. agoraphobia.

16. People often have more than one anxiety disorder or an anxiety disorder plus a mood disorder like depression. Why do these disorders tend to co-occur? Among the causes, which one of the following stands out?
    a. Neuroticism
    b. Narcissism
    c. Evolution
    d. Genetic predisposition

17. Personality disorders are
    a. more easily remedied than anxiety disorders because they tend to be superficial and of short duration.
    b. of little interest to mental health professionals since there is not much you can do to alleviate such patterns of behavior.
    c. inflexible and enduring patterns of behavior that impair social functioning.
    d. Both b and c above.

18. Narcissism, as James Masterson points out,
    a. is not necessarily pathologic; there is no life without healthy narcissism.
    b. can be so destructive that he recommends children avoid involvement with sports until they are 15 or older.
    c. is part of the eccentric cluster of disorders.
    d. cannot be treated effectively.

19. Brain scans of murderers show _____ activation in the frontal cortex, an area where impulses and aggression are _____.
    a. increased; controlled
    b. reduced; generated
    c. double the; generated
    d. reduced; controlled

ANSWER KEY FOR THE ACTIVE REVIEW EXERCISES

1. exaggerations; [1] Video 19
2. frequency; social; occupational; dysfunctional; [1] Video 19
3. standards; time; homosexuality; distress; [1] Textbook
4. religion; diagnosed; symptoms; therapy; [2] Textbook; Video 19
5. See table below; [2] Textbook, Video 19

Biological influences	Psychological influences	Social-cultural influences
Genetic predisposition	Stress	Roles (gender-linked)
Brain structure and chemistry	Mood-related perceptions and memories	Definitions of normalcy and disorder
Evolutionary emergence	Trauma	Expectations
	Learned helplessness	

6. 400; prevalence; behavioral; reliability; [3] Textbook, Video 19
7. communication; research; artificial, categories, brain; [3] Video 19
8. schizophrenia; affective; bipolar; [4] Video 19
9. normal; ill; cause; bias; [4] Textbook
10. stigma; treatment; less; help; [4] Video 19
11. normal; scaredy cats; evolved; persistent; maladaptive; reduce; [5] Textbook, Video 19
12. worry; adaptive; continually; sleeplessness, muscular tension, trembling, perspiring, and nervous twitches; [5] Textbook, Video 19
13. no bear; strikes suddenly; disappears; flight; heart pounding, shortness of breath, choking sensation, numbness and tingling, mouth dry, heard to focus, trembling; [5] Textbook, Video 19
14. objects, activities, or situations; irrational; does; fear of animals, heights, blood, flying, closed-in spaces like elevators or caves; [7] Textbook
15. repetitive; actions; neutralize; impossible; [8] Textbook, Video 19
16. nonsensical; overactive; repeating or playing; [8, 11] Textbook, Video 19

17. control; post-traumatic stress disorder; avoidance; [9] Textbook, Video 19
18. 10; 20; psychological preparedness; exposure; [9] Textbook, Video 19
19. conditioning; generalization; maintain; observing; [10] Textbook, (DVD Find Out More, *Is Fear of Snakes Inborn?*)
20. survival; evolution; dangers; contribute to; [11] Textbook
21. genetically; identical twin [11] Textbook
22. chronic; amygdala; mood disorders; neuroticism; [11] Video 19
23. social; developmental; long-; individual; [12] Textbook, Video 19
24. avoidant; anxiety; eccentric; [13] Textbook, Video 19
25. impulsive; narcissistic; sports; is not; healthy; [13] Textbook, Video 19
26. antisocial; conscience; 15; feel *and* fear; do not; [14] Textbook, Video 19
27. decreased; aggressive; gene; genetic predisposition; environmental; [14] Textbook

ANSWER KEY FOR THE SELF TEST

Item #	Answer	Learning Outcome #	Source	Item #	Answer	Learning Outcome #	Source
1.	d	1	Textbook, Video 19)	11.	a	6	Textbook, Video 19
2.	b	2	Textbook, Video 19)	12.	a	9	Textbook, Video 19
3.	a	2	Textbook, Video 19	13.	d	7	Textbook
4.	b	2	Textbook, Video 19	14.	b	8	Video 19
5.	c	2	Textbook, Video 19	15.	a	10	Textbook
6.	b	2	Textbook, Video 19	16.	a	11	Video 19
7.	a	2	Textbook, Video 19	17.	c	12	Textbook, Video 19
8.	b	3	Textbook, Video 19	18.	a	13	Video 19
9.	d	4	Textbook, Video 19	19.	d	14	Textbook
10.	c	5	Textbook, Video 19				

Lesson 20 (Mood Disorders and Schizophrenia)

Going to Extremes

Assignments

Reading: "Mood Disorders," "Schizophrenia," and "Rates of Psychological Disorders" in Chapter 16 of *Psychology* by David Myers (Modules 50 and 51 in the modular version of *Psychology*)

Video: Episode 20, "Out of Balance"

LEARNING OUTCOMES

Familiarize yourself with the Learning Outcomes for this lesson before you begin the assignments. Return to them to check your learning after completing the Steps to Learning Success. Careful work on these materials should equip you to accomplish the outcomes.

Mood Disorders (Module 50)

1. Describe the characteristics that differentiate **mood disorders** from the ups and downs of normal everyday living.

2. Discuss the incidence, demographics, and constellation of symptoms that characterize **depression**.

3. Contrast **bipolar disorder** with depression, indicating differences in the ways the illnesses manifest themselves and who tends to be affected.

4. Identify the three stages of **mania** and the behaviors, feelings, and actions typically connected with each stage.

5. Recognize the demographics related to suicide and the particular risk associated with severe mood disorders. Take into account the perspective of the person who takes his life as well as survivors.

6. Summarize the factors researchers must consider in developing a viable theory of depression that will

encourage the development of more effective ways to prevent and treat it.

7. Relate the incidence of severe mood disorders to DNA, to distinct brain patterns, and to the social-cognitive environment.

Schizophrenia (Module 51)

8. Specify how the cluster of psychoses called **schizophrenia** affects cognition, thinking, emotion, perception, and behavior.

9. Distinguish between chronic and acute schizophrenia, and between positive and negative symptoms, recognizing that schizophrenia itself has various subtypes.

10. Identify the brain abnormalities researchers have uncovered in their attempts to learn just what creates vulnerability to schizophrenia.

11. Discuss the genetic and environmental factors that predispose a person to schizophrenia.

Rates of Psychological Disorders (Module 51)

12. Recognize the statistical frequency of **psychological disorders** and the risk and protective factors associated with them.

ACTIVE REVIEW

Each item in this section is based on material presented in the video or the textbook assignment for this lesson, or both. Complete this section, referring as needed to your notes or the source materials themselves. Answers are provided at the end of this lesson.

Mood Disorders

1. **Depression**, one of two major forms of mood disorders, is the leading cause of _____ worldwide, and the number *(one / two / three)* reason people seek help from mental health professionals. David Myers refers to it as the _____ _____ of psychological disorders.

2. Depression *(is / is not)* the normal ups and downs of mood that everyone experiences as part of life. It's getting stuck in a down mood, not because of a medical condition or _____, and staying there for _____. Then you're not just down, you're depressed and need _____.

3. Evidence suggests the rate of depression is *(increasing / decreasing),* and the age at onset may be getting *(higher / lower)*. Before puberty, depression is more common in *(boys / girls)*. In adolescence it switches, and *(boys / girls)* become more vulnerable. This gender difference *(remains constant / changes back and forth)* throughout life, with _____ being almost twice as vulnerable.

4. Depression itself is a constellation of symptoms. It includes loss of _____ in things that you value, feelings of profound _____, and a lack of _____; what your textbook characterizes as psychic hibernation. People who are profoundly depressed find it hard to _____, even to shift positions in a chair.

5. In addition to depression, which is _____, is **bipolar disorder**, which has not only a down phase, but an up phase as well. As Kay Redfield Jamison describes it, the depression she experienced was offset by periods of mild _____ when

she would get *(enormous amounts of / very little)* work done and life was *(unbearable / fabulous)*.

6. Throughout history, the creativity associated with mild mania has been linked to some of our greatest artists, _____, and _____. But in general, the incidence of bipolar disorder is *(greater / less)* than the incidence of major depression and affects *(more men than women / more women than men / the same number of men as women)*.

7. In describing the three stages of **mania**, Stephen Hinshaw notes that they tend to *(be discrete / meld into one another)*. In the first stage, called hypo mania, a person is _____ and _____, doesn't need much sleep, and is hyper _____. For about *(25 / 50 / 75)* percent of the people with bipolar illness it's an incredible rush, almost like a _____ high.

8. In most cases without _____, people with bipolar disorder move into the second stage of mania. At this point they become so deluded by their grand ideas and self-importance that they act _____ and use poor _____. In the final stage of mania, people become totally irrational and _____, often losing control of bodily functions.

9. During the later stages of mania and profound depression there is a high risk for suicide. The statistics tell the story: *(30 / 40 / 50)* percent of people with bipolar disorder attempt suicide at some point and *(10 / 20 / 30)* percent succeed. This generally occurs at what point in the cycle?_____ _____.

Recall Kay Redfield Jamison's poignant recounting of her thoughts and feelings at a point when she considered suicide.

10. Suicide is addressed in a Close-up section of this text chapter. Recall information from this article by either circling or filling in the answers in the chart:

	White Americans	Black Americans
(a) Who are more likely to kill themselves?		
(b) Who are more likely to attempt suicide?	Men	Women
(c) Who are more likely to succeed at suicide attempts?	Men	Women
(d) Among which of the following groups are suicide rates higher?	Married	Single, widowed, or divorced
(e) Among which of the following groups are suicide rates higher?	Religious	Nonreligious
(f) Among which of the following groups are suicide rates higher?	Rich	Poor
(g) Is suicide necessarily an act of hostility or revenge?	Yes	No
(h) The suicide act is sometimes triggered by social _____		
(i) In what two demographic categories are suicide rates increasing?		
(j) Of the English-speaking and European countries mentioned, name the two with the highest rates of suicide.		
(k) Of the English-speaking and European countries mentioned, name the one with the lowest rate of suicide.		

11. In developing a theory of depression that will allow us to more effectively treat and prevent it, researchers must find the basis for factors common to the illness, including some we have not yet discussed. One factor is the link between depression and _____ life events. Many behavioral and _____ changes accompany depression. Most major depressive episodes are self-_____. The fact that the disease is so widespread suggests that its causes, too, must be _____.

12. From a biological perspective, depression is considered a _____-_____ disorder. As your text notes, "It involves _____ predispositions, biochemical _____, negative _____, and melancholy _____."

13. We know that **mood disorders** run in _____, and the search for genes that put people at risk is underway. Gene hunters are primarily using two techniques to do this: linkage _____ and association studies. Genetic researcher Robert Plomin talked about this research in video Episode 4,

Codes of Life, when he talked about gene/environment interaction. It is likely that *(many / a few)* genes have *(large / small)* effects that in combination with one another and with environmental factors put some people at greater risk.

14. In searching for the causes of mood disorders, researchers have uncovered abnormalities in brain structure and function. During depression the metabolism of the brain is *(increased / diminished)*, the neurotransmitters norepinephrine and serotonin are *(more abundant / scarce)*, activity in the left frontal lobes is *(slowed / quickened)*, and the amygdala is hyperactive. Stress-related damage to the hippocampus also *(increases / decreases)* the risk of depression.

15. Researchers have also isolated social and cognitive factors that contribute to mood disorder. Loss of a _____, particularly a _____ has been shown to be a powerful predictor of eventual depression. Once depression starts, a vicious cycle of _____ thoughts and moods seems to take over.

Schizophrenia

16. **Schizophrenia** is a *(single disorder / group of disorders)* that typically strikes during _____ _____ after an apparently normal childhood. It tends to affect slightly more *(women / men)* than *(women / men)* in *(a few / most / all)* cultures. Schizophrenia affects _____ percent of the population worldwide.

17. Symptoms of schizophrenia include disorganized, **delusional** _____, a restricted range of _____ expression, hallucinations (_____ experiences that no one else can perceive), and inappropriate _____.

18. When schizophrenia develops slowly over a long period of time, it is said to be _____. When someone who has been healthy and well adjusted develops schizophrenia rapidly it is termed _____.

19. Some schizophrenia patients exhibit _____ symptoms. They may hallucinate, talk in ways that reflect their disorganized thinking, and exhibit inappropriate laughter, tears, or rage. Those with _____ symptoms speak without inflection, show no expression, or are rigid and mute.

20. Of the subtypes of schizophrenia listed in your text, the two that are more likely to fall into the negative category are _____ and _____. Of the two categories, *(positive / negative)* generally responds better to therapy.

21. Schizophrenia is *(one of the most heavily researched psychological disorders / receives little research attention)*. This cluster of disorders is thought to involve *(few / multiple)* genes with *(small / large)* effects. Robert Plomin suggests that the genes are latent until the brain goes through its last stages of development in _____.

22. In the general population the odds are 1 in 100 that a person will be diagnosed with schizophrenia. A person with a parent or sibling who has the disorder has odds of _____ for developing the disease. If that sibling is an identical twin, the odds become _____ even if the twins are raised

apart. As Dr. Plomin comments, "There's no way to explain that genetically. It has to be _____ because genetically they are clones."

23. In looking for links to schizophrenia, researchers are beginning to zero in on the _____ environment. Name at least two complications during this period that appear to increase the risk for schizophrenia. _____ _____. After birth, people who are at risk for schizophrenia seem to be *(less / more)* biologically sensitive to _____ when it occurs.

24. With advances in neuroimaging technology, researchers are also uncovering small but significant _____ abnormalities in people with schizophrenia. There is evidence of smaller brain _____, particularly in the region of the hippocampus. *(Diminished / Increased)* brain function can be detected by a PET scan or an EEG brain map, particularly in the _____ regions of the brain.

25. Researchers have also found a biochemical link in autopsies conducted on schizophrenia patients. Particularly startling was the excess of receptors for _____. Drugs that block these receptors lesson the _____ symptoms of schizophrenia, but not the _____ symptoms.

Rates of Psychological Disorders

26. A recent U.S. National Institute of Mental Health study estimated that one in *(five / seven / ten / twelve)* Americans suffered a clinically significant mental disorder during the prior year. One predictor of mental disorders is _____, although it is unclear whether this condition is responsible for the disorders, or the disorders contribute to the condition.

27. Other than the generic "any mental disorder," which disorder listed in the table "Percentage of Americans Who Have Experienced Selected Psychological

Disorders in the Prior Year" in your textbook affects the largest percentage of people in the United States? _____. Look carefully at the "Risk and Protective Factors for Mental Disorders" table and relate the items listed to your own family. Which risk factors are you concerned about?_____

_____

_____
_____

What factors do you consider your protectors?

_____
_____
_____

SELF TEST

Read each question and circle the letter of the best answer. When you have completed the Self Test, check your answers against the key at the end of this lesson. If you have answered any items incorrectly, review the appropriate materials to correct misunderstandings and cement your knowledge.

1. Depression, one of two major forms of mood disorders, is
   a. the number two reason people seek help from mental health professionals.
   b. the leading cause of disability worldwide.
   c. what David Myers calls the "common cold of psychological disorders."
   d. b and c above.

2. Before puberty depression is more common in boys. In adolescence and the years following what happens?
   a. Male adolescents and adults continue to maintain the statistical lead.
   b. Girls take the lead during adolescence, but beginning in young adulthood the percentages are even.
   c. Girls take the lead during adolescence and the gender difference remains constant throughout life.
   d. Boys continue to lead during adolescence but women take over in young adulthood and maintain that position throughout life.

3. Depression exhibits a constellation of symptoms. Which of the following is <u>not</u> among them?
   a. Feelings of profound worthlessness
   b. Periods of mild mania
   c. Loss of interest in family, friends, and activities
   d. Lethargy

In describing the three stages of mania, Stephen Hinshaw notes that the stages tend to blend into one another. Link the stages with the characteristics that are common to that particular stage.

   a. First stage
   b. Second stage
   c. Third stage

4. Grandiose optimism and self esteem that lead to reckless acts and poor judgment

5. Irrational and psychotic behavior

6. High energy, creativity, sexuality

7. In developing a theory of depression that will allow us to more effectively treat and prevent it, researchers must find the basis for factors common to the illness. Which of the following is <u>not</u> a factor related to depression?
   a. The rate of depression is increasing with each new generation, but the age at onset tends to be occurring later in the life cycle.
   b. Stressful life events–job loss, death of a loved one, marital crisis–often precede depression.
   c. Most people suffering from major depression tend to return to normal for periods of time, even without professional help.
   d. The fact that depression is so widespread suggests that its causes, too, must be common.

8. Gene hunters are using two techniques to search for genes that put people at risk for mood disorders: association studies and _____.
   a. trait analysis
   b. linkage analysis
   c. correlation study
   d. changes in brain chemistry

9. Linkage analyses of mood disorders point researchers to
   a. life situations and stresses that give rise to mood disorders.
   b. demographic factors connected to incidences of major depression and bipolar disorder.
   c. chromosome neighborhoods where further research can be done to find the culprit genes.
   d. medical conditions and drugs that tend to be associated with mood disorders.

10. Researchers have isolated social and cognitive factors that contribute to mood disorder, such as
    a. inability to perform up to personal standards in school or in sports.
    b. loss of a parent, particularly a mother, early in life.
    c. a distorted self-image—feelings of being too short, too fat, or unattractive.
    d. the tendency to prefer one's own company to having a host of friends.

11. During the prodrome, the period one or two years before the clinical onset of schizophrenia, an individual commonly begins to
    a. experience delusions.
    b. withdraw from social activity.
    c. speak in strange and unintelligible ways.
    d. a and c above.

12. A delusion is
    a. a false belief that is not based on logic or rational thought.
    b. a false belief that is based in fact but distorted by sensory experiences that no one else perceives.
    c. related to childhood memories too disturbing for conscious memory.
    d. is the same as hallucinations.

13. The most common hallucinations are
    a. wildly colored.
    b. auditory.
    c. dream-like images.
    d. related to the sense of smell.

14. When a person is delusional or hallucinates about being a victim of persecution, he or she suffers from a subtype of schizophrenia known as
    a. paranoid schizophrenia.
    b. residual schizophrenia.
    c. disorganized schizophrenia.
    d. catatonic schizophrenia.

15. In the general population the odds are 1 in 100 that a person will be diagnosed with schizophrenia. What are the odds if you have a parent or sibling with the disorder?
    a. 1 in 50
    b. 1 in 25
    c. 1 in 10
    d. 1 in 5

16. Drugs that block dopamine receptors do not seem to help the _____ symptoms of schizophrenia.
    a. hallucination-type
    b. delusional
    c. positive
    d. negative

17. Which disorder does your textbook indicate is most prevalent in the United States?
    a. Schizophrenia
    b. Obsessive-compulsive disorder
    c. Alcoholism
    d. Phobias

ANSWER KEY FOR THE ACTIVE REVIEW EXERCISES

1. disability; one; common cold; [1] Textbook, Video 20

2. is not; drugs; weeks; treatment; [1] Textbook, Video 20

3. increasing; lower; boys; girls; remains constant; women; [2] Video 20

4. interest; worthlessness; perspective; move; [2] Textbook, Video 20

5. unipolar; mania; enormous; fabulous; [3] Video 20)

6. writers; musicians; less; the same number of men as women; [3] Textbook

7. meld into one another; productive, creative; sexual; 50; drug; [4] Video 20

8. treatment; recklessly; judgment; psychotic; [4] Video 20

9. 50; 20; as they begin to emerge from depression's depths and have more energy; [5] Textbook, Video 20

10. (a) White Americans; (b) Women; (c) Men; (d) Single, widowed, or divorced; (e) Nonreligious; (f) Poor; (g) No; (h) suggestion; (i) older men, older teens–especially males; (j) Finland, Lithuania; (k) Portugal; [5] Textbook

11. stressful; cognitive; terminating; common; [6]; Textbook

12. whole-body; genetic; imbalances; thoughts; moods; [7]; Textbook

13. families; analysis; many; small; [7]; Textbook, Videos 20 and 4

14. diminished; scarce; slowed; increases; [7] Textbook, Video 20

15. parent; mother; negative; [7] Textbook, Video 20

16. group of disorders; late adolescence; men; women; all; 1 to 2; [8] Textbook, Video 20

17. thinking; emotional; sensory; behavior; [8] Textbook, Video 20

18. chronic; acute; acute; [9] Textbook

19. positive; negative; [9] Textbook

20. catatonic, residual; positive; [9] Textbook

21. one of the most heavily researched psychological disorders; multiple; small; adolescence [11] Textbook, Video 20

22. 1 in 10; 1 in 2; environmental [11] Textbook, Video 20

23. prenatal; oxygen insufficiency, maternal rubella, exposure to viruses such as flu, maternal stress, or famine; more; stress; [10] Textbook, Video 20

24. brain; volume; Diminished; pre-frontal; [12] Textbook, Video 20

25. dopamine; positive; negative; [10] Textbook

26. seven, poverty; [12] Textbook

27. phobias; *personal answers*; [12] Textbook

ANSWER KEY FOR THE SELF TEST

Item #	Answer	Learning Outcome #	Source	Item #	Answer	Learning Outcome #	Source
1.	d	1	Textbook, Video 20	10.	b	7	Video 20
2.	c	2	Textbook, Video 20	11.	b	8	Video 20
3.	b	2	Textbook, Video 20	12.	a	8	Textbook, Video 20
4.	b	4	Video 20	13.	b	8	Video 20
5.	c	4	Video 20	14.	a	9	Textbook
6.	d	4	Video 20	15.	c	11	Textbook
7.	a	6	Textbook	16.	d	10	Textbook
8.	b	7	Textbook	17.	d	12	Textbook
9.	c	7	Textbook				

Lesson 21 (Therapy)

Getting It Together

Assignments

Reading: Chapter 17, "Therapy" in *Psychology* by David Myers (Modules 52, 53, and 54 in the modular version of *Psychology*)

Video: Episode 21, "Getting It Together"

LEARNING OUTCOMES

Familiarize yourself with the Learning Outcomes for this lesson before you begin the assignments. Return to them to check your learning after completing the Steps to Learning Success. Careful work on these materials should equip you to accomplish the outcomes.

The Psychological Therapies (Module 52)

1. Contrast early methods of treating psychological disorders with approaches used today.

2. Be aware of the role that improved diagnoses and a breadth of effective treatment options have played in improving outcomes for people with psychological disorders.

3. Briefly describe the methods used in **psychoanalysis** and the reasons this approach has lost favor.

4. Differentiate between **psychodynamic therapy** and psychoanalysis.

5. Recognize the goals of the **humanistic therapies**, and the nondirective techniques used to promote client growth.

6. Describe the category of therapies known as **behavior therapies**, and relate these approaches to the treatment of anxiety disorders.

7. Differentiate between behavioral techniques based on **counterconditioning** and those based on **operant conditioning** principles.

8. Explain the role **cognitive therapies** play in treating various psychological disorders, by themselves and in combination with other therapies.

9. Discuss the advantages derived from **family** and **group therapies**.

Evaluating Psychotherapies (Module 53)

10. Account for the tendency of clients and clinicians to overestimate the effectiveness of **psychotherapy**.

11. Recognize the importance of **outcome research** in judging the effectiveness of psychotherapies and provide examples of recent studies.

12. Indicate the importance of the psychotherapist in the **therapeutic alliance** and suggest criteria for selecting a therapist.

13. Explain the term **cultural competence** and what it means in the therapeutic relationship.

The Biomedical Therapies (Module 54)

14. Discuss the increased use of **psychopharmacolgy** in the treatment of psychological disorders.

15. Trace the development of **psychotropic** medications for the treatment of schizophrenia from its accidental discovery until today.

16. Describe the attributes, relative success, and side effects of **antianxiety** drugs, **antidepressant** drugs, and **mood stabilizing** medications.

17. Summarize the factors that influences an individual's reaction to drugs of any kind, and why following the recommended **biomedical** regimen may be critical.

18. Be aware of the limited use of **electroconvulsive therapy** and **psychosurgical** procedures in treating certain psychological disorders.

19. Recognize directions of ongoing research that will influence the treatment of psychological disorders in the future.

ACTIVE REVIEW

Each item in this section is based on material presented in the video or the textbook assignment for this lesson, or both. Complete this section, referring as needed to your notes or the source materials themselves. Answers are provided at the end of this lesson.

The Psychological Therapies

1. In the mid-1930s, at the age of 16, Stephen Hinshaw's father experienced the first in a series of episodes that would later be diagnosed as bipolar disorder. He was *(confined to his home / institutionalized)* for six months. During that period of time, which of the following treatments did he receive? *(psychotherapy / restraint [chained to his bed]) / custodial-only treatment / psychotropic drugs).*

2. Today there are a host of treatments for psychological disorders, including _____ and _____ **therapy.** As Charlotte Witviliet says "There is no _____-_____-_____-_____ therapy." It is important to _____ the therapeutic approache to the _____ the person is having.

3. Using techniques collectively called _____, Sigmund Freud attempted to discover the origins of his patients' illnesses, thought to be deeply buried in the *(hippocampus / unconscious).* He had developed some general ideas about how people "work" that he thought were applicable to *(everyone / people who were ill).* As a scientist he was interested in the commonalities rather than individual _____.

4. During **psychoanalysis** the therapist is *(out of view of / looks directly at)* the patient. The patient is asked to free _____—to say whatever comes to mind. A pause or a shift in the direction of the patient's monologue is thought to indicate

_____, a defensive attempt to block a sensitive memory.

5. The therapist calls the patient's attention to such instances when they occur, and _____ their meaning. Clues are found in _____, which are also subject to the therapist's interpretation.

6. Patients who exhibit strong feelings about their therapist, positive or negative, are said to be _____ the emotions felt toward someone important earlier in life. Recognizing this with their _____ help was thought to help the patient with current relationships.

7. Critics of psychoanalysis point out that there *(are / are no)* systematic, long-term studies that prove its effectiveness. It is all subject to the therapist's interpretation. Traditional psychoanalysis lasts for several *(hours / months / years),* is _____, and *(is / is not)* covered in its entirety by managed health care plans.

8. In contrast to psychoanalysis, the **psychodynamic** approach, as James Masterson illustrates, involves _____-_____-_____ conversation. It *(is / is not)* based on loving the patient, taking care of him, *(and / nor)* making him your friend. When crises occur, the emphasis is on creating an atmosphere that helps the patient's _____ _____ emerge.

9. This approach tends to be *(less / more)* expensive and time-consuming. It focuses on a patient's *(early / current)* conflicts by searching for_____ that are common to both past and present relationships. By staying the course and working with the patient's defenses in the initial stage, Dr. Masterson says, the patient and therapist eventually form a

therapeutic _____ in which the therapist's task is to keep the patient (*on / off*) the main trail.

10. **Humanistic therapy** concentrates on the _____ and _____ more than the past, on _____ rather than unconscious thoughts, and on promoting _____ rather than curing illness. It encourages clients to take responsibility for their feelings and _____.

11. Carl Rogers' _____-**centered therapy** relies on the _____'s perception rather than the _____'s interpretation. It combines active _____ with a therapeutic environment that is _____, _____, and _____.

12. **Behavior therapists** (*support /doubt*) the healing power of "talk" therapies. They are interested in _____-oriented techniques, particularly in the treatment of (*anxiety / dissociative / mood / personality*) disorders. As Albert Bandura says, "People need to _____ the problems they face.... Mastery experience has a (*powerful / negative*) therapeutic effect."

13. If you are afraid of elevators because you have a learned aversion to confined spaces, behavior therapists will help you through a technique called _____, the pairing of the trigger stimulus with a new response. Two techniques commonly used are _____ and _____ _____ _____.

14. **Exposure therapy** trains people to (*tense / relax*) and then (*gradually / suddenly*) exposes them to the objects they fear, like the _____ example in the video. Albert Bandura describes the process step by step. First you _____ the behavior. Then you break it down into small, manageable tasks. If your client still can't handle the anxiety-producing situation after going through this process, you do it _____, gradually (*fading out / increasing*) the therapist's participation.

15. **Aversive conditioning** connects a(n) _____ response (like a foul-tasting finger nail polish) to a troubling stimulus (like nail biting). Aversive techniques work for a while, but _____ may eventually override the results.

16. **Operant conditioning therapies**, such as _____ _____ procedures enforce desired behaviors by providing or withholding _____. Critics of this therapeutic approach object on both _____ and practical grounds. They question just how long these preferred behaviors will _____ when the rewards are taken away.

17. People with obsessive-compulsive disorder, as Susan Mineka describes, think they're going to go off the planet with anxiety if they can't perform their _____. But if they can hold off their patterned response for 30 minutes when they are exposed to the things that provoke their obsession, then for an hour, then two, their urge begins to (*escalate / subside*).

18. Jeffrey Schwartz' issue with the behavioral approach is that people with OCD already understand that these thoughts and urges do not make _____. And so it's only logical to use that knowledge as part of the _____.

19. Not all therapy is conducted on an individual basis. **Group** and _____ **therapy** can add a valuable dimension. Social contact within a group allows people to get feedback and _____ as they try new ways of behaving. They also come to realize that others have _____ similar to their own. Group sessions generally cost (*less / more*) than individual therapy.

20. **Family therapy** recognizes that problems occur not just _____ individuals but also _____ individuals. The fact that one person in a family is depressed impacts the _____ family. The dynamics of the family may also be associated with the _____ itself.

Inside Out Course Study Guide

Evaluating Psychotherapies

21. Whatever therapeutic approach is used, the larger question is "Does psychotherapy really work?" Most people who seek therapy judge it to be *(effective / ineffective)*. They are often in _____ when they enter therapy. Like anyone, they want to believe that they've invested their _____ and _____ wisely. And when questioned, their comments about their therapist tend to be *(positive / negative)*.

22. Therapists may also *(overestimate / underestimate)* their client's progress in therapy. What is reported as improvement may simply be **regression toward the _____**, the tendency for behavioral extremes to moderate to a more normal level. Another factor that may skew results is the _____ effect, the improvement that occurs as a result of expectations alone.

23. Michael Otto stresses the importance of *(psychotherapy / research)*. Without it we never know what the ultimate _____ is. **Outcome studies** are clinical trials in which people on a waiting list *(choose to receive / are randomly assigned)* to either therapy or no therapy.

24. By combining and analyzing the results from numbers of studies, a technique termed _____-_____, researchers have concluded that people who do not receive therapy often *(get worse / improve)*, but those who do undergo therapy are _____ _____ to improve. **Psychotherapy** is also cost *(effective / prohibitive)* when compared to the *(lesser / greater)* costs of medical care for psychologically-related complaints.

25. **Meta-analysis** studies reveal that *(only a few types / no one type)* of therapy can be considered most effective. Even group therapy is as helpful as _____ therapy. Some therapies, however, seem particularly well-suited for certain disorders. For example, which three types of therapy are recommended for depression?

_____, _____, and _____.

26. Daniel Weiss cautions against the word _____. It is not appropriate in connection with posttraumatic stress disorder (PTSD) any more than it is for diabetes. Treatment does work, however, to relieve the _____ of the disorder and allow someone to function with *(no / little / moderate)* difficulty.

27. Outcome studies of group therapies comparing various therapy techniques have shown that it's not the nature of the technique that determines whether or not there's a beneficial outcome. As Margaret Kemeny states in the video, it's the nature and style of the _____.

28. In choosing a good therapist, the sense of a _____ between the client and the therapist is all important. This relationship is also called the _____ _____. Jeffrey Schwartz describes this link: it involves finding someone you can talk to, who listens to you and helps you understand what's going on.

29. James McGee recommends choosing a therapist who is _____ and properly credentialed. But even that, he cautions, is no _____. You need to do your _____. Talk to two or three therapists before you make your selection. Try to gain an insight into their approach, their values and beliefs, and the _____ they charge.

30. The _____ _____ of therapists is becoming a larger issue for the field. This *(does / does not)* mean belonging to the same cultural group. But for the therapist it does mean understanding the culture of the people you are working with, and how the group and its value systems may _____ from your own. Janet Helms encourages therapists and clients to deal with the "elephant in the room." By that she is referring to relevant _____ issues.

The Biomedical Therapies

31. In recent years _____ **therapies** have joined psychotherapies and revolutionized the treatment of severe mental disorders. These new discoveries in _____ have reduced involuntary hospitalization and confinement *(by one-third / by one-half / to a fraction)* of what it was 50 years ago. For some unable to care for themselves, this freedom has resulted in _____.

32. Any new drug that is introduced is subjected to _____-_____ studies. Such studies call for *(one-third / one–half)* of the participants to receive the drug, and *(two-thirds / one-half)* to receive the _____. To date, *(none of the drugs / several types of drugs / all drugs)* tested have proven useful.

33. The revolution in drug therapy for psychological disorders began with a(n) _____ discovery. It was found that Thorazine, a drug used to control allergies, also reduced the *(negative / positive)* symptoms of _____ such as hallucinations and delusions. In addition to blocking the chemical called histamine, it also blocks _____, a neurotransmitter associated with the disorder.

34. These first generation **antipsychotics** produced disturbing side effects such as sluggishness, tremors, and _____ disorders. Newer medications have *(more / fewer)* unwanted consequences, and are also effective in dealing with schizophrenia's *(positive / negative)* symptoms.

35. **Antianxiety** drugs such as Xanax or Ativan depress central _____ _____ activity and ease the apprehension and fear experienced by people with anxiety disorders. These drugs are often used in combination with _____ to help people learn to cope with frightening situations.

36. As is true of behavior therapy, **antianxiety** drugs are often criticized for reducing _____ without resolving the underlying _____. The drugs themselves can be both psychologically

and physiologically _____. Today the standard drug treatment for anxiety disorders like OCD is _____.

37. If **antianxiety** drugs calm people, _____ drugs such as Prozac, Zoloft, and Paxil energize people and help them cast off their state of depression. These drugs *(increase / decrease)* the availability of norepinephrine or serotonin, which is *(abundant / scarce)* during depression.

38. **Antidepressant** drugs help elevate a person's mood, but not immediately. It often requires four *(hours / days / weeks)* to produce the full psychological effect. This delay may be because *(increased / decreased)* serotonin seems to promote neurogenesis, the birth of new _____ cells to replace the stress-induced loss of _____.

39. Beyond **biomedical therapy**, _____ is effective in countering the symptoms of mild to moderate depression. **Cognitive therapy** is quite useful in helping to reverse the _____ style of thinking associated with depression. It also reduces the risk of _____.

40. For years, the simple salt _____ has been prescribed by psychiatrists to stabilize the _____-_____ mood swings of bipolar disorder. About *(30 / 50 / 70 / 90)* percent of people benefit from taking lithium. When Kay Redfield Jamison first started taking lithium to get her mania in line, she remembers feeling _____. She is on a much *(lower / higher)* dose today, which is considered standard care.

41. Samuel Barondes, author of *Better than Prozac*, points out that the effect of a medication *(is the same / varies)* from person to person. These effects depend on the individual's _____ when they are taking the medication, specific _____ structures in the brain, and the person's innate body _____. The net effect for *(some / most / all)* people is desirable and that's why they are prescribed.

42. Dr. Jamison points out that drug therapies are
_____-_____. Someone diagnosed with
cancer doesn't hesitate to take drugs that are
absolutely devastating because "you want to save
your life and that's your only _____." The
_____ rate is extremely high in cases of
schizophrenia, bipolar disorder, and depression. "It's
either take the medication or be _____ or be on
the back wards."

43. But as James McGee advises, medication *(is / is not)*
enough. Well-controlled, multi-site field studies by
NIMH verify that "the best outcome is the combination of good _____ and
_____ for virtually any disorder
you want to look at."

44. "Getting people into treatment is one of the hardest
things there is in psychiatric and psychological
practice," Dr. Jamison says. "_____ people
in treatment is almost harder." Sometimes, Andrew
Leuchter comments, the patient is the *(first / last)*
person to know they're getting better.

45. If left _____, there is a tendency over
time for a psychological disorder to get *(better / worse)*,
for the episodes to become *(more / less)* frequent and
extreme, and *(more / less)* difficult to treat. Not to stay
on medications is to invite serious biological hits to
the _____ (the stress-induced neuron loss
mentioned earlier).

46. "The great thing about these medications is that when
they're working they prevent future _____
and the _____ aspect of the disease.
And some of the medications—lithium, Depakote,
and some antidepressants—seem to _____
some of the damage and actually cause neuronal
growth."

47. **Electroconvulsive therapy** is the *(treatment of choice
/ last-resort treatment)* for people with severe
_____. Today neurosurgeons rarely
perform brain surgery to treat psychological
disorders except in life-threatening conditions
because the effects are _____.

48. In the future, with the aid of neuroimaging technology, therapists may be able to not only optimize
_____ choices for their patients and
_____ their progress, but also target the
chemistry of the brain areas involved in specific
systems.

49. Think about Stephen Hinshaw's father and his treatment as you listen to Diego Pizzagalli in the video,
talk about the soon-to-be-realized ability to supple-
ment informed treatment decisions with information
gathered from genetics as well as neuroscience. In a
sentence describe your thoughts and feelings.

_____

_____

_____

SELF TEST

*Read each question and circle the letter of the best
answer. When you have completed the Self Test, check
your answers against the key at the end of this lesson. If
you have answered any items incorrectly, review the
appropriate materials to correct misunderstandings and
cement your knowledge.*

1. Early treatments for psychological disorders
   included all but one of the following. Identify the
   <u>incorrect</u> item.
   a. Beating the "devil" out of people who were ill
   b. Applying restraints so patients would not hurt
      themselves
   c. Arranging sunny, serene environments for
      patients
   d. Enrolling patients in classes so they could learn
      about their disorder

2. What are the two predominant categories of therapies used today to treat people with psychological disorders?
   a. Psychotherapies and biomedical therapies
   b. Electroconvulsive and behavioral therapies
   c. Aversive conditioning and cognitive therapies
   d. Biomedical therapies and psychosurgeries.

3. The first of the psychological therapies was
   a. Carl Rogers' client-centered therapy.
   b. Abraham Maslow's hierarchy of needs.
   c. Sigmund Freud's psychoanalysis.
   d. Aaron Beck's cognitive therapy.

4. When Jill begins to display feelings of anger and distrust toward her therapist that are similar to the emotions she felt for her mother as a child, she is engaging in what psychoanalysts call
   a. transference.
   b. avoidance.
   c. scapegoating.
   d. a false message.

5. In comparison to psychoanalysis, humanistic therapies focus on
   a. the past more than the present or future.
   b. taking personal responsibility for one's feelings and actions.
   c. unconscious rather than conscious thought.
   d. curing illness rather than promoting growth.

6. Read the following exchange between a therapist and a client:

   Client: *I can't stand it when she puts me down in front of my friends.*
   Therapist: *Just how does it make you feel?*

   The therapist is using which of the following active listening techniques?
   a. Paraphrase
   b. Invite clarification
   c. Reflect feelings
   d. Confront

7. Behavior therapies are used primarily in the treatment of
   a. mood disorders.
   b. anxiety disorders.
   c. personality disorders.
   d. dissociative disorders.

8. José gives his daughter a dollar each time she earns an A on her report card. If she gets a C or lower she has to do the dishes without help from her brothers and sisters for a week. What type of therapy enforces

desired behaviors by providing or withholding rewards?
   a. Cognitive therapy
   b. Exposure therapy
   c. Operant conditioning therapy
   d. Aversive conditioning therapy

9. The type of therapy that teaches people new, more adaptive ways of thinking and acting is called
   a. behavior modification.
   b. aversive therapy.
   c. transference.
   d. cognitive therapy.

10. Cognitive behavior is often combined with _____ to alter the way people act and think.
   a. psychodynamic therapy
   b. behavior therapy
   c. interpersonal therapy
   d. operant conditioning therapy

11. In the context of group and family therapy
   a. members learn that others have problems similar to their own.
   b. being with other people allows members to discover things about themselves and get feedback as they try new behaviors.
   c. costs are multiplied because of the number of people in the group.
   d. both a and b.

12. The improvement that occurs primarily because of a client's strong belief in the treatment he or she is engaged in is termed
   a. the dependent variable.
   b. extrinsic motivation.
   c. the placebo effect.
   d. predictive validity.

13. Outcome studies are
   a. "the rest of the story"—detailed anecdotal accounts of what happens after therapy is concluded.
   b. clinical trials in which people on a waiting list are assigned randomly to receive or to not receive therapy.
   c. scientifically-conducted studies that poll people after therapy to see if their opinions have changed regarding the overall value of the experience.
   d. competitive research wars between the various forms of psychotherapy to see which approach can achieve positive results in the least time.

14. Combining and analyzing the results from numbers studies is called
    a. a correlational study.
    b. meta-analysis.
    c. statistical reasoning.
    d. survey research.

15. Some therapies are particularly well suited for certain disorders. Which three types of therapy are recommended for people with depression?
    a. Cognitive, behavioral, and interpersonal therapies
    b. Cognitive, traditional psychoanalytic, and behavioral therapies
    c. Traditional psychoanalytic, behavioral, and group therapies
    d. Behavioral, cognitive, and humanistic therapies.

16. In choosing a good therapist, it's important to choose someone
    a. you have a connection, or therapeutic alliance with.
    b. you can talk to and feel that you're heard.
    c. who helps you understand what's going on, and works in partnership with you to alleviate the difficulty you're having.
    d. a, b, and c above.

17. In recent years what type of therapies have joined psychotherapies and revolutionized treatment, especially for severe mental illnesses such as bipolar disorder and schizophrenia?
    a. Brain stimulation techniques
    b. Systemic desensitization
    c. Biomedical therapies
    d. Light exposure therapy

18. The introduction of drug therapies
    a. revolutionized the treatment of people with severe psychological disorders.
    b. Has reduced involuntary hospitalization and confinement to a fraction of what it was 50 years ago.
    c. was greeted with enthusiasm. But in recent years that interest has faded as drug therapies failed to achieve the results that were touted.
    d. both a and b above.

19. Typically, antianxiety drugs
    a. ease apprehension and fear.
    b. are psychologically but not physiologically addictive.
    c. are physiologically but not psychologically addictive.
    d. both a and b above.

20. What is the new standard drug treatment for anxiety disorders like OCD?
    a. Mood stabilizing medications
    b. Antipsychotic drugs
    c. Antidepressant drugs
    d. Placebos

ANSWER KEY FOR THE ACTIVE REVIEW EXERCISES

1. institutionalized; restraint, custodial-only treatment; [1] video 21
2. psychotherapies, biomedical; one-size-fits-all; match; problem; [2] Textbook, Video 21
3. psychoanalysis; unconscious; everyone; differences; [3] Textbook, Video 21
4. out of view of; associate; resistance; [3] Textbook, Video 21
5. interprets; dreams; [3] Textbook
6. transferring; therapist's; [3] Textbook
7. are no; years; expensive; is not; [3] Textbook, Video 21
8. face-to-face; is not; nor; real self [4] Textbook, Video 21
9. less; current; themes; alliance; on [4] Textbook, Video 21
10. present, future; conscious; growth; actions [5] Textbook
11. client; individual's; therapist's; listening; genuine, accepting, empathetic [5] Textbook, Video 21
12. doubt; action; anxiety; confront; powerful [6] Textbook, Video 21
13. counterconditioning; exposure therapy, aversive conditioning therapy [7] Textbook, Video 21
14. relax; gradually; spider; model; together; fading out [7] Textbook, Video 21
15. negative; cognition [7] Textbook, Video 21
16. behavior modification; rewards; ethical; last [7] Textbook
17. ritual; subside [7] Video 21
18. sense; treatment [8] Video 21
19. family; reassurance; problems; less [9] Textbook, Video 21
20. within; between; entire; depression [9] Video 21
21. effective; crisis; time, money; positive [10] Textbook
22. overestimate; mean; placebo [10] Textbook
23. research; outcome; are randomly assigned to [11] Textbook, Video 21
24. meta-analysis; improve; more likely; effective; greater [11] Textbook

25. no one type; individual; cognitive, interpersonal, behavioral [11] Textbook
26. cure; symptoms; little [11] Video 21
27. therapist [11, 12] Video 21
28. connection; therapeutic alliance [12] Textbook, Video 21
29. licensed; guarantee; homework; fees [12] Textbook, Video 21
30. cultural competence; does not; differ; racial [12] Video 21
31. biomedical; psychopharmacology; to a fraction; homelessness [13] Textbook, Video 21
32. double-blind; one-half; one-half; placebo; several types of drugs [13] Textbook
33. accidental; positive; schizophrenia; dopamine [14] Textbook, Video 21
34. movement; fewer; negative [14] Textbook, Video 21
35. nervous system; psychotherapy [15] Textbook
36. symptoms; problem; addicting; antidepressants [15] Textbook
37. antidepressant; increase; scarce [15] Textbook
38. weeks; increased; brain; neurons [15, 17] Textbook, Video 21
39. aerobic exercise; negative; relapse; [15] Textbook
40. lithium; manic-depressive; 70%; blunted; lower [15] Textbook, Video 21
41. varies; mood; protein; chemistry; most; [15] Video 21
42. life-saving; chance; suicide; dead [16] Video 21
43. is not; psychotherapy, medications [16] Video 21
44. Keeping; last [16] Video 21
45. untreated; worse; more; more; brain [16] Textbook; Video 21
46. episodes; progressive; reverse [16] Textbook, Video 21
47. last-resort treatment; depression; irreversible [17] Textbook
48. biomedical; track [18] Video 21
49. answers vary; [19] Video 21

ANSWER KEY FOR THE SELF TEST

Item #	Answer	Learning Outcome #	Source	Item #	Answer	Learning Outcome #	Source
1.	d	1	Textbook, Video 21	11.	d	9	Textbook, Video 21
2.	a	2	Textbook, Video 21	12.	c	10	Textbook
3.	c	3	Textbook	13.	b	11	Textbook
4.	a	3	Textbook	14.	b	11	Textbook
5.	b	5	Textbook	15.	a	11	Textbook
6.	b	5	Textbook	16.	d	12	Textbook, Video 21
7.	b	6	Textbook, Video 21	17.	c	13	Textbook, Video 21
8.	c	7	Textbook	18.	d	13	Textbook, Video 21
9.	d	8	Textbook, Video 21	19.	a	15	Textbook
10.	b	8	Textbook, Video 21	20.	c	15	Textbook

Lesson 22 (Social Psychology)

People to People

Assignments

Reading: Chapter 18, "Social Psychology" in *Psychology* by David Myers (Modules 55, 56, and 57 in the modular version of *Psychology*)

Video: Episode 22, "People to People"

LEARNING OUTCOMES

Familiarize yourself with the Learning Outcomes for this lesson before you begin the assignments. Return to them to check your learning after completing the Steps to Learning Success. Careful work on these materials should equip you to accomplish the outcomes.

Introduction (Module 55)

1. Name the three areas of study that are the primary focus of this lesson in social psychology.

Social Thinking (Module 55)

2. Differentiate between explanations for behavior that are linked to situations and explanations related to an individual's disposition. Be aware of just how often these **attributions** play out in everyday situations.

3. Explain how the **fundamental attribution error** can distort our judgment about a person's behavior.

4. Recognize the relationship between attitudes and actions, and cite instances in which **attitude** exerts more influence over behavior and instances in which it exerts less.

5. Give examples of research studies in which attitude adapts to behavior rather than behavior following attitude.

Social Influence (Module 56)

6. Briefly enumerate the ways in which social influence wields its power, recognizing that the influence of a single individual can alter the course of events.

7. Explain the **chameleon effect** and look for examples of it in your own surroundings.

8. Relate Solomon Asch's experiments on **conformity** to the reasons people comply to a group's judgment.

9. Recognize the conditions or situations that are likely to produce obedience to the will of the group or an individual.

10. Give examples of situations in which **social facilitation** and **deindividuation** have an impact.

11. Discuss the factors that encourage **social loafing** and those that motivate active participation in a group activity.

12. Contrast two forms of group interaction—**group polarization** and **groupthink**.

Antisocial Relations (Module 57)

13. Define **aggression** as recognized by the field of psychology

14. Describe three biological influences that set the stage for the emergence of aggression.

15. Discuss the psychosocial factors that in combination with biological influences trigger aggression.

16. Define conflict and describe how **social traps** and mirror-image perceptions can intensify the discord between two or more people.

Prosocial Relations (Module 58)

17. Recognize the influence of proximity, physical attractiveness, and similarity on interpersonal attraction.

18. Differentiate between **passionate** and **companionate** love.

19. Relate **altruism** to the norms for helping and to emotions that incline people toward collective principles and support for others.

20. Discuss ways of reducing social conflict and encouraging peaceful cooperation.

ACTIVE REVIEW

Each item in this section is based on material presented in the video or the textbook assignment for this lesson, or both. Complete this section, referring as needed to your notes or the source materials themselves. Answers are provided at the end of this lesson.

1. At the beginning of the video, David Myers, Jim Blscovich, and Mahzarin Banaji focus on just what **social psychology** is. In your own words, summarize what you gleaned from their comments: _____
   _____
   _____
   _____
   _____
   _____

2. Psychologists explore these social connections by _____ studying how people _____ about, _____, and _____ to one another.

Social Thinking

3. Think about the people you meet in a single day. What judgments are you making about them and, more importantly, on what basis? Daniel Gilbert notes that human beings have become very good at looking at someone's _____ and using an _____ process called _____ to figure out their thoughts, motives, and feelings.

4. But such judgments aren't always true, as James Jones notes. Many times we *(over- / under-)* estimate the influence of personal factors and *(over- / under-)* estimate the role of context. This

_____ _____
_____, as it is called, can distort judgment.

5. **Attitudes** are _____ based on beliefs that predispose people to respond in a particular way to objects, _____, and events. They are most likely to impact behavior when social influence is *(strong / weak)*, when attitude is *(closely connected / not connected)* to the behavior, and when individuals are *(strongly aware / not aware)* of the attitudes they hold.

6. Mahzarin Banaji talks about the inferences an immigrant must make on his first day in New York City. The very thing that makes us _____, she observes, may also be that which causes us to fall prey to certain biases. When assumptions are made about people that we *(do / do not)* see, we are _____ them.

7. Several decades ago, in a well-known laboratory study, male students at Stanford University volunteered to spend time in a simulated _____ devised by psychologist Phillip Zimbardo. They were randomly assigned to roles as _____ or _____. After a day or two the simulation became *(all too real / boring)*, as you saw in the video.

8. Guards mocked the prisoners and treated them in _____ ways they would not have conceived of prior to the study. The prisoners broke down, _____, or became passively resigned. Dr. Zimbardo called a halt to the experiment after only six days. Years later, an example of this same scenario played out for real in _____'s Abu Ghraib Prison.

9. Another example of actions affecting attitudes can be found in studies related to the **foot-in-the-_____ phenomenon**, a way of convincing people to act *(in line with / against)* their beliefs by getting them to agree to a *(small / large)* action. Those who agree to a small concession are much more likely to later *(resist / comply with)* a greater demand.

10. When individuals become aware that their attitudes and actions don't mesh with each other, they are troubled and experience what is called _____ _____. In order to relieve the tension and justify the action, they often adjust their _____ to align with their _____.

Social Influence

11. "Social psychology's great lesson," says David Myers, "is the _____ of social influence." What three major areas illustrate this premise? _____, _____, and group _____.

12. The influence of the social context *(is / is not)* just an add-on, says John Cacioppo. It is fundamentally *(reinforcing / changing)* the mixture of the cake we thought we were studying initially. And yet, a single individual can make *(very little / an enormous)* difference, as we saw. List two such examples:

_____

_____

_____

13. The _____ _____ is our tendency to mimic others around us *(without realizing / with full knowledge)* that we're doing it. John Bargh describes one such study. Write down other examples that you have witnessed recently.

_____

_____

_____

_____

14. In a series of experiments, Solomon Asch showed that people *(will / will not)* conform to a group's judgment even when it is clearly *(correct / incorrect)*. In fact, says Susan Fiske, "people are quite distressed when they don't have a socially shared _____ with other people."

15. **Conformity** *(increases / decreases)* when individuals feel incompetent or insecure, when they admire the group's _____ and are being observed by the _____, when they come from a _____ that strongly encourages respect for group standards, and when they are in a group with at least _____ members who are _____ in their opinion.

16. Why do people conform? Membership in a group is of *(great / minor)* significance to individuals. Often they conform in order to avoid _____ or gain social _____, as Claude Steele illustrates in discussing music with a student. In such cases individuals are responding to what social psychologists call _____ **social influence**. That type of conformity occurs even in a virtual _____.

17. People also conform because they want the information others provide, what is referred to as _____ **social influence**. Robert Baron and his colleagues demonstrated that this is particularly true when the information is *(important / insignificant)* and the decision is *(easy / complex)*.

18. In Stanley Milgram's controversial experiment, allegedly on the effect of *(reward / punishment)* on learning, people playing the role of teachers were ordered by an experimenter to administer varying levels of _____ to those playing learners. The question was whether or not the teachers would _____ the experimenter's command when the learners cried out in pain and begged them to _____. In reality, the learners *(were / were not)* being hurt.

19. People were most likely to obey in such instances as when the person giving the orders was *(nearby / at a distance)* and considered a legitimate _____ figure supported by a prestigious institution, when the victim was *(nearby / at a distance)*, and when no other person modeled defiance by _____.

20. How does the presence of others influence behavior and performance? When people are performing a well-learned task, the presence of others *(improves / inhibits)* performance. If they are unsure of the routine or if it's a new task, their level of performance before others *(increases / decreases)*. In social psychology, studies that probe the effect of group arousal on performance are termed _____ _____ studies.

21. The presence of others may cause people to yield to the mob's mentality. Losing one's self regulatory capacity is called _____. It often occurs when people feel not only aroused but _____ in the midst of a group.

22. When people have the chance to work not just in the presence of others, but with others toward a shared goal, research shows that they tend to do *(more / less)*; a phenomenon termed _____ _____. Because they are part of a group, they feel *(more / less)* accountable and worry *(more / less)* about what others think. They may also view their contribution as *(vital / dispensable)*.

23. Given the fact that **social loafing** is common, Franscesca Polletta asks, why then do people choose to participate in social movements at all? She's found several reasons. One is the sense of _____ they feel toward others in the movement. Sometimes the movement itself is the lure. The more they learn about it, the more _____ it becomes. Finally, people gain benefits from _____ itself, giving those who are involved a sense of _____ and purpose they didn't previously have.

24. When people in the group discuss attitudes that most of them either favor or oppose _____ _____ can be seen at work. Dacher Keltner notes that like-minded people on one side of an issue think their counterparts on the other side are _____ _____.

However, studies show that people of different political groups often share certain fundamental _____.

25. Nothing pulls diverse factions together as much as a common _____. The desire for a united front, however, can impede careful judgment. There is a tendency to engage in a *(quick / thorough)* analysis of the facts and not show respect or devote time for _____ points of view. The results can be catastrophic, as seen when the *Challenger* _____ _____ exploded.

Antisocial Relations

26. Psychology's definition of **aggression** is "any _____ or _____ behavior intended to hurt or destroy." It doesn't matter whether the behavior is committed _____ out of hostility or _____ as a calculated means to an end, it is still aggression.

27. Biology *(influences / is the dominant factor in)* the emergence of aggression. It is in three primary areas that biology plays a role: _____, _____, and _____ influences. Psychologists *(consider / do not consider)* aggressive behavior instinctual.

28. Genes influence aggression by the effect they have on _____. Researcher Jean Chen Shih has been studying the link between *(a missing / an extra)* gene called the MAO-A gene and aggression, first identified in connection with a number of males from a single Dutch family who committed violent criminal acts. When this gene was removed from mice in the lab how did the mice react? _____ _____

29. Human brains have neural systems that when stimulated _____ or _____ aggressive behavior. Does this mean that the brain has a violence center? *(Yes / No)* Aggression is a *(simple / complex)* behavior that occurs in particular contexts. If the _____ _____ of the brain (the system that inhibits aggression) is damaged, aggression is *(more / less)* likely to occur.

30. Studies of the effect of the _____ testosterone confirm that _____ influences also contribute to aggression. Testosterone

not only *(increases / decreases)* dominant and aggressive behavior, but acts of dominance or aggression *(boost / lower)* the levels of testosterone as well. For both _____ and _____ reasons, people who drink alcohol are *(more / less)* prone to violent behavior.

31. As David Myers writes, "_____ factors influence the ease with which aggression is triggered. But what _____ factors pull the trigger?" _____ events such as social rejection or the environmental factors Astrid Heger describes can create frustration that leads to angry and hostile feelings. This trend is called the _____-_____ principle. Reinforcement for aggressive behavior creates _____ that are *(easy / difficult)* to change.

32. Children also _____ aggression when they are exposed to violence in their homes and neighborhoods. Boys who see the men in their lives deal with their frustration and need for power by brutalizing family members learn to _____ this behavior. Girls who grow up in such an environment think that it's *(okay / unthinkable)* for a woman to be abused.

33. Media violence also plays a role in the equation by providing _____ _____. Whether the violence is delivered through immersive technology, movies and television, or videogames, there is a *(small / large)* number of children who are _____ to its message and will act on it.

34. **Conflict** is defined as situations in which people view their _____, _____, or _____ to be incompatible. Many real-life situations contain _____ _____, as individuals pursue personal interests *(with /with no)* regard for the effects they may have on others. The challenge is to find a path that can incorporate both. A second way conflict is sustained is through **mirror image perceptions**—distorted or unsavory images enemies have of each other—that tend to *(fuel / diminish)* the hostility between them.

Prosocial Relations

35. Three ingredients tend to bind us together in special friendships. The first is _____. Nearness tends to be friendship's most *(powerful / illusive)* predictor because of the mere _____ _____. Evolution has hardwired us to _____ with those who are familiar and to be *(gracious to / wary of)* those who are unfamiliar.

36. The second ingredient is _____ _____, which influences everything from initial impressions of someone's _____ to feelings of popularity. The third element is _____. The more alike people are, the more their friendship endures.

37. Occasionally friendships move into the more intense and complex realm of romantic love. The beginning of a love relationship is characterized by a couple's intense absorption in one another, what Elaine Hatfield terms _____ love. As love matures, the deep affection transitions to _____ love. Two keys to a gratifying and enduring relationship are _____ and _____-_____.

38. Altruism is the unselfish regard for the welfare of others. Jot down notes about someone you know and what they have done that exemplifies this type of behavior. _____ _____ _____.

Why do you think they acted the way they did? Was it because of the _____ _____ _____? Did the _____ of helping outweigh the costs? Did it have anything to do with feelings of social _____, helping those who are _____ on us?

39. Dacher Keltner talks about his study of the emotions that seem to prompt people to do things for other people. One, he says, is _____, which has its own physiological response. Another is _____, the sense of beauty, wonder, and inspiration that seems larger than the self. This emotion, his

research suggests, gets people to commit to _____ principles and become devoted to their group and their culture.

40. It is because of this devotion to group and culture, and sincere attempts at _____ and _____ that we can begin to chip away at the antagonisms built by years of aggression and conflict. James Jones provides just such an example, sharing his experiences in the country of _____ _____, where _____ is being forged on the

basis of *ubuntu* which says one person's wellbeing is contingent upon another.

41. Dr. Jones explains this ancient African word *ubuntu* further. "You can't be good by yourself. You have to be in relationship to other people. And my humanity is defined in part by my relationship to you." And it was that principle that allowed them to bring people together who had historically been in conflict. "Even though you have done these things in the past, we are creating a new society in which we all have value, we all have humanity and we must move forward."

SELF TEST

Read each question and circle the letter of the best answer. When you have completed the Self Test, check your answers against the key at the end of this lesson. If you have answered any items incorrectly, review the appropriate materials to correct misunderstandings and cement your knowledge.

1. What three areas of concentration generally comprise the scientific study of social psychology?
   a. Social roles, social class, social order
   b. Individual rights, group differences, common good
   c. Family, community, country
   d. Social thinking, social influence, social relations

2. When Roberta goes to the public assistance office to try to get some financial help, the case worker makes certain assumptions about her based on her impoverished state. This human tendency to explain someone's behavior by their disposition or their situation is called
   a. deindividuation.
   b. belief bias.
   c. attribution.
   d. egocentrism.

3. The tendency to overestimate the influence of personal factors and underestimate the role of context, James Jones says, is an example of how _____ distorts a person's judgment in explaining the behavior of others.
   a. the fundamental attribution error
   b. free association
   c. belief perserverance
   d. a false message

4. Feelings based on our beliefs that predispose us to respond in a particular way to objects, people, and events are called
   a. projections.
   b. attitudes.
   c. stereotypes.
   d. generalizations.

5. What occurred during the 1971 role-play study known as the Stanford Prison Experiment?
   a. The students couldn't get past their self-consciousness related to the roles they were asked to play, even into the second week.
   b. The simulation became almost too real, with guards mocking the prisoners and treating them in ways that were extremely cruel.
   c. The prisoners, without exception, broke down and became passively resigned to the ill-treatment they received.
   d. Both b and c above.

6. When Julio became aware that he was not living up to the religious codes of his family, codes he had accepted as a child, he was troubled. He experienced what psychologists term
   a. cognitive dissonance.
   b. the misinformation effect.
   c. the fundamental attribution error.
   d. generalized anxiety disorder.

7. Despite the preponderance of studies that illustrate the human tendency to obey authority and conform to other people's behaviors, if _____ say(s) no, conformity breaks down.
   a. one person
   b. two people
   c. three people
   d. five people

8. The research of John Bargh and Tanya Chartrand that established the chameleon effect began with students engaged in an experimental task quite separate from the real focus of the study. When the leader, a confederate of Bargh and Chartrand, began to shake her foot or pull on her ear, the student
   a. obviously distracted, asked her why she was doing it.
   b. was so intent on the task that she didn't notice.
   c. unconsciously mimicked the behavior.
   d. made more mistakes than normal on the experimental task.

9. All but one of the factors below tend to strengthen a person's conformity. Identify the <u>incorrect</u> response.
   a. The person is made to feel incompetent or insecure.
   b. Other members of the group are unanimous in their opinion.
   c. The person has little regard for other members of the group.
   d. The group has at least three people.

10. The force of informational social influence is particularly strong when
    a. the information is significant.
    b. it is a group rather than an individual decision.
    c. the decision is complex.
    d. both a and c above.

11. The presence of others not only arouses people, it can also cause them to yield to a mob's mentality. Losing one's self-regulatory capacity to a group is called
    a. loss of self control.
    b. social influence.
    c. deindividuation.
    d. social abandonment.

12. One of the reasons that people abandon their self-control in the presence of a mob is because they feel
    a. they are responsible for leading the group.
    b. exhilarated and all-powerful.
    c. absolutely vital to the success of the effort.
    d. aroused and anonymous.

13. Whether you are a Republican or Democrat, a New York Yankee or Boston Red Sox fan, support pro-choice or pro-life, when you get together with a group of like-minded people and discuss your viewpoints, your ideas become even more firmly entrenched. This is a theory in social psychology called
    a. group polarization.
    b. group dynamics.
    c. belief bias.
    d. social feedback.

14. Studies have shown that like-minded people on one side of an issue view their counterparts on the other side as
    a. irrational extremists.
    b. dedicated, if misguided, partisans.
    c. well-intentioned but ignorant dupes.
    d. thoughtful people who just happen to have different points of view.

15. Groupthink results in
    a. judgments that tend not to be based on a thorough analysis of the facts.
    b. judgments being are reached without respect for alternate points of view.
    c. a process that is both deliberate and time-consuming; there is no rush to judgment.
    d. both a and b above.

16. Which of the following people would be considered aggressive using psychology's definition of the word?
    a. Gillian, who verbally abuses her family when she has had too much to drink.
    b. Chip, the persistent salesman at the Fritz Ford dealership who keeps trying to convince you to buy a Mustang convertible.
    c. Gregg, the physical therapist who inflicts pain each time he manipulates your injured leg.
    d. Bill and Amy, who "ground" their teenagers for failing to meet the established curfew.

17. Aggression is a complex behavior that occurs in particular contexts. If Craig experiences damage to the _____ of his brain, that system which inhibits aggression, he is _____ to become aggressive.
    a. frontal lobe system ... more likely
    b. frontal lobe system ... less likely
    c. occipital lobe ... more likely
    d. occipital lobe ... less likely

18. The link between alcohol and aggressiveness is the result of both biological and psychological factors. All but one of the following statements refers to a specific study and its published findings. Identify the <u>incorrect</u> item.
    a. Alcohol sets free aggressive responses to frustration.
    b. Just thinking you imbibed alcohol when you have not has no effect.
    c. If alcohol is slipped into your drink without your knowledge it still has an effect.
    d. People who have been drinking commit 4 in 10 violent crimes and 3 in 4 acts of spousal abuse.

19. If biological factors influence the ease with which aggression is triggered, which of the following are psychosocial triggers?
    a. Aversive events–environmental factors, social rejection
    b. Reinforcement for aggressive behaviors that makes it difficult to change
    c. Models for violence within childrens' homes and neighborhoods
    d. All of the above.

20. In social psychology, a situation in which two or more people view their actions, goals, or ideas to be incompatible is called
    a. conflict.
    b. divergence.
    c. variance.
    d. cognitive dissonance

21. People tend to view their enemies as more treacherous and evil than they are. Their enemies view them in the same way. In social psychology this is called
    a. mutual dislike.
    b. binocular vision.
    c. mirror image perception.
    d. manifest destiny.

22. Which of the following statements about physical attractiveness, one of the three primary factors in forming a close friendship, is true?
    a. Most people cling to the notion that appearances can be deceiving.
    b. Men are more likely than women to say that another's looks don't affect them.
    c. People's physical attractiveness predicts their frequency of dating, their feelings of popularity, and others' initial impressions of their personalities.
    d. People's physical attractiveness is closely related to their self-esteem and happiness.

23. Rex and Melinda cannot stand to be apart. They are totally absorbed in each other, physically and emotionally. How would you categorize their feelings for each other?
    a. Puppy love
    b. Romantic love
    c. Passionate love
    d. Companionate love.

24. Carl Wilkens, the missionary described in your textbook, stayed behind in Kigali, Rwanda, to help the people who were being attacked by Hutu militia. In social psychology, his unselfish regard for the welfare of others is termed
    a. altruism.
    b. a mental set.
    c. resistance.
    d. near death experience.

25. Dacher Keltner's research has identified two emotions that are involved in altruistic acts. They are
    a. compassion and pity.
    b. happiness and awe.
    c. goodness and mercy.
    d. compassion and awe.

ANSWER KEY FOR THE ACTIVE REVIEW EXERCISES

1. *Comments will vary;* [1] Video 22
2. scientifically; think; influence; relate; [1] Textbook, Video 22
3. behavior; inferential; attribution; [2] Textbook, Video 22
4. over-; under-; fundamental attribution error; [3] Textbook, Video 22
5. feelings; people; weak; closely connected; strongly aware; [4] Textbook
6. intelligent; didn't really; stereotyping; [4] Video 22
7. prison; prisoners, guards; all too real; [5] Textbook, Video 22
8. cruel; rebelled; Iraq; [5] Textbook, Video 22
9. door; against; small; comply with; [5] Textbook
10. cognitive dissonance; attitudes; actions; [5] Textbook
11. power; conformity; compliance; behavior; [6] Textbook, Video 22
12. is not; changing; an enormous; *examples*: helicopter pilot protecting Vietnamese family against his own troops at My Lai; Rosa Parks refusal to sit at the back of the bus; [6] Textbook, Video 22
13. chameleon effect; without realizing; *individual answers;* [7] Textbook, Video 22
14. will; incorrect; understanding; [8] Textbook, Video 22
15. increases; status; group; culture; three; unanimous; [8] Textbook
16. great; rejection; approval; normative; casino; [8] Textbook, Video 22
17. informational; important; complex; [8] Textbook
18. punishment; shock; obey; stop; were not; [9] Textbook
19. nearby; authority, at a distance; disobeying; [9] Textbook
20. improves; decreases; social facilitation; [10] Textbook, Video 22
21. deindividuation; anonymous; [10] Textbook, Video 22
22. less; social loafing; less; less; dispensable; [11] Textbook
23. obligation; important; participate; dignity; [11] Video 22
24. group polarization; irrational extremists; beliefs; [12] Textbook, Video 22
25. enemy; quick, alternate; space shuttle; [12] Textbook, Video 22
26. physical, verbal; reactively; proactively; [13] Textbook
27. influences; genetic, neural, biochemical; do not consider; [14] Textbook
28. temperament; a missing; the mice displayed aggressive behaviors; [14] Video 22
29. facilitate, inhibit; No; complex; frontal lobe; more; [14] Textbook
30. hormone; biochemical; increases; boost; biological, psychological; more; [14] Textbook
31. Biological; psychological; Aversive; frustration-anger; patterns; difficult; [15] Textbook, Video 22
32. learn; model; okay; [15] Textbook, Video 22
33. social scripts; small; sensitive; [15] Textbook, Video 22
34. actions, goals, ideas, social traps, with no; fuel; [16] Textbook
35. proximity; powerful; exposure effect; bond; wary of; [17] Textbook
36. physical attractiveness; personality; similarity; [17] Textbook
37. passionate; companionate; equity, self-disclosure; [18] Textbook
38. varied answers; social exchange theory; rewards; responsibility; dependent; [19] Textbook, Video 22
39. compassion; awe; collective; [19] Video 22
40. cooperation, communication; South Africa; reconciliation; [21] Textbook, Video 22
41. [21] Video 22

ANSWER KEY FOR THE SELF TEST

Item #	Answer	Learning Outcome #	Source	Item #	Answer	Learning Outcome #	Source
2.	c	2	Textbook, Video 22	15.	d	12	Textbook, Video 22
3.	a	3	Textbook, Video 22	16.	a	13	Textbook
4.	b	4	Textbook	17.	a	14	Textbook
5.	b	5	Textbook, Video 22	18.	b	14	Textbook
6.	a	5	Textbook	19.	d	15	Textbook, Video 22
7.	a	6	Video 22	20.	a	16	Textbook
8.	c	7	Textbook, Video 22	21.	c	16	Textbook
9.	c	8	Textbook	22.	c	17	Textbook
10.	d	8	Textbook	23.	c	18	Textbook
11.	c	10	Textbook, Video 22	24.	a	19	Textbook, Video 22
12.	d	10	Textbook, Video 22	25.	d	19	Video 22
13.	a	12	Textbook, Video 22				